ANDEAN LIVES

ANDEAN LIVES

Gregorio Condori Mamani and Asunta Quispe Huamán

Ricardo Valderrama Fernández and
Carmen Escalante Gutiérrez, Original Editors

TRANSLATED FROM THE QUECHUA
AND WITH ANNOTATIONS AND
REVISED GLOSSARY
BY
PAUL H. GELLES
AND
GABRIELA MARTÍNEZ ESCOBAR

INTRODUCTION
BY
PAUL H. GELLES

PHOTOGRAPHS BY
EULOGIO NISHIYAMA

UNIVERSITY OF TEXAS PRESS
AUSTIN

Translation from Ricardo Valderrama Fernández and Carmen Escalante Gutiérrez, eds., *Gregorio Condori Mamani: Autobiografía,* Edic. Bilingüe Quechua-Castellana (Cuzco: Centro de Estudios Rurales Andinos "Bartolomé de las Casas," 1977).

Library of Congress Cataloging-in-Publication Data

Condori Mamani, Gregorio, 1908–
  [Gregorio Condori Mamani. English]
  Andean lives : Gregorio Condori Mamani and Asunta Quispe Huamán /
Ricardo Valderrama Fernández and Carmen Escalante Gutiérrez,
original editors ; translated from the Quechua and with annotations and
revised glossary by Paul H. Gelles and Gabriela Martínez Escobar ;
introduction by Paul H. Gelles. —1st ed.
    p.   cm.
  Includes bibliographical references and index.
  ISBN 0-292-72491-8.—ISBN 0-292-72492-6 (pbk.)
   1. Condori Mamani, Gregorio, 1908– .   2. Quispe Huamán, Asunta.
3. Quechua Indians—Biography.   4. Quechua Indians—Social conditions.
5. Poor—Peru—Cuzco—Biography.   6. Cuzco (Peru)—Social conditions.
I. Gelles, Paul H., 1957– .   II. Escobar, Gabriela Martínez.   III. Title.
F2230.2.K4C66313   1996
985.37004983—dc20   95–32444

We dedicate this work to the people of the Andes
and to the hope for a better future.

CONTENTS

ASUNTA QUISPE HUAMÁN

ACKNOWLEDGMENTS

This translation would not have come about without the kind support of many individuals and institutions. The teachings offered during the National Endowment of the Humanities Summer Institute "Recreating the New World Contact: Indigenous Languages and Literatures of Latin America" at the University of Texas at Austin in 1989 have proven important to this project. In particular, we would like to thank Margot Beyersdorff, Luis Morato, Dennis Tedlock, George Urioste, and especially Francis Kartunnen and Bruce Mannheim. The Anthropology Department at the University of California at Riverside is another institution that supported this work, for which we are grateful. We would also like to express our appreciation to the many others who have helped this translation through its successive incarnations, including Alicia Arrizón, Phil Boise, Kit and Bev Boise-Cossart, Dante Caissie-Martínez, Diana Carr, Wayne Costigan, Alexis and Brandt Deeds, Steve Gravely, Robbie, Debbie, and Marley Jarvis, Washington La Torre, Pat Lyon, Viviana Martínez, David and Pia Maybury-Lewis, Ellen McLaughlin, Bethany Morrison, Richard Norgaard, Ramona Pérez, Craig Spjüt, Chris Steiner, Darlene Suarez, Chuck Walker, and Phil Wilke. Thanks are also due to Barbara Cummings and Theresa May at the University of Texas Press for their editorial assistance and many suggestions; they helped shape the present work in important ways. Thanks go as well to Neva Smith, who prepared the index. We are also much obliged to Eulogio Nishiyama, a renowned photographer from Cuzco, who allowed us to use his beautiful photographs, several of which have never before been published. A few individuals have gone far beyond the call of academic duty, friendship, and even kinship in their help with this book. Here we would like to thank our mothers, Marina Escobar Moscoso for her help with some of the Quechua words and Lyn Humphreys for her many useful comments on the manuscript. So, too, the kind suggestions offered by Gene Anderson, Roberto

Calderón, Piya Chatterjee, Andrés Chirinos, Michael Kearney, and Jeff Tobin are much appreciated. Frank Salomon critically reviewed part of an earlier version of the translation, and his generous and insightful comments helped improve it. Bart Dean's careful read of a later version did the same. Eric Deeds' keen eye for detail, his many suggestions, the chronology of events that he mapped out, and his comments on the notes, helped extirpate many errors. Thanks, Eric. The translators would like to send a very special thanks to Soledad Gelles for all of her help and encouragement throughout this long and arduous process. Her abilities with language and the general support she offered us are greatly appreciated. Our final thanks goes to Ricardo and Carmen, the original editors and co-authors of the present text, for their consultations and for being so patient. Translation, as others have noted, is an act of interpretation, and while we acknowledge the support we have received from many people, we accept responsibility for any errors of translation or interpretation.

ANDEAN LIVES

INTRODUCTION

OVERVIEW

In the early 1970s, Gregorio Condori Mamani and Asunta Quispe Huamán developed an enduring friendship with young anthropologists Ricardo Valderrama and Carmen Escalante. The two couples were neighbors in a shanty town, Coripata, on the outskirts of the highland city of Cuzco, Peru. The creation of the narratives that follow grew out of their friendship, and also out of Valderrama's ethnographic research on "strappers"—the burdened-down porters who, like human pack animals, transport goods through the streets of highland cities.[1]

These two testimonial narratives illustrate a wide range of the rural and urban experiences lived by indigenous peoples in the Andean highlands of Peru, Bolivia, and Ecuador.[2] Although their words and life worlds are mediated by the transcription, editing, and translation processes, the narrators nevertheless provide a rare insider's view of Andean history and society, an alternative and complement to histories, ethnographies, and novels about the highlands. Told with stoicism, humor, and anger, Gregorio's and Asunta's accounts are vivid testimonies to the beauty and the brutality of everyday life in the Andes.

Gabriela Martínez and I have tried to provide a readable and inviting translation, and the following introductory material is not essential reading. It does, however, supply background information on the history and social context of the narratives, on several concepts and institutions presented therein, and on some of our translation goals and decisions. Supplementary material is provided in the Glossary and notes.

1

LANGUAGE OF THE NARRATIVES

Gregorio and Asunta, monolingual Quechua speakers, told their stories in a language that is spoken today by over ten million people in Peru, Bolivia, Chile, Ecuador, and Argentina. The lingua franca of the Inka Empire, Quechua was a hegemonic tool used to help consolidate the largest indigenous political system ever to develop in the Americas. After their invasion in 1532, the Spanish attempted to colonize the hearts, minds, and tongues of the native inhabitants. While the Spanish were successful in many regards, the Andean highlanders forged a unique synthesis out of their own concepts and institutions and those foisted upon them by the invaders. Although highland peoples were repressed in many ways during the colonial period, the colonizing practices of the Spaniards also helped to spread Quechua.[3]

Today, the variant of Quechua that Gregorio and Asunta used, Southern Peruvian Quechua, is spoken by 90 percent of the population of Cuzco and five other departments in the south-central Peruvian Andes area of Peru (Mannheim 1991:27) and is mutually intelligible with the Quechua spoken in Bolivia and Chile. Yet, while Quechua is one of the few growing indigenous languages in the Americas today, it remains very much an "oppressed" and "fenced-in" language.[4] Despite the fact that the current Peruvian constitution recognizes the country as a bilingual nation, the native language is starved of institutional support. Indeed, Quechua remains a spoken and generally unwritten language. This condition prevails in spite of its increased diffusion through radio and despite the fact that a good many of its speakers live in urban areas and speak, read, and write Spanish. With a few important exceptions, lengthy works are rarely published.[5]

As such, the original 1977 bilingual Quechua-Spanish edition of these narratives, and the many subsequent editions and translations of this work, are noteworthy in several respects. First, these narratives are some of the only indigenous testimonials to be published in Quechua and are among the most widely diffused written texts in the native language.[6] Subsequent bilingual editions of both narratives (1982a, 1992), as well as a recent bilingual edition of just Asunta's narrative (1994), make this work a forerunner in efforts to promote written Quechua and indigenous literacy in the native language.

Second, in terms of literature from or about the Andes, the Spanish translation of the original edition benefited from Valderrama's and Escalante's intimate knowledge of Quechua and Andean lifeways and their sensitivity to the peculiarities of the Andean Spanish spoken by bilinguals in the highlands. The original bilingual edition presented voices seldom heard in Spanish-language publications, in either Peru or abroad.[7] Indeed, after the original publisher issued a second, less expensive, monolingual edition of the Spanish translation in Cuzco (1979), other Spanish editions were issued in Spain (1983a) and Cuba (1987). The two narratives have also been translated into Norwegian (1981), German (1982b), and Dutch (1985), and Asunta's narrative appeared in a German compendium on Latin American women (1983b). The narratives, though never previously translated into English, have also been referred to and excerpted in many English-language publications regarding Quechua language and culture (e.g., Allen 1988, Harrison 1989, Mannheim 1991, Sallnow 1987). The text, then, is one of the most widely diffused pieces of Quechua literature in either the native language or in translation.

TESTIMONIAL NARRATIVES AND THE PROCESS OF AUTHORSHIP

Gregorio's and Asunta's voices, while relatively "authentic," do not come to us unmediated.[8] Testimonial narratives such as theirs and autobiography are hardly native genres in Quechua culture. While there is some prefiguration of the former in the highland cultural experience, autobiography, that is, a written genre concerned with a specific notion of selfhood—the unique individual developing over time—is a Western literary form (see, e.g., Watson and Smith 1992). The testimonial mode is not native to the Andes either; yet it at least offers the possibility for a different notion of self than that found in autobiography.[9]

Testimonial narrative, or *testimonio*, is a form of collective autobiographical witnessing that gives voice to oppressed peoples. As such, it has played an important role in developing and supporting international human rights and solidarity movements. *Testimonio* can be defined as "a novel or novella-length written narrative . . . told in the first person by a narrator who is also the real protagonist or witness of the events he or she recounts, and whose unit of narration is usually a 'life' or a significant life experience" (Beverley 1992:92). Yet, while *testimonio* is an affirmation of the individual subject and even of its growth and transformation through time, such a narrative is always linked to marginalized and oppressed social groups. If the narrative loses this connection, it is no longer *testimonio* but becomes autobiography, that is, "an account of, and also a means of access to, middle and upper class status, a sort of documentary *Bildungsroman*. . . . [*Testimonio*] always signifies the need for a general social change in which the stability of the reader's world must be brought into question" (1992:103).

Moreover, and as seen in the transcription and editorial processes described below, *testimonio* is a multiauthored text, one that "replaces the 'author' with two aspects of an authorial function: the 'speaker' who tells the story and 'listener' who compiles and writes the narrative that is published" (Kaplan 1992:123). Indeed, because the narrator of a *testimonio* is often a person who is illiterate or, if literate, not a professional writer, the production of a *testimonio* usually involves the tape-recording, transcription, and editing of an oral account by an interlocutor, often an anthropologist, journalist, or a writer. This relationship is potentially fraught with the contradictions of "high and low culture, dominant and emergent social formations, dominant and subaltern languages" (Beverley 1992:99). Because of its collaborative and intersubjective nature, "*testimonio* is difficult to classify according to standard bibliographic categories. To what section of a library or a bookstore does *testimonio* belong? Under whose name is a *testimonio* to be listed in a card catalog or data base?" (1992:111).[10] Authenticity and artifice combine in complex ways in such works, and the present text is no exception.

Gregorio's and Asunta's spoken words were first mediated by a tape recorder and by their relationship with their interlocutors, Ricardo Valderrama and Carmen Escalante, with whom they clearly enjoyed great trust. Indeed, there is an intimacy between the narrators and their interviewers not often found in the production of indigenous literature or testimonials.[11] Carmen, who met Asunta and Gregorio in the early 1970s, explains this relationship in the following words:[12]

> About the interviews with Gregorio and Asunta. The most important thing was a long and disinterested friendship between Ricardo and them, which dates from 1968. Ricardo was a university student and had gone to live on a lot in Coripata that his father had bought so that his children could live in Cuzco, since traveling from San Jerónimo to Cuzco used to take much longer in the past.[13] A sincere and affectionate friendship developed, and Ricardo also helped them with a few of their problems. We developed a solid relationship with them because life had given us the opportunity to meet, to become friends, and to help each other; we never gave a thought to, or even dreamed of, editing their autobiographies.
>
> The interviews in themselves went in two stages. In 1970, Ricardo was an anthropological assistant of Luis Figueroa in the short film *The Strapper*, and he interviewed a number of strappers, among them Gregorio. To the questions asked of the strappers, Gregorio responds with great lucidity and poetic beauty, providing us with tremendously tragic situations as well as comical anecdotes. We put those tapes to one side, and our friendship with Gregorio and Asunta continued. That short film was successful, and Gregorio and Ricardo appear in it as actors, playing the same roles as they do in real life: Gregorio, a humble strapper exploited by the system, and Ricardo, a poor, provincial student who, instead of using a car or a tricycle cart to move his furniture (a bed and strips of wood for a bookshelf, that is, the few things that a poor student has), hires a

strapper, and they talk as they walk the ancient streets of Cuzco. Both are carrying things: Ricardo, his own possessions, and Gregorio, of course, the possessions of someone else. This is the scene in which they appear, but the short feature shows many other scenes of strappers in the imperial city. The short film won the Oberhausen prize in Germany (from a workers' union). Luis Figueroa received a monetary prize that he shared with all who participated, and that's why Gregorio received a sum of money, which Eulogio Nishiyama (a famous Cuzqueño photographer) administered. Nishiyama is such a kind person that even when this money ran out, he kept giving Gregorio small amounts from his own pocket.

In 1974 we went to Cotabambas, to some cattle-rustling communities, with the goal of collecting several life histories.[14] Ricardo had finished his B.A. degree in anthropology by then and was working as a third-level school teacher with a very low salary (I took my degree in 1975). So, in 1975, while I was taking my final exams and needed to be in Cuzco, Ricardo dedicated himself to his thesis on the ideology of the strappers. He renewed his interviews with Gregorio—and for the first time began interviewing Asunta as well—with the urgent necessity of doing their autobiographies; this time the interviews were oriented to reconstructing their life histories. After some weeks of doing nothing but interviews, we began the translation in June 1975. We did more interviews while, at the same time, advancing with the transcription and translation. In the interviews, it helped that we had them provide more detail on certain passages, amplify certain themes, return to others that they had quickly passed over, or further explain those things that *runas* understand but which people from an urban habitat do not, and who have to have it explained to them.

Carmen and Ricardo then edited some forty hours of interviews with Gregorio and fourteen with Asunta to produce the present text. The narratives were first transcribed textually, after which the interviewers' questions and many repetitions were excised from the text; it was then edited to present two chronologically ordered narratives. Sentence and phrase boundaries, as well as the paragraphs, were made at the moment of transcription according to the narrators' pauses and the units of meaning discerned by the editors. Paragraphs often mark places where a question previously existed in the tape-recorded originals.

Clearly, then, Gregorio's and Asunta's accounts were summoned forth, mediated, and in a sense "authored" by the interview and transcription process and the editorial decisions—which range from punctuation to the selection of themes and passages for inclusion—made by Valderrama and Escalante. The production of testimonials such as those presented here is thus a complex, heavily mediated, collaborative process. And yet, the stories, words, and witnessing are those of the narrators themselves.

TRANSLATION GOALS AND GLOSSES

The translation of the narratives into English is a further and perhaps more drastic mediation and refiguration, given the cultural distance between the Quechua-speaking narrators of peasant origin and a North American and European readership. Gabriela and I had as our principal goal an idiomatic translation of the narratives, one that is accessible to a general public and at the same time useful to specialists in Andean and Latin American studies. To this end, we have kept to a minimum the number of untranslated words in the narratives themselves, while at the same time providing supplementary information on the text in the Glossary and notes.

Another translation goal was to capture in English, at least to some extent, a taste of Quechua verbal art (see Beyersdorff 1986, Harrison 1989, Mannheim 1991, Salomon 1991), that is, the "ethnopoetic" dimension of their spoken words (see Tedlock 1983). To achieve this, we have generally—but not always—respected sentence boundaries, as well as parallelisms and other linguistic conventions, found in the Quechua transcription. Strict adherence to this was suppressed, however, when attempts to ensure fidelity made for a more cumbersome and less accessible, more literal and less idiomatic, translation. Again, our main goal has been to provide a text that flows and that communicates in English the ease and naturalness with which the narrators imparted their lives to their interlocutors. In sum, the text effects a compromise between a strict ethnopoetic standard and a relatively "free" translation.[15]

A further objective was to translate as much as possible and to find English equivalents wherever they did not completely distort the meaning of the original. Here again we compromised, leaving certain words in Quechua and explaining these in the Glossary. This was especially true with those terms that refer to institutions (e.g., *ayni*), foodstuffs (e.g., *oca* and *chuño*), and social categories (*wiraqucha, runa,* and *misti*) that are unique to the Andean region. A number of notes that provide greater detail on both translated and untranslated concepts and institutions appear at the end of the text. A few of these concepts and institutions invite further discussion.

Running throughout both Gregorio's and Asunta's narratives is the social dynamic between "Indians" (*indios*) and mestizos, that is, relations between *runas* and *mistis* (the Quechua terms). As Allen, in a sensitive ethnography about the Cuzco region,[16] puts it, "Indian-Mestizo interactions are stylized, with language and demeanor emphasizing the power and superiority of the Mestizo and the subservience of the Indian. The Mestizo, for example, calls the Indian 'Hijito,' equivalent to 'Sonny' or 'Boy'; whereas the Indian, head bowed and shoulders bent, addresses the Mestizo as 'Patrón,' 'Señor,' or 'Wi-

raqucha' ('Sir')" (1988:28). The narratives presented here graphically illustrate these kinds of utterances and status distinctions, as well as the racism and asymmetrical nature of social relations that prevail in much of the highlands.

For example, the term *wiraqucha,* as used by Asunta and Gregorio, could be glossed as "good sir," "mister," "master," "higher-up," "gentleman," "Lord," "mighty," or "wellborn," depending on the context and whether it appears as adjective or noun. These would be poor translations, however, if the reader did not take into account that they must be read in terms of the *runa-misti* hierarchy and the images of power, dominance, wealth, and whiteness that *wiraqucha* calls up. Because of this, and because of the different valences of *wiraqucha* in the narratives—as well as the need to differentiate this term from others such as "master" (*patrón*) and "mister" (*señor* or *don*)—we retain *wiraqucha* in the text (see Glossary) and in the notes elaborate upon some of its different meanings.

Perhaps even more problematic than those terms left untranslated are those that we have translated for the sake of readability. Mannheim, who discusses the problems of "exuberances" and "deficiencies" when translating Quechua texts, explains that a "deficient translation" is one in which "the categories of the interpreter's language fail to account for significant patterning in the original" (1991:129). And although "exuberances and deficiencies of one kind or another are inherent in any cross-linguistic interpretation" (ibid.), a few of our more "deficient" glosses require further explanation, in particular, those terms repeated throughout the text that carry more meaning than conveyed by their English translations, such as "village," "villager," and "town."

The words "village" and "town" (we also use "family village" and "hometown") are our translations for the Quechua terms *ayllu* and *llaqta,* respectively. The meaning of these problematic terms varies over time and space, and as Allen explains in the case of *ayllu,* "different usages can co-occur in a single community, and any given use of the word seems to make sense only in a limited context" (1988:104). While the original editors, in their Spanish translation, translated *llaqta* as "town" (*pueblo*), they left *ayllu* untranslated and defined it in their glossary as follows: "Andean socio-economic unit constituted by a group of people joined by kinship and occupying a common territory" (Valderrama and Escalante 1977:119).

Salomon, in his introduction to the Huarochirí Manuscript (Salomon and Urioste 1991), a Quechua document that dates from the late sixteenth or early seventeenth century, defines *ayllu* for that period as a "named, landholding collectivity, self-defined in kinship terms, including lineages but not globally defined as unilineal, and frequently forming part of a multi-*ayllu* settlement" (Salomon 1991:21). He adds, however, that "*ayllu* is the name of a concept of relatedness and not an entity with any specific dimensions. It has no inherent limits of scale" (1991:22). The same is true for contemporary *ayllus*. While *ayllu* is often used in the literature to describe a bilateral kindred, *ayllus* are spatially localized in many communities and must be understood in terms of "the personal and intimate relationship that bonds the people and the place into a single unit" (Allen 1988:106).

Moreover, while there are often several "neighborhood *ayllus*" that make up a highland town or village, the latter can also be thought of as an *ayllu*; indeed, Allen's glossary definition of this term is an "indigenous community or other social group whose members share a common focus" (1988:257). Whether speaking of a village in Cuzco or of its constituent "neighborhood *ayllus*," Allen finds that what is key is that "*ayllu*-mates derive their well-being from the same locality, and through this shared relationship they are set apart as a distinct social unit" (1988:107). Thus, the term *ayllu* has a strong connotation of affinity and membership and signifies for the individual *ayllu* member deep emotional ties to the collective. It may help the reader to think about the Andean "village"—our translation of *ayllu*—as having a "clannish" quality, in the colloquial sense of clan defined by *Webster's* dictionary: "a group united by a common interest or common characteristics." In sum, the term *ayllu* describes a relationship between people that can be expressed through locality, descent, or political factionalism.[17]

Llaqta is also a fluid concept. While in everyday speech it can refer to a hamlet, village, town, city, people, or country, *llaqta* is generally used in the narratives to mean a "town characterized by nucleated rather than dispersed settlement" (1988:260). Salomon shows how the use of the term in the early colonial period expressed a strong bond between what he calls a "place-deity" or "deity-locale," the territory it was imagined as controlling, and the group of people that depended on this territory and who were favored by the local deity. Fuenzalida (1970) has shown how such an identity was reconfigured through the colonial period and through the fusion of Andean and Iberian beliefs, practices, and institutions. The way in which the Roman Catholic saints were incorporated into this communal dynamic is important: today, towns are represented by a patron saint and other lesser saints, and these play an important role in defining personal and communal identities in the highlands.

In terms of the glosses that we have chosen, we believe that when Gregorio uses the word *ayllu*, which is absent from Asunta's account, he is generally referring to a village type of *ayllu*, rather than a neighborhood-based *ayllu*, and we have translated it accordingly ("village"). When it is clear that he is talking about a family unit or neighborhood *ayllu*, we have translated it as "family" and have provided a note. When the narrators use *llaqta*, they are generally talking about a strongly nucleated settlement, and we have translated this as "town." While these glosses are, in the terms reviewed above, "deficient," we have been consistent throughout the text in distinguishing the terms *ayllu* and *llaqta* by translating them as "village" and "town," respectively.

The reader needs to keep in mind that implicit in the narrators' use of these terms is a sense of kinship, belonging, and participation *in terms of the place itself,* a spiritual connection that bonds together a people, the town they live in, the surrounding landscape, and the deities that reside there. Andean towns and villages, like their subunits (e.g., "neighborhood *ayllu*"), provide a strong local sense of identity for their members and are often closely identified with particular saints, as well as with ancestral spirits, mountain deities, and the earth, which are viewed as having both benevolent and malevolent qualities. As providers of fertility and life as well as of disease, death, and destruction, these different protector spirits and emblems of communal identity must be placated by ritual offerings, libations, and religious celebrations. Indeed, the prosperity of each family, village, and community is to a large degree seen as depending on these frequent "gifts." This dynamic, then, is a key feature of ritual practice, social life, and ethnic identity in the Andes.

In much the same way as "village," our translation of the Spanish loanword *paisano* as "villager," "fellow villager," or "country villager" (and alternatively, where appropriate, as "comrade" and "one of our people") should be read as expressing a kind of cultural, ethnic, class, linguistic, and geographic affinity between the speaker and the person he or she describes. *Paisano,* as used by the narrators, is in many respects synonymous with *runa,* that is, a Quechua-speaking indigenous person of peasant origin, except that in general *paisano* refers to a *runa* who lives in, or comes from, a rural town or village.

While not all *runas* live in *ayllus,* the only people who live in *ayllus* are *runas.* As Allen (1988) has shown, only *runas* have the special sense of place and connection to the land that *ayllu* connotes: only they—not *mistis*—are constantly involved in ritual exchanges with the earth and mountain spirits. Here, then, is the correspondence that we are making between our use of "village" and "villager": villagers (*paisanos*) are rural-based *runas* who generally live in villages (*ayllus*) or in the neighborhood family *ayllus* that make up villages and towns. Yet, what this correspondence glosses over is that some villagers in the narratives live on haciendas (see Glossary), some live in towns (*llaqtas*) with no *ayllu* affiliation, and some, like Gregorio, have moved to and reside in large cities. Indeed, a *runa,* or a "villager," can have several of these affiliations at the same time. What is important for the reader to remember is that, implicit in the narrators' use of the word "villager," is an intimate sense of relatedness with their fellow *runas.*

As mentioned above and as Asunta's and Gregorio's narratives richly illustrate, "land is experienced as animate, powerful, and imbued with consciousness—a parallel society of Earth Persons with whom one is in constant interaction" (Allen 1988:24). Our glosses for particular deities and religious concepts from native Andean religion are usually explained in the notes. Here it bears mentioning that, while the earth and mountain gods that the narrators speak of are an everyday part of their existence, we have put these Andean deities in capital letters (e.g., Earth Mother, Earth Shade, Sun Father, etc.) to accord them the same status as the Christian God and saints.

Another translation decision concerned the terms *qhari* and *warmi*, which mean "man" and "woman," respectively, but which are also used to signify "husband" and "wife" in the sense of common-law marriages. The issue was how to differentiate the status that inheres in these terms from that of formalized, church-consecrated marriages. To this purpose, we have translated *qhari* and *warmi* as "husband" and "wife" where appropriate and have translated the status conferred by church-consecrated marriages as "lawfully wedded" wife or husband or as those people "married by the church." The reader should keep in mind that Gregorio and Asunta were each legally married by the church *just once*—to one another—and that mention of their other "husbands" or "wives" in the text should not be taken as legal, church-sanctioned marriages, but rather as common-law marriages. The same is generally true when they speak of other people's husbands or wives.[18]

Finally, it is important for the reader to keep in mind the topography and environment of the highlands. The city of Cuzco is nearly 11,000 feet above sea level, and Gregorio and Asunta, like millions of other highlanders, live out their lives between altitudes of 7,000 and 15,000 feet. From the small herd steads of the "high reaches" (*puna*), often flanked by snow-capped peaks reaching 20,000 feet, descending past the agricultural towns and villages at half that altitude in the "warm valleys" (*qhiswa*), and further down the eastern slopes of the Andes to the tropical rain forests of the "jungle valleys" (*yunka*), the vertical environment of south-central Peru provides many contrasts. In their travels, Gregorio and Asunta traverse this precipitous landscape under the watchful eyes of Sun Father (Inti Tayta) and Mother Moon (Mama Killa), passing lakes (*quchas*) and crossing plains (*pampas*), treading in the shadows of the mountain lords (*apus*), and paying their respects to the earth shrines that mark the high passes (*apachitas*). Theirs is a sacred landscape.

The reader can find additional information on these and other glosses, as well as on other concepts and institutions, in the notes. The latter, however, by no means represent a complete inventory of our translation decisions. Nor do we pretend to be exhaustive in our explanations of different terms or in citing relevant bibliographical sources. Rather, the notes are meant to signal—and provide some "thick description" about—a limited number of concepts, institutions, and themes presented in the narratives, as well as to suggest where the interested reader can find more information.

TRANSLATION CONVENTIONS AND CRITICAL APPARATUS

Many of the problems of translating Quechua—known as *runa simi* or "the *runa* tongue" in the native language itself—to English have been outlined by Harrison (1989), Mannheim (1991), and Salomon (1991), among others; for more detailed discussions, the interested reader should consult these works. Here I will just indicate a few of the conventions that we have followed, as well as signal the ways in which the critical apparatus that accompanies the present translation differs from that of the original bilingual edition.

Because a principal goal of the translation was to translate as much as possible, we have produced a new Glossary, one that has one-third the number of terms as that of the original bilingual edition. We have accomplished this by replacing many of that edition's glossary terms with idiomatic expressions in English and by providing notes. When we do keep Quechua terms or Spanish loanwords (e.g., *compadre, cargo*) in the narratives, they are italicized the first time they appear and defined in the Glossary; an extra word or two is occasionally supplied in the text to evoke the meaning of the term. A full half of our Glossary terms appear in the first chapter.

Notes that expand on important themes and translation decisions are provided at the end of the text. Where we have drawn on the glossary of the original edition for our Glossary and notes, these contributions are cited as "Valderrama and Escalante 1977." Besides the addition of the notes and a new Glossary, we have provided chapter titles, as well as a Postscript.

The Quechua language "requires the speaker to attach suffixes that clarify his or her relationship to the data conveyed" (Salomon 1991:32). These suffixes indicate whether the information being conveyed has "witness validation" or "reportative validation," that is, whether it was learned through direct experience or is hearsay. As Mannheim has put it, "There is no corresponding grammatical distinction in English, even though we can translate it with a phrase like *it is said that* or *they say*. But the suffixes that mark these categories are ubiquitous. If they were translated consistently, most declarative sentences would begin with either *it is said* or *I vouch that*" (1991:128–129). We have resolved this in the present work by marking only those sentences that have reportative validation, using "I've heard," "it's said," or "they say." In passages that have a great deal of reportative validation, such as when the narrators are recounting stories that they have heard, we usually put the marker ("I've heard," etc.) just once at the beginning.[19]

As these and our other choices make clear, the translation strikes a compromise between fidelity to the original and readability. Thus, in some places we have suppressed repetition by giving different glosses to a single Quechua word. For example, the verb *wikch'uy* is translated as "dumped," "cast," "flung," and "tossed" in different passages, and in some cases, the same passage may employ more than one of these glosses. In other passages where we feel that it enhances the reading and provides a more ethnopoetic rendering, we repeat a term to evoke the cadence, tone, and emphasis of the original.

We have generally followed the paragraph breaks in the Quechua transcription, and only occasionally have we supplied these or suppressed the ones found in the original. To a large extent, we have supplied the section breaks in each chapter.[20] As already mentioned, we have generally—but not always—respected sentence boundaries, parallelisms, and other linguistic conventions found in the original. While we have not translated place names, we have translated the names of saints, except when these identify churches or towns. Quechua words are spelled according to the 1985 standardized alphabet for Peruvian Quechua,[21] except for towns, villages, personal names, and certain words that are already conventionally known by some other Spanish-based spelling (e.g., Cuzco rather than Qusqu, *olluco* rather than *ulluku*). Rather than use the Quechua pluralizer (*-kuna*) for untranslated words, we use the English method (e.g., *runas* instead of *runakuna*).

Occasionally, the narrators switch to a Spanish phrase in the middle of their Quechua, as when they are quoting someone from the dominant culture, be this an army officer, wealthy landowner, or other *misti*. We signal these language shifts in the text itself by putting the phrase in italics. However, because of the many Spanish loanwords that appear in the narratives, we use italicized phrases only when it is clearly an imitation of a power holder and when the entire utterance is in Spanish.[22] Many of these shifts are also marked by use of the imperative, as they are usually orders from superiors of one kind or another.

ANDEAN LIVES

I would like to conclude by returning to the topic of testimonial narratives. Through their accounts, Asunta and Gregorio speak for the oppressed, marginalized, and largely silenced cultural majority of the Andean countries. Their testimonials are distinctly Andean. They take us inside a unique worldview and historical consciousness, transporting us to a society where the colonial experience lingers heavily in both belief and practice, but where the burden of subjugation is constantly subverted by a story, by a memory of resistance, or by a turn of phrase. Different forms of domination and resistance appear again and again in both narratives.

Yet the lives of Asunta and Gregorio also differed in significant ways, and this is also reflected in their testimonials. While Gregorio grew up an orphan and roamed from country village to country village during his youth, Asunta spent hers on the outskirts of a town near the city of Cuzco. Gregorio's early years tending flocks and working the fields of other peasants and *mistis* contrast with Asunta's indentured servitude on an hacienda and her work as a maid in *misti* households. And while her life was spent primarily around the large metropolis of Cuzco, it took Gregorio several years to find his way to the imperial city of his ancestors.

The narratives also differ in that Asunta suffers the double burden of being "Indian" and being a woman. It is also clear from her account that this added discrimination is not limited to *runa-misti* relations, but that women suffer disproportionately and have an added burden within *runa* society as well. One of the strengths of the text is that it shows different forms of domination along gender, ethnic, and class lines in both rural and urban areas. From the free services provided for *misti* landowners, authorities, priests, and educators in the country villages, to the abuses committed by state and church officials in and around the city of Cuzco, the narratives vividly illustrate the discrimination and exploitation to which *runas* are subjected by local power holders. Whether in rural towns, isolated mines, semifeudal haciendas, or in the houses of their powerful *misti* masters in Cuzco, Asunta's and Gregorio's depictions of life in these places bear witness to the violence of everyday life in Peru.

While the reasons for the dirty war being fought in the Peruvian countryside since 1980 are complex and many, one of these is undoubtedly the brutal living conditions described in these two narratives. The social landscape of the Cuzco area has changed dramatically since Asunta and Gregorio, now deceased, told their stories. Were they to speak to us today, they would probably tell us of their increasing poverty, of mind-numbing inflation and the rocketing cost of goods, of widespread bloodshed and their fellow villagers being victimized by both the armed forces and Shining Path, of brutality in the countryside that surpasses even the most horrific passages in these accounts here. Yet, while the people for whom Gregorio and Asunta speak continue to shoulder much of the social, political, and economic burdens of Peru, the testimonials presented here attest to their tremendous resilience of spirit and their ability to survive and give meaning to the difficult worlds they inhabit.

P.H.G. 1995

PRELIMINARY NOTE
TO THE ORIGINAL EDITION

(Translated from the Spanish)

This is the true story of Gregorio Condori Mamani and his wife, Asunta, monolingual Quechua speakers who migrated from their home communities to the city of Cuzco over forty years ago. We met them in 1968 when we moved to Coripata, a shanty town on the outskirts of Cuzco, where they had been living for some time. At present, Gregorio and Asunta live in a tiny shack next to the trash dump, right where the shanty town borders the Southern Railway train station. Their house is one of the few lacking electricity, water, and sewage drains; it occupies less than thirteen square meters of land, on top of which they have built a small adobe room, used as their bedroom and to raise guinea pigs. On one side of the house, other walls have been added to shelter an earthen hearth where Asunta cooks, and in the remaining space she keeps seven chickens and two dogs.

When we met them, Gregorio was already working full time as a strapper, and Asunta was doing her food business on a daily basis. At present, Gregorio continues working as a strapper, but Asunta no longer does business of any kind. She is ill and lives secluded in her house, moving about only with great difficulty. During the years we were neighbors, we developed a deep friendship, which later allowed us to undertake this work; this was initiated in 1973 while I, Ricardo, was interviewing people as an anthropological consultant for the film *The Strapper* (*El Cargador*). Filmed in Cuzco and directed by Luis Figueroa, this short film documented different kinds of strappers, seasonal and full-time ones, old men and boys, with the goal of obtaining data about their situation in Cuzco. Our friendship with Gregorio, his trust in us, and more than

Gregorio and Ricardo in Coripata.

anything, his amazing narrative capabilities led us to renew our interviews with him in 1975, this time with the purpose of reconstructing his life history. We chose general themes that Gregorio—and later Asunta—could freely reflect upon. Many times it was they who chose which themes to talk about, which we then recorded on tape and began translating in June 1975. This process was repeatedly interrupted to carry out other interviews with them, so that they could expand upon certain topics. Gregorio and Asunta know how to sign their names, and Asunta can recognize some letters, but neither knows how to read or write. That is why, in spite of the fact that Gregorio possesses personal documents that note important dates and information, he nevertheless has no memory of any dates, such as his birthdate, which, according to his Conscription Card, was July 6, 1908, in Acopía, currently a municipal district in the province of Acomayo, Cuzco. This same document, dated 1933, establishes that he was called into active service on August 31 of that year, the same date that the government of General Oscar R. Benavides began. In like manner, it is worth clarifying Gregorio's reference to the first time that the airplane, piloted by Enrique Rondán, arrived in Sicuani; his true name was Enrique Rolandi, and he was an Italian aviator who landed in Sicuani on June 7, 1921, while doing the Cuzco-Puno route. We have also confirmed that Gregorio entered the Huáscar cotton textile factory on October 1, 1943, and ceased working there March 11, 1967, when the factory closed. Gregorio worked there as a sweeper for twenty-three years and five months, which he considers to be a short time. He says, "That job didn't last long," a statement that is due perhaps to his conception of time and to his having to rely on that job to assure his economic security for the rest of his life. When the factory closed, his daily wage was thirty-one *soles* and twenty-eight *centavos*, and beginning November 1, 1968, the Workers' Social Security assigned him a monthly pension of three hundred and fifty-eight *soles* and thirty *centavos*, which, although he does not mention it in his account, he still receives at present. We have also been able to confirm that the death of union leader Emiliano Huamantica that he mentions, did indeed occur in a car accident on January 7, 1964, well before the factory closed.

We also feel it necessary to clarify that the Aprista leader mentioned in his account, the one who fled Cuzco dressed as a woman, was not Haya de la Torre; it is possible that Gregorio confused him with General Vargas Dávila, who thus avoided being lynched by the masses during the seizure of Cuzco city by the workers in 1958 (between April 6 and 12). These events began with a strike protesting the rising cost of gasoline and kerosene.

All of these pieces of information have allowed us to confirm the veracity of Gregorio's account.

In Asunta's case, it is impossible to ascertain exact dates, not only because she lacks personal documents—except for a marriage certificate that we were unable to locate—but also because she no longer remembers the name of the mine where she worked. Both Asunta and Gregorio were very pleased when they found out that their accounts had been published, and they offered to retell their stories in greater detail.

With the exception of Asunta and her relatives, the names of the people, including Gregorio, and the places, institutions, and authorities that appear here, have not been changed.

The fact that Quechua, the language of *runas,* is our mother tongue has facilitated the Spanish translation, ensuring that this is as close as possible to the Quechua text, thereby retaining the distinctive way that bilingual Andeans of the region have of expressing themselves. The people who read the Quechua version will be able to take away their own interpretation because we do not consider our translation to be the only one possible or the most perfect. We have retained Quechua words in the Spanish version that require marginal notes, and for that reason a glossary has been added.

We would like to thank Dr. Jorge Flores and the young writer Enrique Rosas, both of the National University of Cuzco. We would also like to thank Dr. Franklin Pease and Dr. Jürgen Riester of the Pontificia Universidad Católica of Peru for reading and making suggestions about the first drafts of the Spanish version. Thanks also go to Rosario Valdeavellano for adapting the Quechua text to the official Quechua alphabet, approved October 16, 1975,* and to my brother Ladislao Valderrama and his wife, Dominga Atayupanki, for their invaluable help and encouragement. We would also like to thank the Center for Rural Andean Studies "Bartolomé de las Casas" and its director, Dr. Guido Delran, for the constant support offered us during the realization of the present work.

Finally, this book fulfills the wishes of Gregorio Condori Mamani and his wife, Asunta, "that the sufferings of our people be made known."

R.V.F. and C.E.G. 1977

*As noted in the introduction, our English translation follows the amended 1985 standardized Quechua alphabet (P.H.G. and G.M.E.).

PART ONE

GREGORIO CONDORI MAMANI

NOTE TO THE READER: *Italics* indicate Spanish and Quechua words defined in the Glossary; in the narratives these words are italicized only on their first occurrence. *Italicized phrases* indicate language shifts from Quechua to Spanish in the original narratives. The notes to the text supply further background information, though the reader need not refer to them in order to appreciate Gregorio's and Asunta's accounts of their lives.

□

ONE

BEGINNINGS

□

I'm from Acopía, and it's now forty years since I came here from my town—my name is Gregorio Condori Mamani.[1] I left my hometown behind because I had no mother or father. A dirt poor orphan,[2] I'd been left in my godmother's hands. It was she who first cut my hair,[3] and one day when I was a bit bigger she said to me:

"Now that you've got the strength and your bones are sturdy, you have to go work. I'm going to pack you a meal so you can go and look for work—let's see if you can bring home some money, if only to pay for the salt in your soup.[4] Your bones are sturdy now, you've got the strength,[5] and I just can't keep cradling you in my arms any longer. Tomorrow you'll have a wife and child, and you may just get a woman who doesn't help you with anything.[6] Then you'd curse me, and I don't want anyone cursing me after I'm dead because I might just be punished and turned into a lost soul, made to wander and suffer.[7] That's why, from this moment on, you must learn to weave your life all by yourself, so when tomorrow comes you'll be able to provide for your family."

That's what my godmother told me. And I said:

"Yes, Mama."

So from that day on I felt a yearning, lodged like a needle deep in my heart, to leave my godmother's house and look for work. I couldn't even sleep. Right about that time a mule driver came to town with many mules and horses loaded down with salt and sugar to barter for *chuño, moraya,* and wool. They told me his name was Mr. Jacinto Mamani and that he often took little boys to Cuzco, to work as servants for his *compadres.* When I heard that, I went looking for him at the corral where he kept his mules. And I told him:

"Papa Jacinto, I want you to take me to Cuzco to work in the house of your compadres."

Hearing that, *wiraqucha* Jacinto looked me over head to toe and said:[8]

"You're still too young."

Well, I don't know where all the tears came from, but I started sobbing, and through my tears I said:

"No, Papa, please! I'm an orphan and on my own—my godmother doesn't want to support me anymore."

So he answered me:

"Well then, this Tuesday wait for me on the road, there next to the river at the Yuraqmayu Bridge."

Even now I can still remember waiting to leave my town and how long those four days lasted. Never have days been so long as the days I spent waiting to go to Cuzco. Just once before, while working shoulder to shoulder at a work party there in the community,[9] did I hear one of the town elders, Laureano Cutipa, talking about Cuzco. Papa Laureano was Staffholder at the time,[10] and while we were working, he told us that when *Inka* was building Cuzco,[11] the home of our ancestors, it was an open *pampa,* completely flat, with no mountains at all, and the wind would come roaring through like a rushing bull, knocking down any wall or house Inka put up. And so they say that one day Inka told his wife:

"Damn! This wind won't let me work; I'm going to lock it away in a corral till I've finished making Cuzco."

Just like that, Inka went to La Raya to lock up the wind, and to do so he built a huge corral. As he was herding the wind in and was just about to shut it away, Inka *Qulla* suddenly appeared. They say the wind belongs to Inka Qulla, and that's why the Qulla region is completely flat and so very windy. Inka Qulla said:

"Why do you want to lock up my wind?"

"So I can build my town," Inka replied.

"If you want to build your town, I'll let you lock up my wind, but just for one day. But if you're not able to finish it that day, you never will, because I'll bring in my wind with so much force it will sweep away everything."

Faced with this situation, Inka tied down the sun, turning time into a very long day. When he'd finished building Cuzco, his wife told him:

"You'd better make lots of windbreaks because when Inka Qulla sets the wind loose, it's surely going to blow again!"

With that in mind, Inka built mountains all around Cuzco, and those are the mountains that've been there ever since.

I was thinking about that story, about Inka building Cuzco and wanting to prolong the day, mindful of Inka Qulla's wind. It was the rainy season; rain and snow were falling day and night, and the hills and pampas were all white with the snowfall. I think it was a Tuesday when we set out, traveling just like that, not even able to see the road. The mules and horses were slogging along, and then late in the afternoon when Sun Father was on his way down,[12] he came out for just a moment—the mountains turned completely white and began to shimmer till they glowed like mirrors. That must've been what burned my eyes, making me snow-blind. It was already night when we reached a stopover on a hill slope where another mule driver, together with his wife and half a dozen mules, had also put up. His wife was big with child, almost due. As we unloaded the mules, the rain began coming down hard, and lightning bolts exploded nearby like dynamite—we were all scared out of our wits. The mules and horses were also frightened and were bucking in the corral, trying to escape, until wiraqucha Jacinto ordered his two workhands:

"Get up on the corral and stop them! And you, Gregorio, grab my mount!"

So there I was, soaking wet in the rain, holding tightly onto the mule. And the mule driver's wife—poor thing!—her belly was hurting, and she was real frightened, screaming loudly between the many thunderclaps and lightning. Never have I seen so much lightning as that night; it seemed as if it was going to turn the mountains into pampas. Right there in the middle of the downpour, with lightning bolts striking all around us, the little baby came out of its mother, wailing as if it too was frightened by the thunder and lightning. Later, as day was dawning, my eyes began hurting as if they'd been pierced with branding irons. I'd never felt such pain, the kind that makes you want to tear out your eyes, and I too began yowling like that woman; as I cried, I felt the fire that was searing my eyes shoot throughout my body. Then the lady's workhand told me:

"Don't be a dumb Indian! Pile up lots of snow, pull down your pants, and sit on it. You'll see that your pain goes away."

I did what he said, and, still holding onto the mule and crying, I sat there on top of the snow. It was really true: little by little the pain in my eyes let up. But the next day my ass was all swollen red, as if the skin had been peeled off with boiling water—I couldn't walk.

That's the bad luck I had on my way to Cuzco to find work as a servant. It just wasn't in the stars for me to reach Cuzco and become a houseboy;[13] instead, I was destined to go round in circles, suffering from one town to the next. My eyes and ass were so swollen I couldn't keep up with the pace of the mule train. They moved on, and I lagged farther and farther behind. The workhands noticed this and told the master, and just like that, he ordered one of them to leave me with some money at a herd stead so they could cure me.[14] So the workhand told me:

"When you're better, you get back home."

But that night, there in the home of those *runa* herder folk, I was very ill, ready to pass into the otherworld.[15] I had a high fever, and my eyes were rolling back in their sockets; my body burned like glowing embers. But the lady in that herd stead saved me. I hope our Lord has that good-hearted woman sitting next to him, because she saved me when I was well on my way to the otherworld. She cured me by making her whole family, from her husband to her youngest son, piss into a large pot. She boiled the urine with lots of salt and bathed my whole body from head to toe with it; then she wrapped me in a large twilled-wool blanket she'd heated by the hearth. That must've done it because the next morning I was all better. So right then and there I felt some hope deep down in my heart, thinking maybe I could still catch up with them. But it was the rainy season, and I didn't know the trails—I saw I wouldn't be able to. When I realized this, I began to cry, hiding my tears from the stead keeper. But since I kept crying and crying, he said to me:

"Stay with us and help tend the sheep."

Since I had nowhere to go, I stayed on with them as a shepherd. So, by the morning of the third day, I was out there grazing the sheep with them. But the stead keeper had lots of kids, devilish little troublemakers, who were always trying to beat up on me. But I wouldn't let them. They'd bother and pester me till I couldn't stand it anymore, and I'd lose my temper. Then I'd make them scream; many times I'd get a whipping because of that:

"You damn bully! You've been hitting my kids!"

Since they and their children mistreated me, and there was hardly any food—there's never much food in a herd stead—I waited for the day I could leave and go somewhere else, anywhere. One day as I was driving the sheep along, my heart now set on going to another town, some mule drivers traveling toward Acopía passed by. So, I left the sheep there grazing on a hill, and I trailed after them.

Following the mule drivers, I found myself back in Acopía. But once there, I had nowhere to go; I was too ashamed to return to my godmother's home. Yet, there was no other nook or cranny I could slip into there in Acopía, so I returned to her house when night fell. I entered the house quietly, walking on tiptoe so her husband wouldn't notice me. But even so, that heartless wretch saw me:

"Well damn! That shifty little smart-ass came back! Mustn't have had enough grub to stuff his gut with."

Those words made me tremble with shame.

"I went away and worked," was all I could say.

But my godmother seemed happy to see me. She said:

"If you were going away to work, you should've told me."

That night in my godmother's house I was so ashamed and scared, I couldn't sleep at all. But the next morning, I was back doing chores for her. Yet, from then on, I wasn't the same person, and all I could think about was leaving to work somewhere else. Even so, I still spent a few more months suffering there in my godmother's house; all this because I was an orphan child—I know nothing about the man who my mother bore me for, if he was married, single, or a widower. The only person who knows that is my mother, and she's dead now. When I was just a baby, still unable to say my own name, my mother handed me over to my godmother, who was childless.

But my godmother's husband was stingy, and he'd give me a bloody beating for any old thing, sometimes just for eating. Only once did my Uncle Luis tell me that Layo was the town where my mother flung me into this world; that's my true birthplace, the town I'm really from. With this in mind, I left Acopía for Layo with a butcher from Cuzco. I traveled all over buying sheep with him. People said that this butcher was a thief because he never slept in town, but always on the outskirts, camping in a tent where he also cooked. The night I went to them it was very cold, and since it was so very cold, I slipped into the tent without their knowing it. When I was inside, they caught me and began laughing, saying:

"There's a thief in here."

They tied up my hands and feet, and that's how I slept with them there in the tent that night. That's what I went through when I was just a little kid.

When my godmother found out I'd left, how she must've cried and cried; never again did she hear from me after I left Acopía that time. Perhaps I'd lost my way climbing toward heaven or entering the underworld,[16] and my godmother surely looked for me.

"Where's my poor baby?" she'd have asked.

"Where's my Gregorio?"

"Where has he gone?"

"Could the river have taken him?"

"Could a boulder have crushed him?"

"What has happened to my Gregorio?"

That's how my godmother must've cried as she searched for me, because she loved me. But I was already long gone with the butcher, herding his sheep and traveling all over. We'd be behind them, trodding along at the same pace as those critters. That's how they'd make me walk, and they'd also give me some of their food; there was plenty of food back then, not scarce like it is now. So one day, on one of the trips with those butchers, I fell asleep at Languipampa, a flat plain that's all covered with rushes and reeds. And while I slept, the butchers moved on, deserting me. Abandoned there on that pampa, I found myself all alone in the world. So I began running all over, up and down from one herd stead to another, asking for my companions. The runa folk there told me:

"They passed through here a while ago."

I was walking through the rushes, sobbing and crying about my bitter luck and wretched life, when a good-hearted woman had me follow her home, saying:

"Cry no more; they passed through here a long while ago."

I stayed for two months in that lady's house, tending her sheep. One day she traveled to Sicuani for wheat flour. At that time white coins were in circulation, and only some time later did Benavides bring out the yellow coins we use today.[17] And so later, there in that town, the lady gave me over to some wheat buyers, and they brought me to Sicuani on a donkey.

"He wouldn't be able to walk it," they said.

So I arrived in Sicuani, where I again worked for a butcher. But as before, this butcher was a real demon. He beat me too much. My ear wasn't an ear anymore, my back wasn't a back—he'd beat me black and blue. I tended the cattle there. Just like any boy, I'd often fall asleep while tending the cattle. Other times I'd come back late. He'd flog me for those things, hanging me by a rope from the rafter and making me drink fermented urine mixed with soot.

"This is what you like, so drink up!" he'd say.

Out of fear, and so he wouldn't whip my back bloody, I drank it.

That's what this Christian did to me;[18] he's probably dead by now. How he must be trying to explain it all to the Lord our God! He did all that to me because I was a motherless child, an orphan. On another occasion, when we were living at Acotapampa in Sicuani, he left me in charge of the house. At that time, there was a powerful wiraqucha named Valdivia who owned a large *hacienda*. That land baron had parcels of land all over the place, and that's why my master would say:

"If nothing else, we'll at least be little Valdivias."

With that in mind, he bought many small plots of land, which were cheap back then. One time, they all went to discuss land deals and didn't return for several days; I stayed home all by myself. And so, being a silly ass, I forgot to feed the guinea pigs.[19] Since they didn't eat for many days, they all died, and then the cats ate them. So, when they came back three days later, they realized the guinea pigs were missing. They began to beat me.

"Speak up, you little sneak! You must've sold them. Tell me, and I won't hit you."

So he wouldn't hit me anymore, I lied:

"Yes, I sold them."

"And how much did you sell them for?"

"No, it's not like that, I just traded them for four pieces of bread."

"So you went and traded them, did you? You no-good, shifty Indian . . ."

Then came the real punishment. He hung me up . . . and whipped my back bloody, leaving it all black and blue.

Other times, on my way to the pastures with the sheep, I'd fall asleep while playing around, and the sheep would go and do damage to the crops. They'd eat the potatoes and wheat that were just coming up. That Christian would punish me for the damage done by those innocent sheep by making me bathe in the Willkamayu River at five in the morning during the dead of winter.

The butcher never stayed home; he was always traveling. So I'd stay home all by myself and watch over the cattle. When he wasn't on the road, I'd look after his little donkey, which used to go to Suyupampa flat to feed. One day the donkey disappeared for good. I was so afraid of the beating he was going to give me for that, I left his house, never to return. Next to the butcher's home, there was a fenced lot with a large pile of rocks where I crouched down and hid in a cranny. At that very moment, I saw my master pass by with a huge bull-whip in hand, huffing and puffing with anger. I was very lucky—our Lord surely hid me—because my master passed right by me, looking everywhere, and didn't see me. So he wouldn't find me, I entrusted myself to God the Father:

"Hide me, Lord, so this Christian devil doesn't see me."

So that night I left Sicuani heading toward San Pablo, keeping to the banks of the Willkamayu River, avoiding the road, so I wouldn't run into that devil. While walking along the trail, I came upon a man and a woman who were trout fishing in the dark. I think they got scared, but I was also very afraid. So, frightened and trembling with fear, I approached them.

"Are you of this world or the otherworld?" the man asked me.

"I'm of this world," I replied.

"Who are you? Where are you going?" he then asked me.

"I'm just wandering; I have no parents."

They were just runa folk like me, and good-hearted. They asked me:

"Want to come along with us?"

Digging into a satchel, they offered me a meal they'd packed for themselves, and I ate a little bit. Then we went back to Sicuani. Deep down in my heart, I hoped: now that I've got another master, that devil will have to stop looking for me. I went with Gumercindo Qhuru, which was my new master's name, from Sicuani to the village of Arisa, his wife's people.[20] The people there were good of heart and pure of soul. So that just seems to have been my fate. Ever since I first saw the light of day, I've traveled from one house to the next, upsetting our Lord. That's surely the fate of those who've been flung into this world to suffer. By suffering like that, it's said that we the poor are curing all the good Lord's wounds, and once those wounds are completely healed, the suffering in this world will disappear. That's what a corporal from the Paruro region once told us in the barracks, and we soldiers said:

"What the hell? How big are these wounds that, with all the suffering there is, they haven't yet disappeared? As if they were horse cankers!"[21]

And he answered:

"Don't be heretics, dammit! Stand to! The last four to fall in!"

So it was.

Thinking back, I'd say there's more suffering now than in the past. This life isn't bearable anymore. This life weighs heavier than the loads I carry on my back. And as the days go by, my burden grows heavier. Such is life. In my ignorance I ask, if our good Lord's wounds are the cause of so much suffering, and life is already so short, why don't they find and cure him? That's what I asked my wife some years ago, and she said:

"That's why foreigners have gone to Mother Moon, they say."[22]

And just like that, it was the talk of the town back then: the *gringos* had traveled by plane for a whole week to get to Mother Moon. But I think that's just people talking.

So much for suffering.

In the village of Arisa, this man, Gumercindo, thought highly of me because ever since I was a little kid I've known how to drive a plough and team. I'd carry the yoke when we'd go out to prepare the fields, and they liked me even more. I was doing just fine there, though my clothes were always tattered like they are now. At that time, I still wasn't drinking cornbeer or liquor as I'd go from field to field.[23] But they'd give me lots of food. Sometimes I'd be sent to his compadres, friends, or kinfolk to do *ayni* or *mink'a* labor on his behalf. So I stayed in Mr. Gumercindo's house for more than a year. But one day, bad luck came my way. I think bad luck is stuck to me like a black mole. On that occasion, my master and I loaded two donkeys with wheat flour and I went to Sicuani to sell it. As I was trying to mount one of the donkeys, the other rounded a corner, but when I went after it, it was already gone—it just vanished into thin air. So I returned with only one donkey, saying:

"I left the other in Sicuani."

So I went back looking for the donkey, asking around while going down one trail after another. Back then there were lots of donkeys, and everyone used them because there weren't any cars or trucks, not a single one; nobody even knew about them. While I was searching around near San Pablo, I ran into a *misti*. So that misti asked me:

"Hey, boy! Where are you going?"

"I lost my donkey, and I'm trying to find it," I said.

"Your donkey's got to be long gone! They've probably already hidden it. So then, where will you go now?"

"Well, with the donkey vanishing as if swallowed by the earth, I won't be going back home," I answered.

"Come with me and herd horses," he told me.

So I followed behind this misti and his horse. I don't remember his name because the very next day he handed me over to another misti in Maranganí. The very same morning, there in the house of that other misti, they told me:

"Run along and tend the sheep."

So I was back to being a shepherd. While driving the sheep up to the mountain pastures, I made friends with other shepherd boys, and we'd play around while the sheep were grazing; we made rag balls to kick around, and from the thick branches of the chachacomo tree we'd make spinning tops. I don't know why it is, but even today I just can't stop the habit I have of falling asleep wherever I sit; I've been like that ever since I was a kid. Well, sometimes I'd be playing or sleeping while the little lambs were grazing there in the pastures, and they'd get hurt or a fox would eat them. So one day my master told me:

"You're going to finish off my sheep. Just get out of here; I don't need you anymore. Why would I need someone who's going to finish off my animals?"

He'd given me new clothes before. Now he stripped me of these and handed me back my old tattered ones, saying:

"Beat it! Hit the road!"

And just like that, he kicked me out of his house. So that whole day I walked up and down the streets of Maranganí crying. In the end, I went to the house of that first misti, the one who'd handed me over, telling him:

"That's what happened to me."

While living there at this misti's house, I also herded sheep. This one had burros, sheep, and cows, but now I wouldn't drive the animals from mountain to mountain. He had his own cattle pens and rich pasturelands,[24] and that's where I tended the cattle. I really don't know how, but one day a lamb disappeared. And so, with no compassion whatsoever, he threw me out, saying:

"You shifty little good-for-nothing—out, dammit!"

So I walked up the big trail sobbing, and I came to the house of Leandro Cutipa in the village of Ttiobamba, up past Maranganí. He was one of us—a villager, not a misti[25]—and I stayed on with him there, once again as a shepherd. In that house, I also had to tend the sheep. I was there about a year. Now that I'd grown up a bit, they'd send me away for weeks at a time to work as a manor servant for the priest of Maranganí. In the country towns back then, the townfolk would have to take turns serving the priests. And this was done by the stewards, those runas who were just beginning their religious *cargo* obligations.[26] Well, that didn't suit me, so, without saying a word, I quietly slipped away to the town of San Pablo and the house of Mrs. Agueda Palomino, who was childless and had no cattle. Each day I'd go to the mountains for firewood and to the pasturelands there to gather dung. But those lands belonged to the hacienda owner, and they'd stop me from collecting dung and firewood from the mountains. Since I was older and more wily by that time, I'd have to fight for each piece of kindling or dung those ass-licking overseers tried to take from me. So one day Zavaleta, the hacienda owner himself, seized my nice poncho for gathering firewood in Onocora. So I returned empty handed, saying:

"They took it all."

All was fine there in that house, until I set to thinking with that donkey brain of mine; I told Mrs. Agueda:

"Mama, I'm going to go sell pots at the Lord of Huanca's shrine." [27]

And so I set out for the shrine, hauling the pots on my master's donkey and on another one I rented. I'd bought the pots in San Pedro and was taking them to barter for valley corn. For each pot, they'd give me half a pot of corn. It didn't matter whether the pot was large or small, it was always half a pot of corn. This was common knowledge, and nobody used money to buy things, not even pots. Everything was bartered for food.

Some three or four years ago, I returned to that shrine with my wife. It's not like it used to be in the old days, when people would also come down from the high country, from as far away as Puno Lake,[28] with hundreds and hundreds of llamas, horses, and burros. Nowadays the Lord of Huanca's shrine is scary and enough to make you crazy. Everything is money, money, money, and the cars and trucks swarm there like ants.[29]

The very day I arrived at the shrine market, I traded all the pots. The donkeys were feeding beside the horses and llamas of another pot trader, a villager from the Sicuani area. While the little donkeys were all herded together and feeding there peacefully, I separated mine out from the others and took them over to drink some water. Just past the Lord of Huanca's chapel, there are four craggy outcroppings, and at the foot of these, springs come gushing out of Earth Mother.[30] The water of the first spring belongs to our good mother, the Virgin Mary. When you drink her water, you become a better Christian, and it also heals the weariness of the elders. The second spring is that of Saint Isidore the Farmhand.[31] His water is blessed and is taken away in jugs and bottles, and then it's poured into the mouths of the mountain springs. When this is done, the spring water doesn't dry up; the same amount keeps flowing to the fields, even during a drought.[32] The water of the third spring is that of the Archangel. This water is for children, and when they drink it, it kills their worms and cures their mange. The last spring has the most water by far and belongs to the devilish demon.[33] You mustn't drink this water because it's bewitched. They say that only witches drink from it, and they do that to cast their evil spells.[34]

Well, like any trader from Sicuani who carries his wares by burro, I wanted my little burros to drink the good mother's water, that of the Virgin Mary, so they'd turn Christian and bring luck to the goods they carried. But soon after, the burros came down with a fever, and that was a sign, a bad omen—I wasn't meant to be a trader. So, together with the other villager, I bathed the burros, and we tried as hard as we could to cure them and keep them from dying. But damn if those Christians didn't die anyway. The Lord of Huanca broke my heart that day, killing my donkeys while they were right there beside him. Weeping about my bad luck, my heart drained dry, I started back toward Sicuani, hauling the dead donkeys' saddle pads; then I stayed in Cay-Cay. Since the burros were dead, there was no corn. And how could I return home empty handed? So I stayed on there in Cay-Cay at the house of a misti baker who baked bread twice weekly; I'd help him with the bread. That misti was a good Christian and didn't beat me, but he was a total miser; even though we baked bread twice a week, I ate bread only two or three times during my whole stay there in his house. One day, since the road from Sicuani to Cuzco passes through Cay-Cay, I found myself face to face with my master, Mrs. Agueda's husband, and straightaway he demanded:

"Where's the donkeys? What've you done with them, you slippery little good-for-nothing?"

And I said:

"They died of fever, but those are their saddle pads over there."

So the same day we just happened to run into each other, he took me on back to Sicuani. There in Sicuani, I worked some two years to pay off the dead burros.

Mrs. Agueda had a little sister, and by that time I was a young man. This little sister of hers was called Justinacha, and we used to see each other regularly, talking and making plans together—she was like my girlfriend. Sometimes she'd say to me:

"Take me."

And I'd ask her:

"Where?"

She'd answer:

"You know, to the fields, silly."

So we'd talk while walking through the fields together, and now that we'd gotten to know each other, our bodies came together.

I didn't stay in that house the whole two years my master ordered me to. With two or three months left to pay off the burros, I disappeared. I'd always wanted to go back to Acopía. Although it's true I had no mother or father, I did have some uncles there I wanted to visit. The idea of returning to Acopía ripened in my heart, year after year. I was a young man by this time, and none of my uncles recognized me when I arrived there. I wasn't able to recognize them either, and I didn't even know how many I still had left, but I was hoping they'd still recognize me anyways. So, starting at daybreak, I spent the whole day sitting in front of the old cross in the town square, hoping they'd recognize me. But people just kept passing me by, some saying:

"There's a stranger sitting next to the cross."

I didn't budge the whole day—I just sat there. Later, when the cattle were coming back from grazing in their pastures, I was still just sitting there. Then a villager driving a flock of sheep passed by. He asked me:

"You're still sitting here, young man?"

"Yes, Papa. I'm waiting for one of my uncles to come by and recognize me. My name is Gregorio Condori Mamani, and I'm the son of the late Doroteo Condori Mamani."

That wasn't my father's name, but the only one of my uncles' names I could still remember.

"Oh, Papa Doroteo hasn't passed away yet! He's my compadre, but now he's in the Yanaoca jail. Come on then, let's go to my house."

Once there in his house, I learned that my uncle Doroteo and some friends of his had made off with a bunch of llamas from the village of Totora in Livitaca. They mustn't have been able to cross over the mountains with their llamas because they got caught red-handed near the earth shrine there at Wamani Pass.[35] That's why my uncle was in jail.

When I arrived in Acopía, the harvest season had already begun, and many hands were needed. At first I harvested potatoes, going from field to field. Payment wasn't in money; for one day's help, you'd get a satchel of potatoes, *lisas*, or *ocas*. So I worked hard throughout the harvest and got together enough potatoes to fill a bin. When the harvest was over, a fellow villager said:

"Stay at my house; all you'll have to do is help me tend the sheep."

So I said:

"All right."

Once again I was a shepherd, and the very next day I took the sheep up to a herd stead in the high pastures. And that herd stead was just a little hut on a mountainside. I lived there all by myself, together with three dogs. Since there was no drinking water there at the herd stead, I'd have to go half a league to get water each day, either in the morning or afternoon.[36] From the very moment the sun's rays first crackled on the mountaintops, I'd start cooking, using one little pot for me and my dogs; I'd do that every morning and afternoon. And during the day, I'd gather firewood while herding the sheep. I stayed there at that herd stead till my master, who was a fellow villager of mine, forgot all about me. In the beginning, he or someone else would at least bring me a little food. And besides being stingy, he was a drunk. One day, sometime after my master had forgot all about me, one of his own people asked me to go away with him.[37] And so, while wandering from one house to another, they grabbed me for the military reserves.

☐

TWO

AEROPLANES AND OTHER BEASTS

☐

When I was still just a little fledgling, living there in the village of Arisa, an aeroplane—those they now call "plane"—came by high above.[1] People had already been talking about that: humans will travel on high, up on top of the wind. But how were we going to see humans traveling on top of the wind? We weren't going to see that! Just like today when they announce on the radio or in newspaper publications, that "Such and such will happen," or "This will come to pass," back then, news used to spread by word of mouth: "Humans are going to travel by trotting on the wind."[2] While they were talking like this, that big beast, the aeroplane, arrived. And when the aeroplane came, people said:

"Oh, Lord! What kind of beast have you sent us!"

They'd throw libations to the wind, using the fermented urine they wash hair with, or they'd chew up garlic and spit it out:

"Ptu! Ptu! Bad omen! What kind of Christian is this?"

One day during the threshing season, when some two or three hundred of us were working behind Mount Silkincha, a huge bird that looked like a condor, and which was shrieking like one of the damned, suddenly appeared. All of us working there threshing got scared. And right then, I remembered what Uncle Gumercindo once told me: that a few days before the end of this world, a messenger eagle with a condor's head and llama feet will come and forewarn us runas, we the Inka's kinfolk, to be waiting ready for the end of this world.[3] And my uncle also said:

"*Inkarí* has been living in the underworld ever since Pizarro the priest killed him. And the day this world ends, he'll emerge and join all the runas."

So when the aeroplane came veering in our direction, people said:

"It's a divine miracle coming toward us."[4]

And they quickly knelt down and prayed:

"Oh, Lord, you've arrived at last!"

When I saw that it was truly veering toward us, I was thinking, "This must be a divine miracle." We were all kneeling down and praying to the divine aeroplane. So, I too, from the bottom of my heart, said, "Oh, Lord, I'm no sinner—I've always helped my elders work their fields." While I was saying this, the aeroplane passed overhead, roaring loudly. And so the aeroplane just passed on by without coming down to us, and all of us there praying, and others confessing their sins, fell silent and watched it disappear as it headed down toward Sicuani. Then the diviner, Machaca, said:[5]

"It's going to come down in Sicuani; let's go see what it has to say and why it has come."

So a few people rushed off to Sicuani, and the rest of us returned to threshing the grain. Back then, the aeroplane was the talk of the town. They were saying, "Enrique Rondán is the driver."[6] Even villagers from the high mountain reaches came down to ask if a miracle had truly passed overhead.

And some time ago, people used to talk about the train the same way they did about the plane. But I still hadn't seen it back then, I'd only heard people talking about it:

"Train, train, what's it like?!"

"It slithers along like a worm."

And others would say:

"It's a black beast, like a big snake made of pure iron, and to keep moving it has to open its mouth—that's where the fire is."

When the train first appeared, there were also songs like this one:[7]

> Where, old smoky, are you now?
> you're passing Santa Rosa
> my pushcart
> you're passing Kisa-Kisa.
>
> If now, Rosalina
> you don't love me
> if now, Rosalina
> you won't have me
> may old smoky swallow me whole.

All anybody talked about was the train. So my curiosity grew and grew. Some time later when I was a young man, I saw a train in Sicuani. I didn't get scared when I saw it, but I did almost begin to scream. It was black just like they'd said, and when it moved, it looked just like a worm. I was really impressed at the time by the huge amount of freight it could pull. On just one of its flatcars, it was carrying hundreds of cases of Martínez liquor.

The first time I saw a car in San Pedro was the same. That car was just a tiny little truck used for hauling things. Because, back in those days, people traveled only by foot or on mules, horses, and burros; those who traveled by car had everybody talking:

"Sure, they've got money, they're rich—that's why they travel by car."

That's how they were regarded, and that's why people didn't want to travel by car.

☐

THREE

MILITARY TRICKS

☐

Some months before they picked me up for the military reserves, I'd been wanting to leave Acopía and go find work somewhere else. And one day, when I'd already decided to leave, I ran into Uncle Doroteo's wife on the road outside Acopía; who knows what we were talking about, but, as we parted, I told her:

"Auntie, with a little luck I'll be leaving, and we may not see each other again."[1]

Since by now I was a mature young man ready for a wife, and I was already nosing around the women there, she told me:

"Stay in the village, together with us here in the family.[2] We'll help you get some land, and we'll find you a wife."

So I said:

"All right."

The woman they had their eye on was named Laureana. But her parents were wealthy and had lots of land and cattle.

From the day they pointed her out to me, I'd go help her family each time they'd work their fields, so we could get to know each other and I could woo her. So I kept hovering around her, and my side approached them on my behalf, saying that I was a hard worker and that I wanted her as my wife. But she didn't want to. Instead, she and her parents insulted me:

"What kind of holdings could this nameless wisp of wind have? My daughter's not interested in the lice this unknown drifter has got stockpiled away."

That's what they said. And from that day on, they were mad at me and never let me work their fields again. All this happened right before they grabbed me for the military reserves; you couldn't get out of it because everywhere you went they'd be asking for the slip of paper given to all the reservists, and that way they'd know whether you'd already been drafted or not. Being a reservist meant doing drills and marching "one, two, three." The drills consisted of running, jumping up and down, and carrying wooden poles we pretended were guns. Our trainer was a retired sergeant named Layme. He'd separate us into two divisions: one division would be the Peruvians and the other the Chileans. So every Sunday after finishing our drills, we'd fight till we were bloody, just like soldiers at war. It was too much fighting, and if the Chileans beat us, we'd get punished. The same thing if you didn't go to Sunday drills: you'd get thrown into the governor's jail and fined a day's work in the governor's fields. In those battles, we'd always have to beat the Chileans, and if we didn't, there'd be punishment or fines. So one Sunday as we were doing our usual drills, we saw some policemen coming from Combapata;[3] then, by a trick, they forced all of us reservists to become soldiers.

Sergeant Layme made us line up. While we were falling into line, the policemen suddenly appeared with their guns trained on us—all I could say was:

"Oh damn! These must be the Chileans. Let's get out of here!"

These last words shot from my mouth, but nobody moved—we were all scared, because this time they weren't wooden poles but real guns. That's how we reservists became soldiers. I was drafted during the time of Sánchez Cerro, and he ordered the army to war.[4] There was going to be war on the border. The reason for this war, they said, was:

"*Recapture Tacna-Arica.*"[5]

The Chileans had grabbed hold of Tacna-Arica, declaring war way back in those distant times of Christopher Columbus. That's how they'd grabbed hold of the Tacna-Arica border. Even now, Tacna-Arica doesn't belong to our country. If Sánchez Cerro hadn't thought of making a road through the underworld to catch his Chilean enemies, Earth Shade wouldn't have swallowed him up, and he would've kept on waging war over Tacna-Arica.[6] But we, too, would've died there at the border. During that war, they say the Chileans tried to make it all the way to Cuzco because there were few Peruvian soldiers. So the Chileans were advancing up the coast of the sea lake.[7] Then, who knows how San Martín's fellow comrades thought this up in order to send the Chilean enemies fleeing,[8] but since there were so few Peruvian soldiers, they gathered together hundreds of llama flocks and tied a mirror to each llama's forehead. That's how, after comrade San Martín had already died, we won the war. The llamas' mirrors were shimmering brightly, and as they advanced, they kicked up a cloud of dust that settled over the mountains—the Chileans were frightened and said:

"Oh! So many people! The Peruvian battalion is screaming down like a thundering avalanche."

When you see a herd of llamas from a distance, they look like people walking, and that's no doubt why the Chileans took them to be a battalion. The llamas are the reason the Peruvians won the war. That's why the figure of the llama is a charmed amulet used on coins and matchboxes.[9]

Sánchez Cerro snatched the presidency away from Leguía. In Spain, Sánchez Cerro had said:

"I'm going to be the Government."

And in Spain they gave him an aeroplane as a present so he could come to Lima. But in Spain they'd asked him:

"Are you still sure you're really going to become president? Will you be president?"

"Yes, I'm sure I will," he answered.

So after Augusto Leguía had been the Government for ten years, Sánchez Cerro snatched the presidency from him.

FOUR

EARTH MOTHER, CROPKEEPER, AND THE THREE BROTHERS

Before I went away and became a soldier, I'd go work the fields with all the young men in town. Out there no one can miss even a single day of working the fields—you just can't do it. You can neglect your wife and even forget all about her, but never the land, never Earth Mother. If you forget about Earth Mother, she'll forget about you too. That's the way it is when you till the soil. You'd have to plant the crops, and after the sowing you'd have to weed and shore up the plants. And during the harvest, you'd have to be bustling all over the place, because that's when you really need the help of many people. You'd have to lend a hand to your kinfolk and villager friends, from one day to several weeks of work, and then they'd also come work for you when you needed them. All you had to do was inform them ahead of time:

"Brother so-and-so, we'll work the fields on such and such day."

"No problem. Where?"

And then you'd just tell them which of your fields needed work.

That's the only contract there used to be.

And they'd come help you. Payment was never in money, whether it was you helping them or them helping you. It was done through exchange, by trading labor in ayni.[1] Ever since I first came here to Cuzco, I've seen little ayni. When country villagers like us come here, they forget about this way of helping each other. Many times I've asked my wife and other neighbors:

"Why don't we do ayni? That way our homes wouldn't be such rat holes."

Only a few of us fellow villagers, among family and friends, help each other out by working together in ayni. If we'd all swap our labor, these houses wouldn't be the way they are, like houses of the damned. It must be that once all those villagers come live here in Cuzco, that custom no longer lives in their hearts. That's why here in the shanty towns they work only for money—and there's no ayni.

The fields aren't the only place where people trade ayni favors, it's used in everything: when you get married they help you in ayni, and when someone in your family dies, they'll lend their help for the burial. If you don't have a horse or a donkey to haul your potato harvest from the fields to your bin, the only way they'll get lent to you is through ayni. But one thing's for sure, you have to return each ayni you've received with all your heart. If you've got draft animals and your relatives or friends need them, you've got to lend them out. And if you don't have horses, burros, or other beasts of burden to haul manure, you won't be able to work your fields. Tell me, how are you going to do this if you don't have draft animals to carry your seed and manure? And you also need cattle to shit manure, because if there aren't any cattle to shit manure, there's no way you'll have anything to haul at planting or harvesting time. So no matter what, if you want to get manure and draft animals, you have to help the people who own beasts of burden. That's why the people who own those animals are able to work lots of land, while the poor, in order to get manure or draft animals, have to go help them. People without draft animals who want to work a plot of land in one of the *laymi* sectors, or some years in two of these communal fields, can't work much land unless they give many days of help to the people with animals.[2]

It's a lot of work to plant in two laymis. But that was only done when the Fieldmaster, reading coca leaves or the stars, decided there'd be two sectors.[3] When the coca leaves or stars foretold bad luck or a bad omen, it meant frost or hail, and when the Fieldmaster said, "It's frost," one sector would be sown in advance and another later on.

It wasn't just anybody who could do this, and the Fieldmaster was also the only one who could begin the sowing. But he couldn't begin on just any old day. The first sowing had to always be on a Tuesday, Thursday, or Friday— those are the days when Earth Mother is flush with life. She's just like a woman: it makes her happy when you do it at just the right moment, right when she wants it. So Earth Mother wants seed only on those days and not on the other ones, which are barren. The same thing would happen when the Fieldmaster said, "It's hail."[4]

There were two laymis and in each of these, potatoes were sown in many places, never in just one spot. Because when hail comes sweeping through, it cuts a path in a straight line or zigzags around, and the crops along the edges are the only ones saved.

The poor villagers in town also bear these woes. Sure, those villagers who have lots of draft animals will help you if you're friend or family, but you must always help them in return. They work many fields, have good harvests, and are rich, because lots of villagers come help them in order to borrow their animals. If you want to haul manure to plant your crops and want to bring in your harvest, you must always lend your labor in ayni.

And in the rainy season, you also have to help them tend their sheep and llamas, watching out for thieves and foxes at night; those foxes are wily, coming in to steal your little lambs on the very nights when it rains or snows. For your help, they pay you in meat or with wool to make twilled flannel.

So I also used to tend a compadre's sheep, and at night I'd look after his cattle. He'd pay me in wool for all my help. One time, for a month of herding, he paid me with the wool shorn from a sheep. Another time, to get some meat, I slept over and helped out in their home, and for three months' help, they paid me a lamb that had died. And I ate that meat with my godmother on Carnival Tuesday.

Such is life for the runa peasant:[5] if you don't have a lot of kinfolk, you suffer, and then you're always having to exchange or sell your labor in ayni or mink'a. When you swap ayni favors, you have to put your heart into it, and when they come help you, you've got to treat them right. If there isn't any warmth in your house, few people will come help you, because some villagers go work the fields just so they can drink cornbeer and liquor. That's why being the host of a work party in the fields is a lot like sponsoring a small cargo.[6] It's expensive: for one day's work in the harvest, you'd have to give a bundle of potatoes to each villager who came by and helped you, that is, if the help they were giving you wasn't in ayni. A lot of people are needed during the harvest. If you were working fields in both laymi sectors, you needed even more workers. But usually just one laymi was being worked at a time, and only occasionally were there two.

Each year on Carnival Monday, a Cropkeeper was chosen,[7] and it was like taking on a cargo that lasted the whole year. The Cropkeeper had to watch over the potato patches, protecting them from hail, pests, and frost. To do so, he'd build a small hut on a hill near the potato fields. And he'd have to stay there, watching the sky, every single day of the rainy season. If dark clouds filled the sky, it was sure to hail, and the Cropkeeper would be in his little hut, praying; it's said that Saint Ciprian's prayers make the hail go away.[8] He'd also burn incense and dried onions, and he'd fling libations of kerosene and holy water towards the patches where the black clouds were about to let loose. If the hail still seemed bent on destroying the potatoes, the Cropkeeper would quickly strip, and, naked as the day he came out of his mother's womb, he'd insult the hail, slinging dirt clods sprinkled with the holy water and kerosene toward it.

It's said that three brothers, who are always together, travel in the hail. First, there's Birnaku; he's the most boisterous of them all, always thundering up and down and making a racket. That's the lightning bolt—but he only threatens you.[9] After him comes Elaku, and he's not so bad. When you insult him with Saint Ciprian's prayers, casting kerosene and holy water toward him, he always flees—the kerosene and holy water burn his eyes like chili peppers. The last of the brothers, the baby of the family, is Chanaku, and he's the craziest of them all;[10] he doesn't heed anyone, and he'll strip and glean the fields of everything. When he enters the fields, he steals it all, taking the potatoes, broad beans, and the rest of the crops. He carries off their life spirit. And what's left to harvest if the crops have been stripped of their spirit?

One has to watch out for those wicked ones because they're real thieves. If the Cropkeeper isn't on guard or paying attention when they show up, they can take all the crops, and the village is left with nothing to harvest. That's why, when it was a good year with a big harvest, the Cropkeeper would get a furrow of potatoes from each field, and nobody would complain. He could choose any furrow, large or small, of potatoes, lisas, or ocas. It was up to him, and he'd stock away plenty of seed that way. But if the hail or frost caused a bad harvest, they'd insult the poor Cropkeeper. They'd say:

"You damn dog! Aren't you man enough? While you were stuck there between your wife's legs, it was hailing. Where's the potatoes, dammit?!"

Then on Carnival Tuesday, nobody would treat him to food or drink. But if it had been a good harvest, they'd get him drunk for sure. Those Cropkeepers were always young, recently married men, those who'd just taken up with a woman. Of course, they'd have to be young and very strong to battle the hail in a sling fight. The hail would sling down a lightning bolt, and the Cropkeeper, between insults, would answer back with his sling. When the Cropkeeper was real wily, the hail wouldn't feel like coming in and stealing.

That's the way those three brothers are, always traveling together wherever they go. Their mother is the snow,[11] a white-haired, little old lady with a wrinkled face who's always sitting down. They say that beneath her eyes, there are two furrows that run down her cheeks like irrigation ditches, and bits of sleep drip from her eyes day and night. This constant flow of sleep is the snow melting on the sacred mountains.

One time, I've heard told, a traveler from the village of Pinchimuro was walking through the tall, silent prairie grass of the high plains. The rain started to beat down as he moved through the rushes, and a dark, gloomy night quickly fell upon him. He kept on walking, and then, in the distance, he saw a small light; so he took heart, saying to himself:

"There's a herd stead over there; that's where I'll stay."

So he approached the herd stead. But it wasn't a herder's house, only a useless little tumbledown storeroom with no corral or barking dogs. And when he went to ask for lodging, out came a little old lady whose head was buried beneath her white hair. The traveler said:

"Please, ma'am, put me up for the night."[12]

And the little old lady answered:

"I can't put you up. My children are raving mad, and they'd surely kill you."

The traveler begged her:

"But, ma'am, where will I go now? Please put me up!"

So, with his pleading, the little old lady let him into her house.

"All right, you can stay over there," she said, pointing to a corner. "I'll cover you up with this clay basin—you keep completely still."[13]

So it was.

But it kept raining outside, and soon a huge thunder and lightning storm, strong enough to blow the house to pieces, let loose. Then, right at the doorway, lightning bolts thundered down even harder: "Crack Crack! Boom Boom!" In the midst of thunderclaps and lightning, a man entered the house—it was the snow's eldest child. And soon afterward, again in a flash of lightning, another of her sons arrived; he was cursing angrily. Then even more thunder came down, and between lightning bolts, Chanaku entered the house, grumbling and bitching:

"That fucking so-and-so was dousing me with his little kerosene libations. But damn, I still went and sacked the place!"

The man he mentioned was the Cropkeeper from the traveler's village.

And through a hole in the basin, he saw many mules laden down with potatoes and broad beans, and the ropes tying up the mules were yellow snakes, alive and writhing. The traveler then fell fast asleep. When he awoke, it'd been daylight for some time, and the house he'd been staying at was no longer there—he was sleeping alongside a lake.

The hail's home is Mother Lake.[14] Everything those three brothers steal is there: potatoes, beans, corn. All the best stuff is piled up there, just like a storehouse, and at midnight during a full moon on Saint John's Eve, you can see it.

And when those runas who've been struck and killed by lightning arrive to the otherworld, they turn into the hail's servants.[15] There in the otherworld they spend their whole lives with the hail's loot, loading and unloading the mules. And though these laborers also live there with food piled up around them, they're cursed by the people. Because when there's nothing left to harvest, is there any village that doesn't curse the hail?

◻

THE BARRACKS

◻

When they killed President Sánchez Cerro, Benavides received the Government.[1] I became a soldier during Benavides' time, back when they brought me in as a recruit from my town Acopía. I was stationed at Maruripampa Garrison for three whole years. And during my time as a soldier in the army, I was in Machine Gunners, Third Company. I was a mule driver. My mule's name was Renounceable, and I'd have to take her with me wherever I went, on long-distance marches where we'd rest up every league or so; whether I lived or died, that little mule had to be right there beside me. There used to be mule rations for the mules to feed on. They'd hang sacks from their necks and give them barley grain to eat. During those campaigns, I'd always be with my little mule, morning, noon, and night—we were inseparable. There were loaders for each mule, and they'd pack them up. But I also had to take care of mine, cleaning its hooves as well as the sleep from its eyes; I'd also have to wash off its snot with a little rag, clean its butt with water, and then groom it. Those were my mule duties. The loaders also put on the saddles. In the army I used to handle a Mauser rifle. During my first months there, I used one of the original Mausers. Later came the tiny little mosquito rifles; the helmets arrived with them. We just used little field caps back then. There weren't boots or anything else—we'd just use a wide strip of cloth, like a waistband, to wrap each of our calves.

There inside the barracks,[2] stealing is everything—they'd steal leggings, shoes, buttons, any old thing. Then, when something of yours was missing, they'd tell you:

"I've got one I can sell you. I'll sell it to you for just seventy *centavos*."

When what they were offering was already yours.

We soldiers also had our mess packs rationed to us. They'd steal the knives, spoons, and forks you'd been rationed. All your utensils. So there'd be nothing to eat your mess hall meals with. Without those things, you couldn't have any grub, and you'd just have to forget about eating. Because you'd enter the mess hall by company. When utensils were missing, they'd blame the garrison watchman, saying:

"Why weren't you keeping an eye on the utensils?"

One time they also stole my jacket and shoes from me.

There inside the barracks, stealing is everything; you can't be there without stealing—stealing is everything—they'll even steal your little sewing needle from you. Here on the outside, they're not so bad. But there on the inside, they're always stealing from you: your shoes, your cap, your penknife. If they weren't stealing your jacket, they'd be cutting the buttons off your coat. It was real annoying because then you'd have to buy back or steal the things you were missing. When you're a soldier, you can't be missing a thing; you're just like a tailor with your needle, thread, and everything for sewing all ready to go. And if you were missing something, they'd take you off to the dispensary and give you the things you needed against your cash allowance, docking it later from this allowance.

In the barracks, everyone was always stealing from one another. It was the custom. But what I don't know is how the heck they'd get it out of there. Those things would disappear from our hall at night while we were sleeping. I think they must've cut a deal with the watchman to get the things out. If the army sweater they'd given you disappeared, they'd also dock it from your allowance. And when your day off arrived, there'd be no allowance left. Sometimes just a single one of your shoes would disappear. And damn, they'd do that just to fuck with you; it was also taken out of your allowance, because they'd have to give you another one the same size. On my days off, I'd hear people in the streets cry out:

"Thief! Thief!"

But compared to the barracks, that wasn't really stealing because there on the inside everything gets stolen—they wouldn't leave you a thing. You weren't even able to sleep, because you'd have to go to bed clutching onto your things so they wouldn't steal them from you. But later, you'd take your Sunday leave and meet up with your friends and fellow villagers in the street. They'd say to you:

"How are you doing? We didn't come just to visit. Come on, let's go drink some cornbeer."

And so they'd take you off to drink cornbeer, which didn't cost too much back then; a glass was ten centavos. Sometimes after firing practice, we could leave at midweek, but only if we had good scores. They'd give us our leave with twenty or twenty-five points. I always shot a twenty in firing practice. We did this up on Rodadero pampa. We couldn't wait for our Sunday leave to arrive.

We'd go out strolling with our sweethearts and cook meals with them because those mess hall meals aren't tasty like the ones here on the outside. In there the food is fit for dogs; they'd throw lots of salt in the water, which wasn't good for you. When I was a soldier, I had a girlfriend named Elenacha who was from Pomacanchi. Back then, kitchen maids wouldn't get their Sundays off like they do now; they'd be serving their masters day and night without a break. Who knows how she did it, but every Sunday she'd somehow get away and be there waiting for me at the entry to the barracks. When I was a soldier, I had another one besides Elena, because women would be standing around and waiting there at the entryway for their boyfriends, brothers, and fellow villagers. That's where we'd get to know each other.

After the flag raising on Sunday, we could go out till ten at night. But if you stayed out past that hour, you'd get severely punished. They'd take away your allowance or lock you up in the stockade. There was also another punishment: they'd take away your Sunday leave for a whole month. That's how they'd punish you if you came in late or if you got drunk and lipped off to the police, or if you tried to pick a fight with the noncommissioned officers. All those things were severely punished.

The noncommissioned officers, the corporals and sergeants, were just like judges; the second sergeant was in charge, but the first sergeant was like our father. He'd know if your clothes were spent or not, and when your shoes got old, he'd have them give you others. They'd replace your shoes every seven months. If your jacket, sweater, or pants got worn out, he'd have them give you others; that's why we had to show him our clothes and pass inspection. He'd say:

"Indians, fall in! All of you! Off with your underwear!"

You'd have to completely strip down. Then another corporal or sergeant would come and jot down:

"So-and-so: clothes worn out."

You had to show the sergeants and corporals the same respect as you would your own parents—you couldn't mess around with them. Your leggings had to be tied on properly, and your jacket couldn't be torn or missing its buttons. Everything had to pass inspection. If your jacket was torn—then "Rip! Rip!"— they'd tear it up some more, saying:

"Dammit, why the hell haven't you sewn this? No-good, fucking Indian!"

That's why you'd have to buy buttons, needles, thread, and shoe polish, and you'd also have a toothbrush for cleaning your teeth. You also had to have three clean hankies: one for dancing with your girlfriend,[3] another to lend her if she'd forgotten her own, and another to blow your nose with. There also used to be wool socks. We never wore foreign socks like they do now.

Such was the soldier's life. No matter what you did there, you had to live and die at your post. If you were a sharpshooter or commissary, you'd have to do everything by the book, or damn, they'd give you a swift kick. In the army, discipline is everything: "*Serve country, obey all orders.*" You can't refuse to do anything they tell you to. If you say no or do it halfheartedly, they punish you with jail time or give you a beating. Even if they order you to kill your own mother, well, you've just got to do it because if you don't, you're not obeying your country. There's also an alphabet in the barracks for those who can't read; the wood-block letters are strung up on a wire: *a, b, c, d, j, k, p.* The non-commissioned officers would teach us the alphabet, and when you finished learning it, they'd put you in first grade. When you first entered the army, they'd ask:

"Do you know how to read?"

If you said, "No, I don't," the sergeants and second lieutenants would bring out those letters and make you learn them. Alphabet practice was always after lunch. After alphabet practice, we'd have to brush our mules and sweep up; that was all done in the afternoon. But in the mornings, we'd have to shine the mules' hooves with animal fat the same way we shined our own shoes with shoe polish.

You'd be punished if you didn't get a good score in firing practice. They'd load you down with two rifles and a full pack and make you stand on top of a bench for three or four hours. There was another punishment if you were caught fighting. Those little corporals would pick on you, and when you couldn't take it anymore, your heart aching with pain, you'd have to fight back. Those little corporals would tell you:

"*Stand to, dammit! Dammit, stand to!*"

Then they'd kick you, and your heart would boil over with anger. So you'd tell them:

"Just you wait, dammit. Someday we'll both be out of here. We're just passing through. When we get out of here, I'm going to kill you, dammit!"

What's more, those fellow soldiers of mine were all Indian runas just like me, because there weren't any mistis.[4] They'd be real fuckers when they got promoted to corporal or noncommissioned officer. There inside the barracks, they were just like God himself. And later on at night, we couldn't go to sleep like you normally do, because they'd make us line up outside, and when we were all lined up, they'd tell us:

"*The last four there: this week's sergeant duty . . .*"

So we'd all run off, trampling one another. Then we'd have to instantly undress, and once undressed, right away we'd have to get dressed again. That's why you had to have everything ready beforehand. Your shoes had to be all ready to go, shoelaces already undone. After doing that, we'd have to sleep without moving, our clothes bunched up beside us. If you moved at all, they'd get you up, and you'd have to instantly get dressed and take the reserve watch from ten to twelve. And later on, another relief would come and stay till dawn. It was real boring just standing there, all cold and sleepy, guarding the gate or the tower. I used to ask:

"Why, dammit, does this have to be so carefully guarded? What thieves are ever going to come in here? Instead we should be guarding our own clothes so they don't get stolen so much."

I said that to my friend while we were on watch one night around Independence Day.[5] He replied:

"Gregorio, don't be a dumb ass. The sergeant says the Chileans are on their way to Lima and want to make war in Cuzco because they crave the women here."

And I said:

"So we're going to war over those bitches?[6] Well not me, dammit—I for one am not letting go of my mule."

They wouldn't let you sleep there in the quarters. You'd be in a sweet slumber, and they'd come wake you up and take you off to relieve someone else. And if you weren't doing relief watch at two or four in the morning, they'd have you sweeping the halls and stables. They'd make you sweep just for the hell of it.

When they got promoted to corporal or noncommissioned officer, damn, their feet no longer touched the ground. They'd look down on the common soldier as if he was a dog.

Our Sunday leave allowance each week was two *soles* and fifty centavos. One time they punished me, docking my allowance for a whole month, all because of a little corporal who was always picking on me. So I went and got drunk with some soldier friends of mine, and when I came back real late and totally drunk, I started cursing and chasing that little corporal of mine, wanting to beat him up. I tell you, I really wanted to kill him.

I think that nowadays, life in the army is very easy. Because it's not like in the past when you'd have to be wrapping your legs with strips of cloth, walking to the war drills with a mule dragging behind you . . .

They taught me the alphabet there in the army. I was able to sign my name, and—*a, o, i, p*—I could also recognize some letters of the alphabet on paper. But I didn't have the brains for the alphabet, and I just couldn't learn it. Soon after leaving the army, I forgot how to read the letters I'd learned or how to spell my name. They say that nowadays, whoever enters the army unable to see, comes out with their eyes open and knowing how to read. And those unable to speak also come out with Spanish flowing off their tongues.[7]

So it was. You'd enter the army sightless, and sightless you'd leave because you'd never really get the alphabet right. And just the same, you'd be unable to speak when you entered and unable to speak when you left, Spanish barely dribbling off your tongue. There in the army, those lieutenants and captains didn't want us speaking the runa tongue.[8] They'd say:

"Dammit, Indians! Spanish!"

So the noncommissioned officers would beat Spanish into us.

☐

SIX

"THE ARMY ISN'T CHRISTIAN"

☐

After I was recruited, they brought me by train from Combapata to the Saphi station, and from there they transferred me to Maruri Garrison. And there they examined my whole body: my mouth, nose, eyes, ears, and even my penis. Then they told me:

"Damn good cholo! You pass."[1]

They took away my clothes and gave me an army uniform to put on: jacket, sweater, shoes, and a rucksack.

The day after I became a soldier, we went up above Saqsaywaman to do drills. There they taught us how to march. If we couldn't do it right, they'd hit and kick us. There at the beginning, it was nothing but misery, pure punishment.

I'd been in the reserves before entering the army, so I already knew the drills, and it was easy for me. I wouldn't get beaten as much as the ones who'd just arrived. They'd really get beaten up. Our first corporal's name was Calle, and he taught us how to march and do drills. He was a heartless dog. If he's dead now, I doubt he's under God our Father's sheltering gaze. He must be one of the damned, a suffering soul wandering inside Qurupuna Mountain.[2] Never in my life have I seen anyone who enjoyed hitting people as much as Calle, that little army corporal. When my fellow soldiers weren't able do the drills, that dirty mutt would kick them till they pissed blood, dammit. Damn but he was a dirty dog—he made my blood boil.

I didn't get promoted in the army, not even to corporal, because I never got anywhere with the alphabet. I couldn't pass my classes; they were only for the clever ones. I was always hoping I'd get promoted, and I'd often dream about being corporal and getting revenge, dammit, for all the times they'd beaten me. To this day, I've never run into the people I wanted to get even with. It seems that Earth Shade swallowed them whole for being such heartless dogs.

I was never happy in the army. They haul you off like cattle, throw you in the train's cargo hold like you were livestock, and then in Cuzco they cut your hair, heap some clothes on you, and just like that you're a soldier. Doing those drills each day, being on watch all sleepy and cold, guarding the main gate—damn I hated it. Day and night, even when you just wanted to take a piss, dammit, they'd always be chasing after you with "The last four there":

"All right, cholos, off with your shoes, the last four to the bathroom!"

That's the army for you; it was always the same thing, an endless "The last four there." The army isn't Christian.

Nowadays, while I'm lugging goods around as a strapper,[3] I hear people talking: "The Government, Velasco in Lima,[4] has said, 'Everyone must serve the country.' Only Indians were soldiers in the old days. Life in the barracks today isn't the way it used to be," they say.

When I was discharged from the army, I didn't want to go back to my hometown wearing soldier's clothes; your fellow villagers see army clothes and say:

"He'll be a little misti only as long as those state clothes last him."

So when I got out, I went looking for a job and found one in the cemetery, making adobe bricks for two weeks. We made those bricks to repair a wall that had fallen down. And after making the bricks for about a month, we opened the burial niches and removed the dead; we'd take them out and dump them in a hole. In that hole, we'd douse them with kerosene and set them on fire. That's what we were doing with the dead corpses, but one day I asked my work partner:

"Why are we disturbing these poor souls? God our Lord might get angry with us because of these things we're doing."

And he answered me:

"Don't be afraid, Gregorio. Our Lord knows that these souls are behind in their payments. I heard they haven't been paying their space here."

Ever since the time I burned those corpses, and even now, I often tell myself, "I shouldn't have done that." Because, to this day, I still dream about some misti wiraquchas, old ones, young ones, ladies dressed in black shrouds pulling along some little kids by the hand—they all come weeping to the door of my house. These mistis have appeared in my dreams many times: men, women, and small children dressed in black with faces white as paper. They all wail together like the dead, and from the door of my house, they ask me:

"Gregorio, why have you burned us? Our bodies are covered with open wounds."

But in my dreams, I've yet to see them enter my house. They always just talk to me from the doorway:

"Gregorio, Gregorio, why have you burned us? Our bodies are covered with open wounds and festering boils."

So my wife told me:

"The day they enter our house, we'll surely die."

That's why, to cure myself of that, I went to a healer several times, and he'd make offerings to those souls.[5] But the healer said:

"Didn't work. Those souls are all misti wiraquchas, and they don't want to accept the offerings."

My first wages and all the wages I earned working as a hired hand came after I was discharged from the army. My friend Bernaco Tito and I would have Mrs. Teodolinda Baca hold onto all our wages for us. Even now I still remember her name. She was a good person and owned a cornbeer tavern up on Pampa del Castillo Street.[6] We boarded there without having to pay for our lodging; we just helped her wash her large straw strainers in the mornings or afternoons. She was very honest and used to keep the money we'd give her in a napkin, mine on one side and Bernaco's on the other. That way there'd never be even a centavo missing.

You can make money doing all kinds of things in Cuzco, working as a hired hand or hauling goods. So, in order to return to my town after I got out of the army, I bought myself a lot of clothes with the money I'd earned: two pairs of pants, a vest, a coat, a shirt, and two pairs of those white socks people used to call "German style." They were real nice and rode up to the knee like those of soccer players. All of that cost me eight soles. It was like having a suit. With all those things, I couldn't get used to living back in my town again.

Back in those times, like today, I'd also carry people's goods in the mornings or afternoons. At that time, there wasn't any small change like there is now. It was only every once in a while they paid you with money—five centavos a load—and that was only when it was from the train station into town or from the market to the edge of town. Good pay was ten centavos. Payment was almost always in chili peppers or *rocoto,* and we'd take them to the people selling cooked corn.[7] For just five centavos, you could lunch on three heaping plates with nice, big chunks of meat. Back in those days, you ate well. Ah, but those were good times for eating meat!

SEVEN

INKAS AND SPANIARDS

T úpac Amaru was from Tungasuca; he was one of our people, son of Inkas,[1] but one day those Spanish enemies killed him. They ripped his tongue and eyes out by their roots. That's how Túpac Amaru was killed by his foes. Túpac Amaru's enemies were the very same ones that our ancestors, the Inkas, used to have. They tell this story about Inkaríy; it was way back then in those distant times of our ancestors.

Our God used to travel from town to town, asking:

"What kind of work would you like me to give you?"

And Inkaríy replied:

"We don't want any of your jobs. Our hands can do any kind of work if we need to work."

That's how he answered.

"We know how to make stones walk, and with a single throw of a sling, we can build mountains and valleys. We don't need anything at all; we know everything there is to know."

Well, then this two-faced God went to Spain, to the enemy of our ancient Inka forefather, where he also went from town to town, asking:

"What would you like? I'll give you work. Ask me and I'll give you anything you want."

Where Inkaríy had scorned him, all the people in Spain were ambitious and greedy, and they asked him for everything:

"We want this, that, and the other."

That's why today we runas don't know how to run engines, cars, or those machines that travel high above like birds, the helicopters and planes. We don't know how to build any of those machines, but those Spaniards are clever and know how to do everything. A wiraqucha Spaniard invented electricity by just watching water, and with some pieces of glass, he invented the light bulb. Even right now, this light here comes from the waters of Calca.[2]

So the Inka, our Inkaríy, was proud and scornful and didn't want the jobs. But those Spaniards asked for all kinds of work, saying, "We want it." That's why today they can build cars, engines, iron pots—all the things we don't know how to make. That's the way it is, all because God himself gave those jobs to them and not us, the ones who spurned the good Lord's gifts.

We are Peruvians, native people,[3] and they were Inka runa; but we're their children, and that's why those Spaniards also killed Túpac Amaru.

They say that, just like those nuns today there in Santa Teresa Convent and in San Pedro, the Inka used to have women like that back then. The Spaniards took those women out of there and married them, and those women bore them children.

It's said that when those Spaniards were about to kill the Inka, he told them: "Don't kill me."

And he had golden ears of corn given to their horses.

"We'll give you gold like this, but don't kill us."

Well, those greedy Spaniards were hungry for power, so they killed our Inka. The Inkas didn't know anything about paper or writing, and when the good Lord wanted to give them paper, they refused it. That's because they didn't get their news by paper but by small, thick threads made of *vicuña* wool: they used black wool cords for bad news and for the good news, white cords. These cords were like books, but the Spaniards didn't want them around; so they gave the Inka a piece of paper.

"This paper talks," they said.

"Where is it talking? That's silly; you're trying to trick me."

And he flung the paper to the ground.[4] The Inka didn't know anything about writing. And how could the paper talk if he didn't know how to read? And so they had our Inka killed. Inkaríy disappeared and has been gone ever since. The Inkas Wayna Qhapaq and Inka Ruka had been his uncles, and Inka Rumichaka was his brother.[5] The Spaniards killed them all.

But now I ask:

"What would the Spaniards say if our Inka was to return?"[6]

Such was life.

EIGHT

STORIES FROM JAIL

A year or so after I left the army, a friend from Pomacanchi and I set out for Quincemil to look for work, because everybody was going to Quincemil and returning with lots of money.

"There's gold in the river, and you can just scoop it up with your hands," they were saying.

Everyone was going. And so my friend and I also got ready to leave. Then we set out toward Urcos. Later on, as night began to fall, we came into the town of Ccatcca, where we stayed in the house of someone my friend knew. We fell asleep. But the owner of the house was in the habit of rustling cattle at night. He was a thief, and around midnight, together with his wife and children, he brought home a cow and, working shoulder to shoulder, they slaughtered it. They put water in a large pot to make stew and began stripping off the meat, some for stew and some for roast. A bit later the whole house began to fill with the aroma of roast beef; we just lay there on two small skins in the corner, not moving, as if we were asleep. So they ate meat all night long.

Just before daybreak, they offered us a tiny bit of stew. Since they'd been up all night eating meat, they hadn't let us sleep either, so after we had the stew, we all just kept sleeping into the day. But the cattle owners and authorities—the governor, together with his lieutenant and subordinates—had gone and followed the cattle tracks to our friend's house. Since the owners had notified the authorities and were accompanied by them and others when they arrived, they just entered the house. Dogs were barking, and they were already searching the place, when we woke up. They discovered the pots full of meat. And then searching around, they came upon even more beef that had been quartered and that they'd put in gunny sacks and hidden in the corral, covering them up with manure. So then the governor of Ocongate also found us there, and he asked us:

"And you, what's your story?"

"No, it's not like that, Papa. We just lodged here overnight on our way to Marcapata."

The governor called over the lieutenant.

"All right, Lieutenant, take these thieves away."

So they arrested us.

But our friend with the house hadn't stolen just one cow, but three. So they took us to the Urcos jail together with many llamas loaded down with meat. Three days after they'd locked us up in jail, they took us out and had us give our statements. So our friend testified:

"Yes, Papa, Your Honor, driven by my sins and to feed my children, I went and stole those cows."

They put everything our friend was saying down on paper. And then the judge said:

"*Lodgers come forward. Gregorio Condori: make statement.*"

First he asked me:

"Now, son, did you bring the cow in with them, or did you see them bringing it in? You're not going to be punished, so come clean, son. Now, did you all go and rustle those cows together? Tell me, don't be afraid."

"No, sir, we weren't involved in it. How could we have rustled cattle that night if we were just staying over? It's true, the owner of the house went out that night, but we didn't see them slaughter the cow."

But then I thought to myself, "We've already lost four days of travel. So I'll tell him that they'd been eating meat all night long."

"Yes, sir, they were eating all night long."

And the judge asked:

"They ate all night long?"

"Yes, sir, they ate all night long."

"And didn't they offer you all even a little bit to eat?"

"No, they didn't give us a thing to eat."

"How could that be? Speak up now, were you all there rustling with them too? Tell me the truth, I'm not going to punish you."

"No, Papa."

"So they didn't offer you any at all?"

"Nothing at all, Papa."

That's how he questioned me. But then he began questioning me again:

"How could that be? Didn't they offer you any at all? Not even a little bit?"

Well, since he just kept on asking and asking, I told him:

"Yes, they did give us a tiny bit of stew, but none of the meat, just a little bit of broth."

And the judge said:

"No, son—for that you're now going to jail. That broth counts; it was the cow's essence. Meat is worthless without the broth; the essence is in the broth. That's why you're going to jail. Because if you were eating stolen meat, you should've informed the authorities—that's what you're guilty of, not notifying them."

So that judge had us thrown in jail, just for sipping some stew offered us at a friend's house. That's justice for you; they make you do six months in jail, just for having a little stew like we did. That's the reason we never made it to Quincemil to get gold from the river. I've always thought about how the judges and all the mistis are eating meat morning, noon, and night, and how that meat comes from stolen cattle. And they know all about it. Like Luis L., a judge in Urcos who makes deals with thieves who steal for him. He doesn't go to jail or notify the authorities. That's justice for you—with mistis, the law looks the other way.

So I was falsely and unjustly put in jail for having sipped some stew a friend offered me.

We spent the first days in jail anxious and worried. There was nothing to eat nor anything to sleep on but our little ponchos, and we had nothing to do. The other inmates just watched us. But by the third day, we began to make some friends; some of them told us:

"Come over here and help us weave."

And others:

"Come over here and help us spin wool."

But I didn't know anything about the craft of spinning or weaving.[1] In my town that craft was only for women. But there in jail if you don't weave or spin wool, you don't eat. So I too began learning how to spin wool. At first I'd just look on. Then, by watching them over and over, I began spinning clumsily, sometimes thick and other times thin, but in the end I became skilled at the craft of spinning wool. The day I learned how to spin, life in jail became a lot easier. We'd spin from the moment they let us out of our cells into the prison yard till lock-up time. We'd keep on doing this in our cells because there was always plenty of work, weaving and spinning, there in jail. They'd bring in sacks full of wool from all over, to spin and weave ponchos, blankets, sackcloth, and shawls. There was never a lack of wool, be it alpaca, sheep, or llama. We'd be spinning that wool day and night. And during the daytime, all the prisoners went about their business, spinning, weaving, having visitors, seeing their lawyers or witnesses. But at night, all of us prisoners, who together numbered around two hundred, counting men and women, were locked up. There was one large cell for women and another for us men. In our room, we men got together every night, and surrounded by candles and oil lamps, we'd form a circle just like at the work party meals back in the community. And we'd keep on working the wool, laughing without a worry, listening to the storytellers spin their tales. I've never heard so many stories as there in jail, and even now I can still remember some of them.

Like the story of a cattle rancher who'd gone to buy cattle over by some communities near mountain lord *Apu* Ausankati.[2] The rancher hadn't found any cattle and was tired, so he sat down on a large craggy boulder in front of the apu. While the rancher was sitting there like that, they say a runa dressed in the local garb of the region approached him,[3] asking:

"Wiraqucha, what are you doing here?"

"I want to buy cattle. I'm a cattle merchant," he told him.

When he heard this, the runa disappeared in the blink of an eye. Later on, when it began getting dark and the rancher was still sitting there on that same rock without moving, the runa reappeared and asked him:

"Wiraqucha, if it's true you buy cattle, then I'll sell you some. I have lots of cattle, as well as daughters who want to get married. If you'd like to get married, I'll marry you to my daughter. My daughter doesn't decide this. I'm the one who decides."

The cattle rancher agreed to marry his daughter.

"Well then, come along and meet my daughter. As I said before, it's not my daughter who decides this—it's me who decides."

While they were walking, a large boulder suddenly opened up like a door right there in the middle of Ausankati Mountain. They went inside. I don't remember if he had the rancher sleep with his daughter that night, but, in any case, the next morning the rancher found himself in a strange town, with herds of cattle, llamas, and alpacas covering the mountains like clouds.

Some days later, the rancher married the daughter of that runa. But this runa was really Apu Ausankati. So, from one mountain to the other, *Awki* Arequipa Maysisku and Apu Khunurana called each other to be the godparents of his daughter's wedding.

After the rancher's wedding, a lot of time went by, till one day he said to his father-in-law:

"Papa, it's been a long time now since I've had any news about my family's village, and I'm going to go visit there with my wife."

The apu accepted. So they went happily on their way, together with a llama saddled with a small pack sack his father-in-law had given them. The sack was probably full of silver coins. Traveling together as husband and wife, they arrived at Cuzco, and, just like all travelers, they were tired and thirsty. So her husband said:

"We'll drink some cornbeer."

But the woman didn't want to drink any. Instead, she wanted him to make offerings of its essence to her.[4] Because before eating or drinking anything, you must make offerings with it, that is, you have to blow its fragrance toward the earth and venerable awkis, who feed on the fragrance of those offerings. Since she was the apu's daughter, she wanted to receive libations from the cornbeer we drink, so she could taste its sweet flavor. But this dimwit didn't understand that. Instead, he just drank it all by himself without making libations to his wife. After a while, he got drunk and begun cursing his wife:

"So, damn you, you don't want to drink the same cornbeer I drink?! Drink it down, dammit! Dammit, drink it down!"

Then that dumb donkey hit her. He threw cornbeer on her. Well, because the rancher went and hit her, she vanished from his side in the blink of an eye, taking the llama and all it carried with her. So the next day when he sobered up, he found himself alone, with no wife, llama, cargo—nothing at all. Once again he left and traveled back to the same rock, there where he'd been sitting before he'd met Apu Ausankati's daughter. The stupid jackass just sat there on the same rock, morning, noon, and night while several days came and went. But one day while he was sitting there, the mountains began to shake and rumble, and then a door suddenly opened up. It was the same door he'd entered before, the one that led inside Ausankati Mountain. But this time, a giant hand suddenly shot out of the door and grabbed him like a fly, whisking him away inside Ausankati Mountain—they say he's been there to this day. Nobody knows if he was punished or killed.

I heard that story there in jail, and on another occasion I also heard about how Apu Ausankati went all the way to Lima to talk with the Government, right there in its own house. For the occasion, the apu got all dressed up in his best clothes, which were beautiful and made of pure gold. He entered the Government's house all shimmering and aglow, and since that kind of garment can't be found anywhere, even the Government envied the apu's clothing, saying:

"Damn nice!"

But the apu had come to tell the Government that its police and compadres were going around killing his vicuñas, and that if they kept on killing them, he'd run all his vicuñas into Ausankati Mountain, and there'd be no more vicuñas left on Peruvian soil.

Later, I thought about why there aren't any vicuñas left today. I've heard they've all disappeared. It's because the Government didn't follow through in telling the policemen, "Don't kill the vicuñas." Or perhaps they were told and ignored it? Anyway, Apu Ausankati must've gotten real mad and herded his vicuñas away. That's why there aren't any vicuñas left on Peruvian soil now.

There in jail, at five in the afternoon, we'd already be standing in line for roll call, and after that, with the sun still up, we'd be locked away in our jail cells. Those cells were huge rooms, one for men and another for women. But during the day, the women inmates would be together with us in the prison yard. They also used to weave and spin wool, as well as cook meals to sell. For all the inmates there in jail, men and women alike, weaving and spinning was everything. Everybody had to work. There were even carpenters and tailors, though only a few of them. The people who go to prison for robbery, like we had, are the ones who'd have to work the most. They'd earn lots of money spinning and weaving so as to have enough for their lawyer and the notary, and for paper as well. Even in jail, money is everything, and if you don't pay your lawyer or buy paper, who knows how many years you'll stay in there.

They'd lock you away very early in your jail cell, which was always dark and gloomy, but there were always lots of things to do. The cell was just one room for all the prisoners, and each person had a little niche to sleep in and to stow their bed and belongings. But since you never had much of anything except your little poncho with you when they carted you off to jail, that's all you found yourself with in there, no sheepskins or blankets, and all hungry and cold. Even today they don't give you food in the town jails, locking you away as if to say, "Die, you damn dog!" And once you're in jail, you have to look out for yourself. You couldn't just sit there doing nothing; you'd have to be weaving or spinning. If you don't know how to weave, you learn how. Because in jail, there's none of that "people will see me doing women's work." Instead, the inmates came out with new skills, and back in their towns they'd keep on weaving, sometimes even doing it in secret. So, while serving time, I too became a skilled weaver. In my hometown, weaving and spinning wool were jobs done only by women. If they saw you doing women's work, they'd make fun of you:

"Poor little llama herder, you little llama herder's wife."

But in jail I supported myself by weaving. Since I didn't have any pots or pans, nor anyone to bring me firewood for cooking, much less any food, I'd take my meals with a woman from the Quiquijana region. I'd pay eighty centavos a week for meals, both lunch and dinner. And I'd make those eighty centavos spinning wool. But I tell you, I'd have to be spinning wool day and night.

At night it was like a wedding in there, the cell all filled with candles and kerosene lamps. So, while spinning and weaving, we'd tell each other stories late into the night. As far as storytellers go, Matico Quispe was really something. He was an inmate from the town of Oropesa and had been living in Huaro, where his wife came from. He'd been a farm servant, tending the drying shed on wiraqucha Díaz's hacienda,[5] and one night three sacks of corn seed disappeared from the drying shed. Matico was innocent, but the estate owner didn't believe it.

Instead, he'd gone to Urcos, where his brother-in-law was a judge, and had accused Matico of robbing his shed; that's why he was now behind bars. Matico was real special, and never since my time there in the Urcos jail have I come across another villager who could spin yarns like Matico. He was such a great storyteller that, in all my time there in jail, I never heard him tell the same story twice; it was all set up in his mind.

So we'd tell stories every night, and one time another inmate told a story about Earth Mother. In other times, who knows how long ago, our Lord ordered that the crops people grow for food should all be on just one stalk with a single root. At the top of the plant, wheat was to be grown; on its sides, five to ten corncobs; and in the roots, potatoes. But here Earth Mother protested angrily:

"I can't bear all these different crops. Instead, each one should have its own plant and roots."

And ever since that time, potatoes, corn, and wheat have each had their own roots. If Earth Mother hadn't protested back then about bearing so many crops on just one plant with a single root, then even today women would be giving birth to five or ten baby boys and girls each time they got pregnant. When we heard this, our voices rang out as one:

"Damn! You mean there'd have been so many of us that we'd be swarming around here like ants?"

And Matico replied:

"You fools, if one plant was going to provide so many crops, then why shouldn't women be able to bear lots of babies?"

There was another inmate who was a storyteller like Matico. He was from the community of Ccamara in the Ccatcca region. This Ccamaran was in jail for stealing a llama herd—he'd gone and done that to his wedding compadre.[6] In jail there were lots of Ccamarans, and they were real tough guys. Some of them were living in jail with their wives, and they'd cook for all their fellow villagers. They all lived there together. I can only remember some of the stuff those Ccamarans used to tell us. They told about how, way back in other times, our God was known as a witch and a thief here in this world. In those times, our God had many enemies chasing him:

"Where's that witch, where's that thief? Has a thieving witch passed this way?"

And the people answered:

"No witch or thief has come by here."

So they looked and asked all over for him. One day, as they were traveling from town to town asking about him, his enemies met up with Saint Isidore the Farmhand while he was sowing wheat. But a moment earlier, our God had come by Saint Isidore the Farmhand's field, leaving him some instructions:

"If they come asking for me, then say, 'Yes, he passed by, but it was a year ago when I was still just sowing the wheat.'"

A little while later, the ones pursuing our Lord came and asked:

"Did a witch or thief pass by here?"

And Saint Isidore the Farmhand replied:

"Yes, a witch passed by here, but, come to think of it, that was a year ago when this wheat was just being planted and—oh my!—the wheat's now ready to harvest."

And so, in the blink of an eye, the wheat Saint Isidore the Farmhand had been sowing was ready to be threshed.

Some time later, on a different occasion, when cows used to be just black, our God got fed up with being persecuted so much and hid his enemies' cows so he could milk them. And just like holy water, he sprinkled that very same milk over the herd. So the cows changed color, and their owners weren't able to recognize them. Then the owners began to travel all over the place, asking:

"What could've happened to my cows? My cows are gone. There's some cows over there that look like mine, but their colors aren't the same."

Ever since that time, our Lord's enemies stopped chasing him, because they now had to travel from one town to the next searching for their cows.

So that's how cattle rustling began, with that prank pulled by our God.

Well, the Ccamarans were real wily rascals and were known as the town whips. You had to watch out for them more than anyone else in jail, because they'd approach you, and I don't how those witches did it, but they'd pinch something from you, even if it was just a little sewing needle or the hankie you used to blow your nose. Yet, since we were also villagers like them and had been arrested for rustling, we sort of became friends. They were well known in the town of Urcos and were never lacking pelts for spinning wool. People were always bringing them wool, and those of us who didn't have any, would help them. But those wily Ccamaran rascals never stopped talking about all the stunts they'd pulled.

One time a Ccamaran was testifying in a court hearing, and the judge told him:

"Listen up, buddy: if you want your freedom, it's your obligation to tell this court the truth."

And the Ccamaran replied:

"No, it's not like that, Papa. As you know, we poor people always have to be traveling. I never stole that cow, Papa. As I left the outskirts of town riding my horse, that cow was feeding on a small rise. And just fooling and messing around, I threw out one end of my lasso and let it drag along behind me, but when I got home that damn cow had followed the lasso behind my horse. At that moment, I was filled with joy and said, 'Thank the Lord! He must be sending this little cow to us.' That's what I thought, Papa, Your Honor, and so I slaughtered the cow and then ate it with my whole family. As you can see, Papa, dear Papa, Your Honor sir, I'm no thief. The cow followed the lasso to my house."

So, according to this smart-ass Ccamaran, the cow had followed him all the way home. That's the star those Ccamarans must've been born with, no doubt, because it's said that when they're out on their exploits, even the damned get fed up with them and flee. One night they told about how a Ccamaran had grown tired during his nightly forays. So he entered an abandoned house in the high plains to rest. There were huge, woolly hounds in that house, and they bolted away when they saw the Ccamaran. So, tired and hungry, the Ccamaran began searching for food, going through the house from one end to the other.

And while looking around, he found a pot full of cooked corn and another of pork rinds. So he started eating. But he wanted more pork rinds, and he looked around, finding other pots full of it—but the rinds were human ears, and the corn kernels in the pots were human teeth. With his eyes almost popping out of their sockets, the Ccamaran stared at the pots he'd been eating from—then far off in the distance he heard woeful crying like a bugle sounding. As the wails came closer and closer to the house, the Ccamaran jumped up on the main rafter and clung to it like a big dark butterfly.[7] And then a person entered, sobbing woefully and stinking of sulfur, its clothes all tattered and torn up, its hands and feet full of open, bloody sores. It was one of the damned. Between its cries and moans, it quickly gobbled up the pork rinds as well as the cooked corn teeth, cracking them like toasted broad beans. Then, while licking the pot, it started sniffing around:

"What's that, what reeks of human hair?"

Still moaning, the wretched soul started looking around everywhere, and with each of its howls, sulfur smoke blew forth from its nose like a strong gust of wind. Then the beam pole started to creak with the Ccamaran's weight. So the Ccamaran jumped down, landing on top of the wretch and shrieking wildly:

"Eeeeeyow! Eeeeeyow!"

He came down on the damned one's head. And that suffering soul fled its house screaming, "Waaaaaaaaaaaaaah!" as its pointed cowl fell to the ground.

After the damned wretch had fled, leaving its house behind, the Ccamaran went and looted everything there. Later, when he got back home with all his loot, the Ccamaran said to his wife:

"But I've had to work damn hard for it!"

The way those Ccamarans told it, they weren't afraid of anything—they'd even rob the houses of the damned.

I wonder whatever became of the Ccamarans. They're probably still following the same path because that's the star they were born with.[8] It was even funny sometimes, like when one of the Ccamarans got jailed three times in just one year. The first time they let him go, less than a month later he was stealing a herd of sheep, and, bad luck, they caught him. So again they sent him from Ccatcca to the Urcos jail. After spending another six months there in the Urcos jail, he got out by posting bail. Then, the very same day they released him for the second time, that cunning rascal ran off with a bull he found above the town of Urcos. The bull's owner must've been a well-known misti from Urcos, because when they went and asked around for the bull, the people told them right away:

"So-and-so has taken it."

In cases of robbery, when the person searching is just a runa peasant with no close friends, nobody will tell him a thing—not even his own relatives will tell him, even if they saw the robbery themselves. Because if the thieves catch word that someone has reported them and that what they've stolen is about to be discovered or already has been, then they go rob the person who's going around blabbing. And who wants to lose cattle and other things! That's why those thieves are always people to watch out for and be wary of.

Well, they say that this Ccamaran entered his town driving the bull and that his fellow villagers were happy with his return home; they slaughtered the bull and right away went and feasted on it. But while they were celebrating his return late into the night, the bull's owner had been asking around and following the tracks. He arrived at the Ccamaran's house while they were still passing around the bottle. So the bull's owner and his companions searched all over the house, but there wasn't even a single piece of meat left because they'd already divided it up; all they found was the hide and a little bit of the innards. So the very next day, the Ccamaran, still drunk and carrying the skin and guts of the bull he'd stolen, arrived back at the jailhouse. They say the judge took his statement before sending him to prison.

"Not even a day has gone by, dammit, and you're back out stealing again! You're going to get it this time, you no-good shifty cattle thief. Because you didn't learn your lesson, I hereby sentence you to ten years. Happy now?"

That's what the judge told him.

"In the end, your Honor, if it's from your mouth, may it be a hundred years. But, sir, what harm have I done you that, again and again, you call me 'cattle thief' and are always sending me off to jail? What did I do to deserve all this hate, Your Honor, steal your wife?"

That's what the Ccamaran replied.

Such was the Ccamaran way of life.

My jail sentence for being an accomplice to a cattle rustler was six months, but they kept me there nine. One day, a Tuesday afternoon in April, they called out:

"Gregorio Condori: Ready your things!"

Since they just called me and not my friend, I didn't think it was to let me out. Instead, I said to myself, "Where the hell are these devils sending me?" When I got to the entryway where all the prison guards were, they saw me and started roaring with laughter; then one of them kicked me so hard it almost sent me sprawling on the ground:

"Get out of here, you fucking Indian! To your woman's legs."

I was thinking, "Dammit, these Christians are taking me out and are going to punish me," and so I walked ahead slowly and fearfully, while behind me they kept on laughing. And so I just kept going without looking back till I lost myself in the streets. As I rounded a corner, I looked behind me to see if anybody was following, and there was no one there. Only then did I believe I was truly out of there. I felt real happy.

I was a stranger there in Urcos, and nobody knew me, so in order to find out if there were any travelers going to Cuzco, I entered a house that had the little cornbeer-for-sale flag outside.[9] There I bought five centavos' worth of cornbeer. It was a lot—two full pitchers—which would now be about six of those large glasses and would cost thirty soles. Before, it used to cost only five centavos. I treated the owner of the cornbeer tavern to one of the pitchers and drank the other myself. Since she accepted the cornbeer I offered her, I told her I was a stranger in town and had just gotten out of jail, and that I wanted to know if there might be people traveling to Cuzco who I could cross the Rumiqulqa Pass with. So the lady told me:

"On Tuesdays and Wednesdays, there's muleteers leaving from Marcapata for Cuzco."

I couldn't travel all by myself to Cuzco that same day because the Rumiqulqa Pass was infamous: thieves there would attack and kill travelers to steal their money or goods. It was crossed only during daytime, with people traveling together in numbers.

It's said that one time in Rumiqulqa around Piñipampa, thieves thrashed and beat a woman to death in order to rob her of a little satchel she was carrying. And then they dumped her dead body into a hole just off the trail. Some days later, the mules of a muleteer from Quincemil had grown tired on the rise there, and, as his workhands were adjusting their loads, they suddenly heard a baby crying. Since they were several people strong, they began searching for whatever was crying like a baby. That pass is full of old dwellings covered by scrub brush, and since that's where the cries of the little baby were coming from, they drew closer, happy with the thought that the crying might be coming from a little gold idol of the ancients.[10] And as they approached, they all threw down their hats together and pissed in them as if they were pee pots so that the little gold idol wouldn't become enchanted and vanish. But when they came closer to the hole and peered inside, they saw a dead woman— the little baby that had been crying was nursing on its mother, whose body was already rotting away.

Another time at that pass, they killed a traveling qulla man to steal his goods, and afterward they cut off his head. That's why this pass was infamous and all travelers were afraid of it.

The attacks there at that pass have stopped now, ever since the road came through and the first passenger cars arrived.

NINE

ROSA, JOSEFA, AND MIRACLE SHRINES

After serving time in the Urcos jail, I went to Cuzco and worked for several months at the convent of La Merced, putting doors and windows in the rooms that opened onto the street, those that are now stores there on Avenida del Sol. During the time I worked there, I used to go have lunch at the Cascaparo Market during my noon break. I was single at the time, but wishing I had a woman who'd cook for me. And so, while going to that market every day for lunch, I met my first wife, Rosa Puma.[1] She was a food vendor and came from the village of Sullumayu;[2] that's up in the high reaches of Urpay, next to Urcos. She was well known there in the market. She'd already been married before I came along, but he'd abandoned her. Since she was a good cook, and since she served me nice portions, and didn't have a husband, I courted her. She was willing, and from that day on she'd come sleep over with me in my house or I'd go sleep at her house. Then one night she came to my house for good, hauling her bed and all her pots. So we began living together as one there in my room, which was barely big enough for both me and her pots.

Two months passed by. Then the potato harvest in her family's village began. And so, using many llamas, we began hauling the potatoes from Sullumayu to Urpay. She'd travel with me on each of those trips, but she mustn't have been used to walking from the warm valley up to the high reaches several times a day. On one of those trips, she caught an ill wind and couldn't walk,[3] as if she were paralyzed. And since she was suffering, I carried her, walking behind the llamas till I got to Huaro. The healers there tried everything they could to cure her. I went to Urcos to buy her medicine and did everything I could for them to cure her. But that's fate I guess—nothing could be done.

Three days later she woke up unable to talk or even recognize anyone. Her illness got worse that same night, and she became very feverish and broke out in chills. In the early morning of the fourth day, sweating a cold sweat, she grew rigid, and, just like that, she died. And so, to pay for the burial expenses, I sold the potatoes we'd gathered together, and we buried her in the cemetery at the Lord of Kaninkunka's Chapel.

She'd left her community when she was still just a little girl, taken away by a hacienda owner to be a little kitchen maid. That's why she knew how to cook, and when her first husband abandoned her, she'd left that house and set herself up in the food business. After that bad luck in Huaro, I went back to Cuzco again, together with one of her relatives who took away her things, her bed and pots. Some days later, I began working on Saphi Street, repairing a wall that was falling down. There was a little cookhouse there in that home,[4] and when I finished the job, the owner told me:

"If you stay in Cuzco, I can give you a room; you won't have to pay rent, you'll just grind corn sprouts for the cornbeer."

Since I wasn't going to have to pay rent and was all by myself again, I accepted. The payment for staying in that room, which was a perfect rat hole and barely big enough for me alone to fit into, was grinding twenty-five pounds of corn sprouts every morning, and twice that much on Saturday and Sunday. Sure, they'd treat me to cornbeer every day, but it was much too much lung-busting work for such a rat hole. Each morning after grinding corn sprouts, I'd have to go to my job. On your noon break, they'd sometimes give you lunch right there at work. Back then, if you worked as a hired hand building or repairing houses, sometimes they'd give you food and other times nothing at all. If there was no lunch, I'd go to Cascaparo Market. That's the little market they now call Croucher's Kitchen. It was while I was going there daily that I met a woman from Pampamarca, and she became my second wife. Her name was Josefa Tupa Quispe, and she was also a food vendor. She already had two little daughters when I met her; her husband, who was from Abancay, had abandoned her and run off with another woman to a different town. My wife Josefa was a very good person, and in order for us to live together, we took a little room on Belén Street, paying three soles a month rent.

But three years later, we moved to wiraqucha Quintanilla's house on Matará Street, a very large house with two patios, and I stayed on there as a doorman. We lived there for many years, and I did all kinds of work, as a hired hand and also carrying goods, even selling food to support us and her daughters. Throwing all of our sins into a single satchel so we'd have enough to eat, my wife Josefa and I made a life together. I know her daughters recognize me when they see me in the street now, but they act as if I'd never existed. It really stinks: now that they're little *mestizas*, they're ashamed of their stepfather. They don't say, "There was a time when this stepfather of mine provided my food." I don't think my stepdaughters ever give me a thought, not even when they're shitting.

After five or six years, Josefa and I left the house on Matará Street because when Quintanilla, the owner, became a little old man, he didn't want me to budge from his house.

"I've got to go work," I'd tell him.

"You just can't do that, you're my doorman," he'd answer.

I worked there as a doorman in exchange for the room we occupied, but I wasn't paid a thing. That's the reason we left and went to live in Puente Rosario, where the owner of a field gave us a tiny little plot on a small rise; I built my house there. It looked like a herder's hut, but it had adobe walls and a roof made of tin slats, sheet metal, and pine poles. I'd collected those construction materials from all the houses I'd worked on. When I finished this house, my only child, Tomasito Condori, was born. When my little Tomasito was three years old, he got a bad case of diarrhea, and since nothing we tried was able to cure him, I followed our neighbor's advice and took him to Lorena Hospital. A doctor there had him put in the children's ward, bed number 21. Three days later he was almost all cured of his diarrhea, but then he caught a bad case of whooping cough there in the hospital, and each time he coughed, it made him faint. One day when his diarrhea was all gone, they gave him an injection in one of his little cheeks; the injection mustn't have spread through his little body, and the place they'd given him the shot started to swell up. A few days later, like a leaky bag, pus began to stream out. The open sore caused by the injection turned into a large welt, and it began to swell up and spread all over his little body. My little Tomasito Condori died from that swelling, there in Lorena Hospital. If he had lived, right now at this very moment he'd be a young man, and I wouldn't be in the state I'm in—my son would always be saying to me:

"No, that's alright, Papa. If you can't haul goods anymore, your son's arms are here for you."

Even if I were a drunkard, he'd look after his father just like any son does; he'd be asking me:

"Do you have enough money for your bread, for your cornbeer, for your liquor? Here, take this, Papa—I'm working now."

But ever since Tomasito died, there's been no one to tell me those things. That's why every time I remember my baby it makes me feel like crying, because little Tomasito was a sweetheart.

My Tomasito Condori isn't in limbo: he'd been baptized, and he was buried in a coffin like a good Christian. That's why he's keeping watch over and tending the good Lord's garden, there where the qantu flowers turn into high-neck jugs, the ones they carry to water the garden blossoms.[5] I doubt he's going to remain silent as he watches his father dragging himself along beneath his burden. He's a little guardian angel in the good Lord's garden, and I'm sure he's always imploring God on my behalf.

Limbo is down in the underworld—it's dark and gloomy, black as night.[6] That's where the souls of the unbaptized babies go. Those little souls are crawling up and down in that total gloomy darkness, miles and miles on end, looking for the rope to the bell clapper. While they're searching, if one baby or several of the babies find the clapper cord, they ring the bell: Bonggggg. And when that bell sounds, it's said that a little ray of light shines down on the babies, and they grow wings and turn into doves, rising through the ray of light as if it were a path. That's how those little souls save themselves from limbo; like doves, they take off for the upperworld and become gardeners.

The only child born of my blood was Tomasito Condori. That's not the way I wanted it, but God's will; there are things that escape our will. He didn't want to give me more offspring because if he had wished us to be fruitful, there could've been any number of babies, even twenty.

When I began living with Josefa, she was still a strong-legged woman and able to bear children, and after Tomasito I wanted to have a baby. So resting now and again, I'd mount her up to five or six times, but my blood would no longer take hold inside her belly.[7] So I went around asking my friends what was good for having children. Some friends would tell me, "Drink beer till you get drunk, then go mount your wife," but other friends burst out laughing and made fun of me when I'd ask them. They'd call me a fruitless aransach'a—that's what they call those who are childless. The aransach'a is a barren little tree with no leaves or branches; it's all stalk and only grows in gullies or on rocky hillsides. On another occasion, after talking with a friend who was also childless, I remembered that four or five months after I began living with Josefa I'd come down with inflammation of the kidneys and was so bad off I was bedridden. I was pissing blood and in a lot of pain, and I wasn't able to sleep night after night. My wife's market friends advised her that, to cure me of this, she should prepare some herbal teas—such as radishes, dog thorn, sharp sowthistle, soft sowthistle, ribwort, and ox tongue—and make me drink them for at least a month.[8] My wife went and gathered those roots and herbs, and since I wanted to get completely cured, I took them not just one but two whole months, which cured me of my illness. But the essence of those herbs must've passed through my bones to the marrow, destroying it.[9] So my blood is barren and can't bear children.

My wife Josefa was always getting sick, either with headaches, bellyaches, or backaches. And since she was from the town of Pampamarca and her family lived there, a week before the Lord of Pampamarca's fair I told her:

"Look, Josefa, I'm working, repairing that house; if I were to go with you to the good Lord's fair, I'd lose my job and again be without work when I returned. Go on now, you go visit the good Lord and pray for us all."

After saying that, I gave her a hundred soles to spend, so she could return home respectably and have a mass said for her health. But when she arrived at the good Lord's side in Pampamarca, she must've found some food or clothes she liked there at the fair, forgetting all about the mass. Four days after the Lord of Pampamarca's octave, she came back to Cuzco with new clothes.[10] Since she'd forgotten the Lord of Pampamarca on his day while being right there beside him, she fell ill a few weeks later. That's how the Lord of Pampamarca punished her.

That wiraqucha is incredibly miraculous, and his story is well known; he's not just plain folk like us.[11] From that day on, her illness grew worse and worse till it had her all huddled in a corner of the house. Since that wife of mine was from Pampamarca and that miraculous Lord is right there in her town, he punished her for having forgotten him.

That Lord of Pampamarca is very miraculous, and that's why people come from all over seeking him out. But that good Lord isn't from Pampamarca itself but from the town of Curahuasi; it's from there that he came to the Pampamarca region. This good Lord grew tired as he was traveling, and he rested at the base of a llaulli tree down in Chhallakacha. A poor little woman from Pampamarca who was gathering wild turnips greeted him:

"Good morning, Papa. Oh, Papa, but you've worn yourself out!"

"Yes, my daughter."

"But, Papa, you've really worn yourself out—you're sweating blood."

"Yes, my daughter, I'm worn out, and that's why I'm shading myself."

Just like in a story, the raggedy little woman took two tiny steps and was already back in Pampamarca with the news:

"There's a wiraqucha wearing silver sandals in Chhallakacha who's all worn out and sweating blood at the foot of a llaulli tree."

The townsfolk all came together to discuss it:

"Sweating blood! Sweating blood! If he's sweating blood, he's no ordinary misti. Let's go bring him here!"

So the whole town went running off behind the raggedy little lady, while others sent a note to the priest of Pampamarca, who was still in Surimana. When the priest received the news, he also came, carrying the processional cross on high and driven along by cracking whips behind his sacristans. Well, when they found him, they carried him off to Pampamarca, bathing him with sweet incense while they sang hymns and chanted prayers. But he didn't want to live there, so he returned to the place where they'd found him. A few days later, they realized:

"That wiraqucha isn't here—he's disappeared."

And again the town went out looking for him, until they found him at the same place as the first time. Finding him once more, they again bathed him with incense, and with great ceremony they brought him all the way back to Pampamarca. It's more than a league from Pampamarca to Chhallakacha. After the whole town had settled back down, the wiraqucha once again disappeared. The priest was barefoot and he carried the processional cross on high in penitence as he led the authorities and all the people of Pampamarca, who were cracking whips and carrying the Peruvian flag to the rhythm of whistles and drums. Just like before, they found him back at the foot of the llaulli tree. Since it was the second time he'd insisted on this nonsense of not wanting to stay in Pampamarca, the priest and all the townsfolk implored him never to leave again, to stay in Pampamarca as if it were his own town. Then the priest bathed him with incense, and, chanting prayers, he washed his feet and carried him barefoot from Chhallakacha to Pampamarca. Ever since then, that wiraqucha has stayed there as the Lord of Pampamarca.

They say that ever since he's been in Pampamarca, he hasn't let any of the fellows there in town gain too much power or money. He alone is Lord of the town. Even now his authorities, all the principal officeholders in town— the judge, governor, and mayor—are just poor little fellows of no account. Being Lord Justice and the high staff of righteousness, he doesn't allow those wealthy little fellows there, only poor ones. Since he won't accept them there, they can't live in that town, and they always leave.

The Lord of Pampamarca also has brothers, five of them. One of them is the Lord of Pampak'ucho. He also had traveled around Acomayo, over Pillpinto way, until he reached the town of Cochirihuay. As he was climbing a rise and nearing that town, he grew tired and approached a little tree to find some shade. And that was the little aransach'a tree. When he was about to sit in the shade of the aransach'a, this tree fled, going far away—the Lord of Pampak'ucho became very angry and cursed it:

"Dammit! Who are you, aransach'a, to make fun of me? From now on, you'll be barren."

So he kept on walking. The aransach'a is now just a spindly little stalk with some leaves stuck to it, which grows in dry, rocky gullies. Before it was cursed, the aransach'a used to be a very leafy tree, like a weeping willow, and it provided shade for tired travelers on the trails coming up from the warm valleys to the high reaches. The Lord of Pampak'ucho didn't rest on this rise, but tired, suffering, and thirsty, he dragged himself along till he came to a hillside spring. There he drank some water from the high reaches, and it gave him pneumonia, probably because the water was too cold for him. Having pneumonia, he spit up blood; even now today that hillside is still dyed with the blood he spit up. That's what happened to the Lord of Pampak'ucho, though his true name is Jacinto Roque. They say he was suffering terribly, with blood spurting from his mouth, when he arrived at the place where the miracle happened. I don't know how they found him, but it must have been the people of Cochirihuay. Nor do I know where the priest who celebrated mass came from; I'm not sure if it was from Nayhua, Cocha, or Paruro. When they learned of the miracle, dancers came from all over; even today they still come and do the Qanchi, Chilean-foe, tilt-step, and windmill dances.[12] Those dancers come from everywhere, from Sicuani, Tinta, and Ocongate with as many as fifteen or twenty groups doing each of the different dances. When they dance there, they play around as if they were really sowing seed, planting potatoes and corn. They even have a yoke and oxen with a Peruvian flag tied to it, and the women driving the oxen also have Peruvian flags tied to their backs, and they walk along singing and sowing the seed. They do the threshing the same way, and when it's over they leave five or six playful little smart alecks to watch over it; fooling around, they light the threshing floor chaff on fire. And when the dancers see the threshing floor in flames, they run to extinguish it, saying:

"Dammit, now you're going to get it, you little devils!"

Saying this, they'd whip the little guys, and that was always funny. The people watching would be roaring with laughter. This Jacinto Roque is in a chapel there where the miracle happened; he's bleeding from the mouth and sweating blood, and his fierce eyes follow you like bullets. He's burdened down with a heavy cross, and that's why the priest used to say in his sermons:

"Look well, my children—our poor Lord can never rest. Because of our sins, he must suffer. The more sin there is in the world, the heavier his load. Our poor Lord."

That's the way the priest pitied him and his burden; they say that this Lord, Saint Roque, has now gone far away, but I have no idea where.

The Lord of Pampamarca's other brother is the Lord of Huanca. It's said that his miracle happened in the community of Huacoto up around the high reaches of Machu Pachatusan. The gap there at Atas is close to Huacoto, and there's a pampa out that way where the little kids of Huacoto would graze their cattle, sheep, and llamas. One day a little misti boy carrying some bread appeared on the pampa, and he made friends with the little shepherd kids. So they began playing and stopped tending the animals, and though they just kept on playing day in, day out, the cattle didn't disappear or get eaten by pumas or foxes—instead, they began to fatten up and multiply. And the little shepherds wouldn't eat the lunches packed for them, but would bring them back home untouched.

"What have you been eating? Aren't you hungry?" asked the little shepherds' parents.

"No, Papa, we've been eating the delicious bread that a little misti boy brings us. That's why we don't even touch our lunches anymore."

So the parents of the little shepherds asked themselves:

"Who could this little misti boy be?"

And one day, one of their fathers went to have a look at the little misti who was playing with their children, but he didn't see anyone there except the kids, who were all playing around while the cattle roamed freely.

Before that time, they say the boy used to dwell right there at the earth shrine on Atas Pass,[13] but it was very cold and the wind would really whistle through there. And the boy, who was still young, didn't like that. He moved down from the earth shrine at that pass to live in a place called Huanca-Huanca. When the boy was a bit older, he took a trip. During his travels, he came across a man on the trail who was very ill with syphilis.[14] His body was one big, festering sore that was oozing with pus. And some days later, they say the good Lord went to his house to cure him. That sick man was Pedro Arias, a wealthy prospector who had two wives.[15] But they didn't treat him like a human being anymore; they'd just leave his food at a distance and run away all scared, as if he was some kind of rabid dog.

The Lord went to his house and said:

"Pedro, what has happened to you?"

"Oh, Papa, none of the healers are able to cure my sickness. What illness could this be, Papa?"

"Let me take a look. I'm going to cure you, my son."

He took out a little flask of water and bathed him with it, and his sores began to dry up—just like the sores from smallpox do—until they were all cleared up. That's how the Lord of Huanca's water purified him. So Pedro Arias, happy and thankful, asked the Lord:

"Where do you live, Papa, so that I may visit you?"

"If you want to visit me, come all by yourself to Pumaq-Waqananpata in Huanca-Huanca."

Since Pedro Arias was a prospector, he had lots of money. One day, he said good-bye to his wives, and, riding a mule and taking another loaded down with lots of money, he traveled from town to town asking everyone:

"Where's Huanca-Huanca?"

And so, traveling all over the valleys and high reaches, he'd ask every traveler he came across where Huanca-Huanca and Pumaq-Waqananpata were, but none of the thousands he asked knew anything. All tired and worn out with no food or money left, he turned away from the jungle valleys and headed up toward Cuzco, thinking:

"Where could he be living?"

When Pedro Arias arrived in Cuzco, he stayed at a rooming house in San Blas.[16] There, in a cornbeer tavern, he met a man who belonged to a community from the Huanca-Huanca region, and he asked him: [17]

"Where are you from, my friend?"

"I'm from Huanca-Huanca."

"Is Pumaq-Waqananpata in Huanca-Huanca?"

"Yes," he replied.

"Can you take me to your town?"

"Well, all right, sir."

Pedro Arias was very pleased and treated him to several large glasses of cornbeer. The next day he had that man take him down the road to San Salvador, and, leaving his mules in that town, he went by foot to Pumaq-Waqananpata. Well, the Lord was living there among the *tumbo* thickets, and as Pedro Arias approached, he said:

"Oh, Papa, I've been looking for you everywhere! So this is where you're living!"

"But, son, I'm sure I told you that I live in Huanca-Huanca!" he replied.

"I've been all over and none of the people I've asked were able to tell me how to find this place."

When Pedro Arias saw that the Lord was sweating blood, he asked:

"Are you going to stay right here, Papa?"

"Yes," he replied.

So, all sad and worried, Pedro Arias went to San Salvador to notify the priest. So the priest and his sacristans went back to that place carrying the processional cross on high. Pedro Arias was the first to arrive back to the place he'd first found him. But the Lord was no longer there at the place where Pedro Arias had met up with him—he'd hidden himself away. But Pedro Arias went looking around and found him:

"Papa, don't hide anymore, we've been looking for you."

The Lord fled when he saw the priest and all the people, but they began to chase after him. When they were just a hair away from catching him, he grew weary and fell over backward—sprawled out and shuddering, he became wedged in the crag of a huge boulder. The image of his body is all that remains on that huge rock.

Well, after that miracle happened, they celebrated mass and prayed for him, and then Pedro Arias built him a small house, which they've now covered with a large monastery. A chaplain priest came all the way from the Chilean side to drive out the bad spirits and bless the chapel that Pedro Arias had built, and ever since that time until now, the chaplain has stayed there in Huanca-Huanca.

After the miracle happened, the Lord appeared to Pedro Arias and called to him:

"Pedro, Pedro, Mr. Pedro—listen, my son—from now on, you must lead your life with just one of your wives, the one you lawfully married. If not, I'll strike you dead."

"All right, Papa, I'll remember what you've said."

That's how he replied. Pedro Arias went happily back to his town, but the wife he'd lawfully married now acted as if he didn't exist, even pretending she didn't know him. But his other wife, crying with joy, received him with lots of food and cornbeer. So Pedro Arias just kept on living with both wives. But a while later, for having disobeyed his order, our Lord killed him with a fever.

That's the Lord of Huanca's story. From all over, people come swarming like ants just to see him. Some come to pray, others to buy and sell, and others to purify themselves with his water. The time I went there as a boy to sell pots, people used to go by foot to get to the Lord, and they'd return just like a parade, carrying little jugs and bottles of the Lord's water. The Lord of Huanca doesn't want dancers there; he says, "They bother me." And he also doesn't like people to drink cornbeer or liquor. That's why, when they drink cornbeer and liquor near the Lord, they say it's milk, milk for their thirst. They don't say it's liquor they're drinking.

Well, his other brother is Quyllur Rit'i,[18] but I don't know anything about his miracle. People say he's miraculous, but why should I tell you, "I know all about it," when really I don't. They say his other brother is also miraculous and is in Akllamayu, but I'm not sure where that is either.

I lived with my second wife, Josefa, for nine years till she died of a lung cold, that which they call tuberculosis, in room number 4 at Lorena Hospital. She'd been in bad shape. Day after day, she grew worse and worse till she had no energy left. Her color kept changing: she was yellow, and then in the end she was part yellow, part black. Her body wasted away, and there was no flesh left—she was pure bones. So I carried her to the hospital again and again to have the doctors cure her. But they'd only check her mouth and eyes each time, and then they'd give me some small pills, saying:

"Bring in next week."

So week after week, I carried her to the hospital, but in the meantime her lungs were freezing up. Finally they told me, "Tomorrow there's a bed free." I brought her the next day, and it was true, they took her in; but by then she was really ill. I myself don't think they were treating her, because every time I'd go to the hospital those young ladies wearing white clothes wouldn't let me visit her. My wife was in the hospital two weeks, and, during this time, they only let me see her on three occasions. But in spite of that, I still went every day, and when I'd ask those ladies, they'd tell me:

"She's fine, she's fine."

So while they were telling me, *"She's fine, she's fine,"* I went there one morning as usual, and one of the ladies in white told me in my language:

"Gregorio, your wife has died—you've got to take her out of here."

Only then did they let me see my wife, and that same lady led me to where she was. She opened a little room, and from the doorway I saw four souls covered with blankets, strewn out on the floor. Then the same lady told me:

"That one over there."

I pulled back the blanket, and there she was. It was true—my wife was dead—and it seemed as if her eyes were fixed on me. Right there my heart turned bitter—in a daze and trembling with rage, I grabbed her by the hair and began desperately shaking her:

"Hey, Josefa! Hey, Josefa!"

But she was dead—and her little body was totally naked—they'd already taken away the hospital clothes they'd given her.

If I hadn't taken my wife to the hospital, I don't think she would've died. Because I found out later that it's very easy to cure a lung cold; all you have to do is warm up the cornbeer's bottommost dregs and drink it with whipped egg whites and liquor.[19] They say the cough from that cold makes holes in the lungs and this medicine plugs up the holes like clay. So, if she hadn't died, she'd still be beside me today.

That poor soul of mine had just been dumped there on the floor of the morgue. Some of them told me, "Get her out of here," and others told me, "To get a corpse out of here, first do this and then do that." Just then a grave digger interrupted, saying:

"That soul is poor; they should just dump her in the common grave."

My heart changed from being bitter to boiling over with hatred. It was like flames were blazing from my eyes to kill that grave digger. Tell me, how could they even think about dumping that poor soul of mine in a ditch if I was right there beside her and able to bury her in a coffin like a Christian? So I told that lady in white:

"No, ma'am, I'm going to bury my wife in a coffin like a good Christian."

But I didn't have enough money to pay for the coffin, which cost three hundred and forty soles. So, without even thinking about it, I went straightaway to the house of a fellow villager from the Sicuani area to borrow the money. May our Lord reward that good Christian. He didn't refuse me. He lent me two hundred and sixty soles, which was all the money he had. I pawned my poncho and her shawl in order to meet the burial expenses. Then I hurried back to the hospital so that they wouldn't toss my poor wife's body into the common grave. But as I arrived to the entrance carrying the coffin, the doormen were already closing the door—they wouldn't let me inside. While I was standing there at the door with the coffin, they must've finished lunch because they opened the door. When I went in, my wife was no longer laid out in that room. They'd taken her to another room, and she was on top of an adobe bench wrapped in a white sheet. Since I was all by myself, I didn't feel like changing her into the clothes I'd brought. Then my wife's relatives arrived, those who were living in Cuzco at the time; drinking the liquor my compadre and a friend had brought, we readied ourselves to change her clothes. When we pulled back the white sheet, I saw that my wife had been quartered like sheep meat. Slitting open her head and chest, they'd mangled her, and they'd also carved open her belly. Right there my spirit died—I couldn't even talk. But, if she was already dead, why did they have to cut her open?

So that same afternoon, accompanied by six of my people, I buried her.[20]

◻

TEN

LIFE WITH ASUNTA

◻

After my wife Josefa died, I lived alone at Puente Rosario for four months, working, and cooking my food all by myself. I'd go down to the Fly Jail Cornbeer Tavern, which was owned by Mercedes Cusi there in Puente Rosario, and I'd drink a little cornbeer so they'd sell me the strained cornbeer slag for my guinea pigs.[1] I met my present wife, Asunta, while drinking cornbeer at that tavern. She was working as a cook there, and since I didn't have a wife and she served up nice portions, I invited her to have some cornbeer with me, trying to strike up a friendship. She accepted, and sometimes we'd kid around with each other. And then one time, she took the day off, pretending she had to go visit her mother. But I took her off to another cornbeer tavern where we drank cornbeer mixed with regular beer till we got rip-roaring drunk, and so, all drunk like that, we went and slept together at my house.

We've been living together ever since that first day Asunta stepped into my house. She was separated at the time and had a little daughter at her side.

But we couldn't keep living there at Puente Rosario. From dawn till dusk, there'd be nothing but fights, insults, and filing complaints at the police station. One of our neighbors worked as an army mechanic. His wife was from Huayllabamba, and she was really possessed by the devil—from the very day she arrived there as that soldier's wife, she destroyed the peace between our neighbor and us. She'd somehow decided that we were her enemies, and every single day she'd be insulting us. My wife didn't just take it—she'd answer back. So they'd keep on insulting each other till they ran out of breath. And then, when words wouldn't do it anymore, they'd flail away at each other till they were bleeding or their faces were all black and blue. That's why we filed complaints again and again, but even with that she wouldn't stop the fighting.

Even before we could get back home after filing a claim at the police station, the insults and the fighting would already have started up again. So the next day, heads all scraped up and faces bleeding again, we'd be back seeking justice there at the police station. One time my wife got sick from those fits of rage, and her tongue became swollen and filled her mouth, like a horse that's been poisoned. When I asked what kind of illness it was, they told me "anger spells."[2] So, thinking about it, I said to myself:

"Well, before this one dies on me too, dammit, I'd better free her of these anger fits."

So I moved here to Coripata. First, we lived there where the army officers' cottage is now. Back then it was just a large fenced lot belonging to Mrs. Baca Rivero. Inside the enclosure was a pigpen, and I repaired the pigpen's little shack, making a roof out of some tin slats I'd always had. I didn't pay a single centavo of rent, but every Sunday I'd have to go do whatever chores the owner ordered me to. One Sunday while we were living there with no neighbors around to bother us, my compadre Leocadio Mamani came by. He'd been the godfather at my Tomasito's baptism. During that visit, he helped me repair the shack, saying:

"Oh, compadre, we're going to fix this up real nice because right now you're living in a pigpen."

So we took down the tin slats and made the house a bit bigger. And when we finished, my compadre and I set ourselves to drinking, and we drank till dawn the next day. But because I hadn't gone to work for the owner that Sunday, she got mad and told me:

"Vacate my lot!"

I must've lived in that field five or six months. Then I moved to a shack in Dolorespata, and we lived there for four years. That shack belonged to a fruit seller in the central market. There in Dolorespata, my wife still wasn't over her anger spells and felt like she was dying. That's why one day my compadre told me:

"Gregorio, since the women at your side always end up short on luck, you should get married by the Church. That'll change your luck."

And I said:

"But, compadre, who knows how much it would cost!"

So that good-hearted man told me:

"We'll help you, compadre. If you don't want to kill this woman, get lawfully married."

"Well, thank you, compadre. But then you'll be my wedding compadre."[3]

I have to say that this compadre of mine, who's now deceased, really came through for me—may our Lord always help him, though by now he's been saved no doubt. He told me:

"Dammit, Gregorio, let's not be dumb asses; we're not out in some little country town where your wedding compadre has to be another runa like you. We're in a big city full of mistis; why shouldn't we be able to find you a misti who can put in a good word for you once in a while?"

But at the time I didn't know which misti to go to.

You see, I had little friendship with mistis. But Asunta used to know a lot of the people who'd go drink at the Fly Jail Cornbeer Tavern,[4] and she'd struck up a friendship with one of the mistis there; the wiraqucha who became my compadre was named José Díaz. He was a brakeman on the Santa Ana train, and his wife, my *comadre*, was also a mestiza.[5] She used to tend the store she had on Avenida Street. I talked it over with Asunta some more, and we began to get things ready to go and approach them. Whether you're here in Cuzco or out in a country town, it always costs a lot to get yourself a misti compadre— it's different with a fellow villager:

"Hey, I'd like you to be my compadre—well then, let's drink a toast, compadre."[6]

And just like that, your compadre would be all ready to go.

In order to approach and ask that wiraqucha, José Díaz, to be our wedding compadre, we went to his house accompanied by my compadre Leocadio, carrying a satchel full of corn on the cob, a side of mutton, a dozen beers, and two big jugs full of milk that we also lugged along. This was all part of the cost. Asunta had brought the corncobs, meat, and milk from her hometown, San Jerónimo, the place she'd been cast into this world.

My compadre, thank our Lord, wasn't like other mistis who make you beg them. He accepted, and later on when we'd had a bit to drink, we set the date. It was to be the month of March; then my comadre said:

"Let it be on Easter Saturday. To marry on a Saturday is to marry good luck."

And we said:

"Yes, ma'am."

Our wedding was supposed to be the first week of April. But it didn't happen that way. It was set back three months while we practiced praying. Neither she nor I knew how to pray, and since you must take confession and Communion to get married by the Church, we had to prepare for that. If you're a runa, the priest makes you pray, and if you don't know how to pray, he sends you back from the confessional, saying "heretic." That's the shame you'd be put through. My wife just couldn't get the prayers, the Lord's Prayer or the

Creed, into her head. But by Saint John's Day, we were skilled at praying, and only then, that very same day, did we marry.

For our wedding, we both bathed the day before the ceremony. And later on that same night, we went for confession to the church in San Pedro. Just as I thought, when we approached the priest, he asked us if we knew how to pray or not. Then the priest ordered us:

"Let's see then: pray."

So I prayed. The priest had nothing to correct me on; everything went fine, and then he spoke again:

"Now tell me your sins."

Since I'd never confessed before, I told him my sins: that I'd slept with married women, as well as with other women who I wasn't married to, and that I'd gotten drunk. But then my mind went blank and, in a daze, I fell dumb; I wasn't able to think of any more sins to tell him about. Then the priest asked:

"That's everything, my son?"

"Yes, Papa."

"How can that be! That can't be all, my son—tell me every little thing!"

So I told him:

"Papa, there's other sins, but my mind went blank."

"Pray, my son."

I began to sweat, but the prayers hadn't left me, and, in a sweat, I saved the confession.

The next day was Saint John's, and our mass took place at six in the morning, there at the church in San Pedro. When mass was over, my compadre hired a taxi from the plaza to take us to his house on Avenida Street, where we'd gotten everything ready. My wife's relatives came from San Jerónimo, bringing cornbeer for the occasion. The only person from my side of the family was my compadre Leocadio. We ate, drank, and danced that day, but I didn't enjoy it—I felt ashamed. My new compadre had invited his brothers, brothers-in-law, and neighbors, and there wasn't enough food to go around. Having a misti wedding compadre is always expensive. Early next morning, my wife and I went to pay our compadres a visit. They offered us some tea and a little bit of bread, but not a drop of liquor or anything else. After our visit, we went back to our shack in Dolorespata, where, together with our relatives, we stayed up till dawn the next day drinking the liquor they'd brought.

Although my wife Asunta isn't as good as Josefa was, we're doing well together. I don't have any children by her, but she has her daughter, who now has a husband and two kids. Her daughter is kind; she calls me "Papa" and doesn't neglect us—she's always there for us. My little wife, Asunta, also treats me well. The very day we began living together, she stopped cooking there at the cornbeer tavern. And since she's a real good cook, she's always had her little food business there at Huánchac Market. She works at her little business twice a week and sometimes makes ten, even twenty soles, though there've been many times she's gone broke; that's because nowadays the cost of all cooking supplies is rising. On the days she's not cooking, she goes and buys bottles from stores in Coripata, Dolorespata, and Santiago. She also goes to the San Sebastián trash dump, combing it for bottles, pieces of metal, and little flasks. She and I wash all that so we can take it and sell it at the Saturday flea market. That, too, leaves a few centavos for our bellies.

Well, we'd been living in the shack there at Dolorespata for four years, and during that time, I'd made sheaves to reinforce the reed walls and had replaced the roof's worn-out sheet metal with my own tin slats. So I'd fixed it up real nice. I was like a caretaker and didn't pay any rent; but whenever the widow sent for me, I'd have to cart fruit from her house in Santiago over to the market. So I had to haul stuff. But one day they began to urbanize Dolorespata, and, without telling us a thing, the lady sold the piece of land with the shack on it. A month after it sold, the owner came by, bringing two workers to tear down the shack. I was working as a hired hand that day, finishing a house in Almudena, when my wife ran up screaming as if she'd lost her mind:

"The house! The house!"

I took off flying, thinking, "It must be on fire." But when I got there, my house had been leveled. Our things were all piled up, and the guinea pigs were running around all scared. And his workers were already carrying off my sheet metal and tin slats. And so, dammit, I started foaming at the mouth with rage. And since I didn't know what to do, to scream or go flying after the workers to get my tin slats back, I said:

"Damn it all! Who the hell did this to my house?"

And a young misti fellow answered me:

"I did. I'm the owner."

I couldn't hold back my anger, dammit, and I punched the little crook— that measly runt tumbled to the ground like an adobe brick. But a little while later, he had some police take me to the Santiago Police Station, where a policeman told me:

"You uppity little Indian, so you went and hit a misti—well, now you're going to prison for this insolence. Here, take this, you fucking Indian!"

And he gave me a swift kick.

But they didn't send me to prison; I was out of there in just twenty-four hours. Meanwhile, my wife had been running around crying, there at the place where the office of Inka Motors now sells cars; back then a misti who raised

lots of dogs used to live there. That misti had seen my wife sobbing as if she'd lost her mind, and, taking pity on her, he'd pointed to an open shed in the middle of a potato patch here in Coripata, saying:

"Live over there."

When those fucking policemen let me go, my house had already been completely leveled. My wife and all of our belongings were gone. So I went to a neighbor who was also caretaking a fenced lot, there next to the eucalyptus grove in Dolorespata, and I asked him about my wife and all our things. And he told me:

"Yes, we carried your things to a shed in Coripata yesterday."

It was true—there was my wife, down and out, just sitting there in that open shed, our belongings strewn out around her. And she told me:

"This is where we'll stay and live; the wiraqucha who owns it says he needs someone to live here and watch over the crops."

I went to thank the owner and to ask him if he wanted us to stay on his land. I said:

"Thank you, good sir, for having called my wife over; may God bless you. We've been left without a home—if you'd like, good sir, I can watch over your field."

That good Christian agreed to my caretaking the crops there in his field. Well, back then Coripata was full of crops: potatoes, barley, and peas. But over to one side, next to a ditch, there where my house is now, the soldiers used to come do drills, and they'd built a little house back who knows when. But by that time, all that remained of the house was the foundation, which was also falling to pieces. So the owner told me:

"Repair that foundation, that's where your house will be."

So I fixed up the foundation and walls with stone and adobe brick, and my compadre Leocadio lent me some poles that I used as beams; then I finished the roof with the tin slats I still had left. That's how I built the house I now live in. At that time, I had a neighbor named Puma living next to my home. He was a brick mason, and his wife was a fruit vendor. My neighbor Puma and I were the first to live here in Coripata; we were like the caretakers of those fields. When that misti's dogs multiplied in number, my job was to bring them food from the Savoy Hotel, which had just begun to operate at the time. I'd go pick up the hotel guests' leftovers every morning at six. It was good food, and there was always a little something for us as well. Because of that, the wife of our neighbor, Puma, began to envy us, and she turned into a real devil. That woman isn't Christian—she'd go around like a haughty little snob, better than the rest.[7] When something happens to her and she dies, she'll be damned, because each and every day that woman used to fight and trade insults with us, and we'd often end up filing complaints at one police station or another, one day in Huánchac, the next in Santiago. Today she's all huddled in her house, old and worn with rheumatism. My wife just says:

"God is just. Those tears of mine weren't mere raindrops falling—my curses worked. That bitch is going to die, just lying there all balled up like that."

But suddenly they stopped cultivating the land. The owner was a foreigner named Repeto, and he'd sold it to an association of people who wanted to develop it. And then, just like a union, those people began to have get-togethers and meetings every single Sunday to divide up the lots. I also went to talk with them, and they told me:

"Since you've already lived here for many years, we can make you a member if you'd like, but the lots are going to be sold, and you'll have to pay your first contribution dues."

We got together a thousand soles by borrowing from the people we knew, so that we'd be admitted as members of the housing development; they gave us a lot next to the grove of trees. But each Sunday, there'd be meetings and more and more dues. There were dues for everything, and since we weren't able to keep up with our dues, I transferred my lot to someone I knew. So I got back the dues I'd paid. Coripata was just like one big work party, with everyone tripping over each other to build their houses as fast as they could. When they were almost all finished paying off their lots and some of them even held titles, the Law of the New Town came around.[8] We were anxious and worried, thinking, "Since we don't belong to the association, they'll no doubt kick us out of here." Then, one Sunday some civil service wiraquchas, a military commander, and a priest came and held a large meeting, declaring Coripata to be a New Town. It was funny, because the members gathered there couldn't do a thing about it; so one of them, all by himself, began whistling and jeering.[9] And that's when it all began: hurling rocks and insults, they sent those wiraquchas flying right out of there. After that, there were lots of meetings, one right after the other. Everyone was saying:

"We can't be a New Town, because we've gotten these plots of land from our sweat—they've cost us—it's not a squatters' colony, it's not a gift. Coripata can't be a New Town."

So they talked that way for about two years, fighting against Coripata becoming a New Town. But now they've been beat—Coripata became a New Town anyway. And no one has said a thing to us yet. Instead, they say that, being a New Town, whoever occupies a lot is already the owner. But our house doesn't appear as a lot, because it's not on the map; according to the map, it's a space on the street that was left open to build a sidewalk garden. That's what the secretary of Coripata once told me when I wanted to have water installed in my house. All the houses here already have water, electricity, and sewer drains; but because my lot isn't registered, I can't have them installed at home. That's why I have to get the water I use from my friends' homes, the ones I haul loads for. But dammit, I was the first person to live here in Coripata, and neither the New Town nor the association will be able to drive me out of here—I've poured my sweat and blood into this soil. They just can't do that to me.

☐
THE FACTORY
☐

The Huáscar factory needed workers to repair a wall that had fallen down, but they were wary and wouldn't accept people they didn't know. You had to be taken in there by someone who knew the powerful wiraquchas who owned the factory. But I had just a single friend, Leandro Mamani Tito, working there as a laborer in the factory; he spoke to them on my behalf, and I think he must've told them:

"This man's a brick mason"—but I wasn't a brick mason, just a regular workhand—"and he knows how to work with adobe."

So the factory accepted me, taking me in as a brick mason. It was easy putting one brick on top of another, and I did my job as a bricklayer well. One day, after we'd been working there for several months, my friend came by and told me I had to go to a workers' meeting. It took place in the afternoon, right there in the factory, and all of the workers, some four hundred of them, were gathered together as one.

At the meeting, they said:

"Comrades, the price of gas is rising, the price of kerosene is rising, and that's no good because it affects the people, all of us. The price of gas goes up and then everything goes up: bread, clothes—everything! But our wages don't go up!"

That same night, we went to central square carrying flags and placards and shouting slogans:

"Down with the price of gas! Down with the price of gas!"

When we arrived at central square, we were strong in numbers. The beer company workers had also joined in and were marching behind us. Once there in central square, the leaders again gave speeches about the same thing: gas. And each and every worker was chanting slogans with all their might. I was also yelling them at the top of my lungs. When they finished their speeches, I headed back to the factory with my friend Leandro, and when we got there he told me:

"I'm going to introduce you to a great comrade."

And I asked:

"Who?"

"Comrade Emiliano Huamantica."

Sure, I already knew who he was. In the square that night, he'd been a gutsy and fearless speaker, a real man. So I was real happy—I was going to be friends with a good-hearted comrade. When I was introduced to Emiliano Huamantica, he offered me his hand:

"How do you do, comrade?"

And shaking his hand, I responded in the runa tongue: [1]

"Gregorio Condori Mamani at your service, comrade."

So it was.

One afternoon, a month after I'd personally met Emiliano Huamantica, they notified all the unsalaried workhands:

"As of tomorrow, you're laid off."

There were about ten of us workhands there, and we got very upset with the news that they were letting us go. Once again we'd be out in the street without a steady job, looking here and there, asking: "Where can I find a job or some goods that need hauling?"

So that same afternoon, when I left the factory, I waited by the entrance to give my friend Leandro the news:

"I'm out of a job starting tomorrow. They're letting us go."

And Leandro immediately said:

"Let's go to Emiliano."

When we approached Emiliano Huamantica, he was speaking with a large group of workers. We waited till he finished, and then my friend told him:

"Comrade, they've dismissed Gregorio here from his job. Can't something be done for him?"

Comrade Emiliano Huamantica looked worried; after a brief moment of silence, he replied:

"Why don't you come back tomorrow."

When I went the next day, he'd already spoken with the factory owners about me working as a steady laborer there. He told me:

"Comrade Gregorio, we've already spoken so that you can stay there and work. Some days ago, a comrade became very ill; he's a sweeper and you'll replace him, at least for now."

Some time later, I learned that this fellow had caught pneumonia, and he'd died of it a few days later. So that's how I ended up taking the place of a fellow factory worker who'd died.[2]

While I worked there, my job was to sweep the entire factory: the yard, offices, machine shop, and hallways. I'd be doing nothing but sweeping and mopping—I barely had enough time to do it all. I was happy sweeping. It wasn't tiring, but there just wasn't enough time to do it all. My job there in the factory didn't last very long, because one day when everything was going just fine, they announced:

"The factory's closing down."[3]

All of us, from office workers to sweepers, out in the street. Once again, dammit, having to worry. "The factory's closing, the factory's closing"— hearing that was the worst fucking thing. A lot of meetings were held in the plaza, but by then it was too late to do anything. The union had already been bought off—the leaders went and covered it up, saying, "There just aren't any raw materials to be worked." The factory bought them a house in Ttio to keep them quiet. The union secretary was blind in one eye, and I've run across him many times in the street when I'm out hauling goods. If I'd had bullets at hand any of those times we've run into each other, I'd have blown away his other eye, because it's that bastard's fault they closed down the factory, booting more than four hundred workers out into the street. If he'd protested the same way that comrade Emiliano Huamantica used to, the factory wouldn't have shut down. Lomellini, the factory owner, said, "How can I bring in more cotton if there aren't any materials or money left?" And the union didn't say a word.

So we all left the factory—there was nothing else we could do. Ever since then I've devoted myself to lugging goods, because it's a sure thing. If Comrade Huamantica hadn't died, I wouldn't be a strapper like I am today. That's because this comrade of mine was a true man of character. He never would've let the factory close down. I'm sure he'd have thought about making a cooperative like they're doing at La Estrella factory. The luck of four hundred workers changed quickly with Emiliano Huamantica's death; he'd been a villager from the Calca region, and he died an awful death. As he was on his way to speak to the Government, the car he was traveling in fell off a cliff, there above Arequipa in Santa Lucía. Yet he managed to stay alive, but because the rich hacienda owners were against him, they gave him sedatives—that's how he died.[4]

Lomellini's sons were responsible for the factory coming to ruin. Their father had built up a good factory, even bringing machinery from abroad. But when old man Lomellini died, his children began taking charge of the factory. They spent money recklessly, and there was no money left to buy materials or pay wages. And so the factory really began to fall apart.

I've heard about women around here who force you to spend money, thousands and thousands, on drinking binges. They get you to dance, and then they all get together, rape you, and grab all your money. That roadhouse first operated in Tullumayu next to the Bay Colt Cookhouse. Later, it moved farther down, over across from La Salle High School. Men such as us used to go there, just like they were celebrating somebody's birthday. There were always lots of drunk roughnecks picking fights. Who the heck knows why they'd go to that house—maybe they didn't have wives, or maybe they'd been fighting with their wives, or their wives didn't want to give it to them. Because it's dirty to go to bed with a woman everyone has slept with. It's much better to have a woman all to yourself, for nobody else. Sometime later that house moved to Quilque, where it's still operating. That kind of house only exists here; they don't have anything like that out in the country towns. Everyone has their own wife to do it with whenever they feel like it. That roadhouse is only for the wealthy, and they spend all their money there. It's said that half the money made by the women in those houses goes to the Government; they're like its employees.

So it was.

Comrade Emiliano Huamantica was always on his way somewhere, to Lima or Arequipa, to make demands on behalf of the workers. And you know, to the different Governments' way of thinking, he must've been a real headache. That's probably why, from the time of Odría to that of Belaúnde,[5] they were always having him arrested. Huamantica used to work together with Dr. Angles, the union lawyer. They were on the side of the poor and were known as communists. That's why they were hated by the Aprista hacienda owners, who were wealthy, treacherous enemies.

Those wealthy Apristas wanted to make Haya de la Torre president. So they dressed him up as a lovely lady and brought him here to Cuzco by night.[6] And he came from the train station to central square all dressed up as a lady, and when he was already in the square, people said:

"That's not a lady, that's Haya de la Torre."

They began hurling stones. So rocks were flying all over, and many bullets whistled by that day. After the fight, there were lots of injured people: some with their eyes all swollen up and others with their faces and heads split open, dripping blood. All kinds of things just kept happening that day, until Haya de la Torre had to flee Cuzco. During the Bustamante Government, everyone was saying: "Haya de la Torre for president, Haya de la Torre for president." But now they've forgotten all about him—you never even hear his name anymore.

Back when five large pieces of bread made of pure wheat used to cost ten centavos and three pieces only five centavos, Odría snatched the presidency away from Bustamante. That Odría snatched the presidency from Bustamante because he raised the price of bread from three pieces for five centavos and five for ten centavos—during Bustamante's time, a single piece of bread had come to cost ten centavos. Worst of all, back then there wasn't any money; there's lots of money now, but it's not worth a thing. At that time, ten centavos worth of bread would last a whole week, and it was even made of pure wheat. Nowadays, we buy five soles worth of bread each day for breakfast. And dammit, those pieces of bread are about the size of the buttons on my old army coat. Back then, who knows, five soles worth of bread was maybe even enough to carry out an important cargo, not like it is now, where five soles of hunger is what you gulp down daily.

That's life, real fucked up. Life really fucks with you, dammit—it fucks with your belly, and this back of mine just can't lift loads anymore.

I don't know if Odría came to Cuzco to proclaim himself Government when he snatched the presidency from Bustamante. I didn't see him, but I did see Bustamante. He came to proclaim himself before Odría snatched the presidency from him. Well, I don't know about these Governments—all they do is snatch it back and forth from each other. They're just like brothers fighting over an inheritance. When someone like Bustamante is in Government, then another like Odría comes along and snatches it away from him. And then another one comes along and snatches it from this Odría, and when the one who snatched it from Odría is in Government, yet another one comes along and puts himself on top of that Government. But then still another comes and puts himself on top of this other Government, like when Velasco snatched Belaúnde's Government. And who knows how long Velasco's Government is going to last? Though I've heard they're not going to sack him, because the armed forces all support him and he's helping the poor by getting rid of the haciendas.[7]

Long before the Agrarian Reform Law was even discussed, people began talking about Hugo Blanco.[8] I've heard that he used to live down the valley in the jungle, just like any other tenant farmer there.[9] It was some time later, when they were forming unions and he made himself one of the leaders, that his name became known outside the jungle. During those union meetings, Hugo Blanco would say:

"The haciendas must all be done away with—the hacienda lands will become village lands and belong to the people."

That's why the hacienda owners were opposed and tried to stop him. But to that, Hugo Blanco replied:

"But it doesn't matter if those little land barons try to block us, because we'll gladly spill our blood for the land."

The hacienda owners were frightened by that threat and asked the police to come in. While people in the jungle were all talking about Hugo Blanco, soldiers and policemen were swarming all over the place like ants, searching around for him. But they say he was holed up in a cave on top of a mountain peak, like an ancestral spirit.[10] His friends would bring him food only at night. During the day, he'd just watch from his cave as the police bumbled around, searching all over for him. But one day a policeman passed near Hugo Blanco's cave and stepped on a mine made of dynamite, which blew the poor policeman to pieces. Other policemen arrived, and they too were blown to bits by dynamite. Then lots more police arrived, and they nabbed Hugo Blanco as he was fleeing his cave.

After they'd caught him, planes and helicopters flew to the jungle to take him off to jail. And so, one day while Hugo Blanco was being held prisoner in the garrison stockade, he tried to escape and was almost past the gate when the lookouts caught him. Since the garrison didn't have the security to hold Hugo Blanco, the Government sent him off to Frontón Prison out in the sea lake.[11] But then they sent him from Frontón to a foreign country.

So today Hugo Blanco is being held prisoner in a foreign country.

TWELVE

WE STRAPPERS

Day in, day out, ever since I first began as a strapper, I've always started my work hauling goods at five in the morning. I haul goods there in the central market itself, or from the market to people's houses, or else I'm carrying out my set contracts. The things I carry are always different, from packages of bread or clothes to large crates; other times, it's baskets of food or sacks full of potatoes. It all depends how much strength you have, though you've always got to push your strength to the limit.

It doesn't pay much, but there's always something to take home; you can make twenty to twenty-five soles a day, and sometimes even up to seventy.[1] But in order to get seventy soles a day, you have to really fly, making twenty or even twenty-five trips, looking all over for anyone needing a strapper. You have to just stay around the marketplace or outside the entrances to the supermarket and stores. Back when I had more than enough strength, I could get jobs at the train station, loading and unloading. But now they don't want me anymore, and they pretend not to recognize me when they see me—when they see you're old, they won't even let you help. That's why I'm always there at central market and out in the streets, looking around for cargo to carry. But there's always some ladies who will shove me away when I step in to shoulder their loads:

"You're too old now, you can't do it, go rest up. Call someone young for me."

It's always those wealthy, well-dressed women who haggle the most. They have you carry their goods from the market or stores all the way to their doorsteps, and then, without even asking how much you charge a load, they toss you two or three soles. That's why, many times I've been so angry, I've felt like taking the goods back where I picked them up. But if you complain, it's even worse—they tell you:

"You're just too old now. Run along, go rest up."

That's what those inconsiderate ladies say, as if your belly could also rest. But other ladies are reasonable and always pay what you ask. Maybe they just do it because they see you're old. But there aren't any of those mishaps when you're portering for a set contract. That's why I wish I had more set contracts; right now I just have six a week. One of these contracts is carrying three blocks of ice from where they make it in Coripata, all the way to central market at six each morning.[2] That contract's with a lady who sells fish and shrimp, and she pays me six soles a trip. And another contract is with a shoemaker; from Rosaspata I carry three large crates of shoes for him, again to the central marketplace. The crates are bulky, but they aren't that heavy; I also have to take those same crates back at six or seven at night. He pays me thirteen soles for the trip there and back. I also have a contract with Mrs. Angélica Salas, from Belén Bridge, again to central market. Every morning at eight I carry over her pots of food. She only pays me three soles, but she also gives me a bowl of soup or plate of food on top of that. She sells that food to the little shoeshine and newspaper boys and to some of the drivers.

Mrs. Angélica has real good luck selling food; by ten in the morning her food's all gone. Because of that, her fellow food vendors envy her. They say:

"That woman has lots of luck—she must be blessed by offerings to have such good sales.[3] The old man also carries good luck. The food his back brings never gets returned, while almost everything my strapper carries gets sent back."

So we strappers bring luck to the people we carry for, and it's the luck of your back that decides whether they want you or not. But some of the other strappers aren't so lucky, and when the food they've carried doesn't all get sold, people say:

"That strapper's back is bad luck."

And then they never have them carry their things again. Ever since I began working as a strapper, I've had a lucky back for carrying merchandise. So while my contracts are few, I've always got some the whole year through. My back is lucky because of the offerings that've been made to my guardian spirit.[4] Those fellow strappers of mine who walk the streets with no one giving them work haven't made any offerings at all, and they're just shouldering their loads any old way.

Other temporary contracts, bringing over goods that are needed by the stores here in Coripata and Rosaspata, arise throughout the week. But when you carry merchandise for stores, you risk getting swindled. A year ago I was lugging along some *pisco* brandy for one of those stores, and as I was going by Limaqpampa some young guys approached me and said:

"Papa, the lady told us there's no need for you to carry that case anymore, now that we've got a car to take it there, along with some other cases."

And stupid me, I believed the message and handed over the case of pisco, when those who took it were really crooks. But the owner thought I'd hidden the case or sold it, and every day she'd demand more than five hundred soles as payment. But since I didn't have it, how could I pay her? After a while, she got tired of trying to collect. But I tell you what, I was at her service for almost a year, and with that I surely paid the price of the pisco twice over.

A few days from now I'll have another daily contract, carrying sprouted corn seed from a cornbeer tavern to the mill and then bringing it back all ground up. I'll get paid seven soles and two large glasses of cornbeer on top of that. According to the tavern owner, the strapper who had that contract carrying corn sprouts for her just took off without saying a thing, and it's been weeks since he's come around. But I've heard that her strapper is sick. Such is the strapper's life. When we get old and keep on lugging, that's when we get sick, but when we stop showing up at the people's houses where we've been portering year after year our whole lives, they never stop to ask about us: "Our strapper hasn't come around; I wonder what could've happened to him?" They'd never ask anything like that. They just want to be served. Even when you're down and out, like some poor stray dog just sprawled out in the street or in the corner of some house, even then they won't ask about you.

When strappers get old and don't have the strength to carry even their own bones anymore, they're rarely taken to a rest home. Because just like everywhere else, they ask you for your papers, your birth certificate, where you're from, your name, and if you've got relatives. If they like your papers, they let you in. But since none of the strappers have papers, they're never accepted. So, looking for handouts up and down the street, that's where they die.

We strappers are always walking around begging when we die. Who knows, maybe that'll happen to me too. I'll get run over by a car, they'll take me to the hospital, do an autopsy on me, and then they'll just toss me in the graveyard.

When a strapper who has no one, nobody at all, dies on a street corner or in some house, the person who finds him notifies the police station, and then the police come and take them off to the morgue. If he has relatives, they come claim the body and have him buried. But if there's no one to claim him, they just dump the poor soul on top of a cold stone slab for two or three days there in the morgue. Then they just take the corpse, with it wearing the same clothes as usual, no shroud or coffin, and heave it into the common grave—then they cover it with a little dirt. They just dump you there like some dirty mongrel. There in the common grave, the children, women, and old ones are all piled up like firewood, one on top of the other. That's where strappers get tossed, there with the people who don't have anybody.

I saw all this recently when a strapper friend of mine named Purificación

Quispe died. His lungs collapsed, no doubt from the burden he'd been carrying, and he died spitting up blood, there at the Santo Tomás and Urubamba bus station on Belén Street. They just tossed Purificación Quispe on top of some straw that they'd unloaded from a truck, and, dead like that, the poor soul was just laid out there most of the day. When night was falling, some officers came from the Santiago Police Station and had him taken to the morgue. So, since none of his relatives showed up there at the morgue for two days, they just heaved him into the common grave.

As an old-timer who has been lugging for a long time, I'd like all of us strappers living here in Cuzco, young and old alike, to get together and form a union so we don't have to live this kind of life.[5] That way we'd be united as one, a single voice. Maybe then justice would open its eyes and help us out, at least with a little something, so we don't have to be dragging along our tattered clothes beneath the loads we carry, dying in the street like dogs.

Such is life for us strappers—we move through the streets and markets like the damned, our tattered clothes dragging along behind us. These rags can still be patched up, but the hunger in our bellies can't be mended. Such is life for us strappers, young and old alike, though the young strappers aren't in the street like us old-timers; they work loading and unloading the boxcars at the train station. When there's no work at the train station, they go to the bus companies where people travel to Arequipa or Lima, and they load buses there or lug goods to people's houses. It's piecework at the train and bus stations; the pay's pretty good, but you have to sweat like a mule. There's a fixed rate there. You're paid between fifty and two hundred and fifty to load or unload a truck. It's the same rate to load or unload a boxcar from a truck. There's often a truck or two to load or unload at those places each day, but sometimes there's none at all.

Some of the other strappers are villagers from the high reaches who come to Cuzco just a few months a year, those after the harvest in July and August. They stay one, two, or three weeks, and sometimes even a month or more. When they aren't working as hired hands, building houses or making adobe bricks, they become strappers. Here in Cuzco, house construction begins in May and goes till September or October. They need workers for the adobe houses being built, especially there in the New Towns. They never accept us villagers on large construction jobs, saying, "They don't know how to work," preferring construction workers instead. During the months of January, February, or March, after their fields have been sowed and the young plants weeded, country villagers fill the streets of Cuzco. During some weeks of those months, there's more strappers than loads to be carried.

For one who has suffered in the street, it's heartbreaking to see those fellow villagers of mine, the ones who don't know their way around the hardships one has to suffer through here in the city. They're nobodies here, just like orphans, and they sleep wherever they can: on the bare ground, in lodging houses or in doorways of the cornbeer taverns, or there in the hallways of the Melgar Boarding House. And when the first rays of morning light are just beginning to show, they're out and about, looking for loads to carry. They come here because they're poor and can't make money in their communities; the land they work grows just enough to feed them. And since without money, one can't buy all the things needed at home—like salt, sugar, pepper, or work tools— they come here looking for work. Since there aren't any steady jobs here in the big city besides lugging goods, they become strappers, and that way they save up the money they need for their purchases.

PART TWO

ASUNTA QUISPE HUAMÁN

THIRTEEN

RUNNING AWAY
FROM THE HACIENDA

Back when I was just a girl, around the time I'd started my bleeding, my older sister Juliana married a man who belonged to the community of Rondobamba, and right after they got married, he took her off to his community.[1] She lived there at her husband's side, working the fields and looking after the cattle. When they'd been married five years, we received word that the people of that community, from one end to the other, were dying of fever. My sister had also died. She'd already had three little babies by that time, and those babies of hers also died of that same sickness. When my father found out, he readied himself to go to Rondobamba, so he could be there for the octave and wash the clothes of the deceased.[2] Two weeks later, my father returned home, and two days after his return, he came down with fever. That plague fever had followed him. That sickness makes the stomach burn, and your head aches all over till you just can't take it. That's how people were dying. My father spread his fever to our little old grandmother, my mother's mother.[3] She died two days after her belly started burning with pain—she just couldn't hold out any longer. After our grandmother died, the fever leaped to Juanico, our older brother, who was a young man by then. He only held out against that deadly fever four days. Juanico died in a crazy fit, shrieking:

"My head's on fire!"

It was my father who fought the fever the longest—he died six days after his belly began burning. Less than a week after those things happened in our home, all our neighbors fled their houses, saying:

"It's spreading!"

They went and lived out in their fields. And others went up to the herd steads. Our house was in Coñipata, there on the outskirts of the town of San Jerónimo, at the foot of the trail going to Pata-Pata Hacienda. Everybody in town knew the plague fever was in our home, and, out of fear, no one took that trail anymore. I remember others also dying of that plague—it spread from our house, no doubt. Yet, people were saying, "It's from the vaccine." Sure, when the plague appeared in our house and people began dying, the vaccinators had come from Cuzco. But then those who'd gotten vaccinated also came down with fever, and a lot of them died. When people saw that those who'd been vaccinated were dying, nobody wanted the vaccine. And then, when nobody wanted it, the police came in and made them get vaccinated, taking people by force as if they were criminals. When they realized what was happening, everybody fled to the high reaches to escape the vaccinators.

When our father and older brother died from the fever, we had no one to work at Pata-Pata Hacienda, which belonged to the Dominican fathers. We were tenant farmers there, with three *tupus* of cornfield and two tupus of wheat. The wheat fields were in the high reaches of the hacienda lands and were sown only in the rainy season. Wheat was grown there every four years, and the other years the land lay fallow. In exchange for those plots of hacienda land, the tenant farmers there in the hacienda all had to do labor service.[4] That is, for each tupu of cornfield, you'd have to work for the hacienda six unpaid days a month, all year round, and for each tupu of corn you'd also have to do a month of manor service each year.[5] If you were working wheat fields, for each tupu you'd have to do three days' labor service a month, as well as a month of manor service each year. Being a manor servant in exchange for wheat fields was easy. There'd be two of those servants, and every morning till noon or in the afternoons, all they'd have to do is cook food for the more than twenty dogs the hacienda had. The dogs, like the priests, had gotten used to eating three times a day, and that's why there were three shifts. So you see, in the hacienda, there were manor servants for everything. When the hacienda had enough servants, they sent you to the monastery in Cuzco, and that's where you'd do your service to the priests. Many tenant farmers would come here to the Santo Domingo monastery and work as servants. Some did the laundry, washing all the priests' clothes. And others were the kitchen help. Still others were sweepers. Those doing their manor service at the monastery would come for the whole month, bringing their beds with them. Everyone wanted to go to the monastery, because they fed you and the work wasn't as hard as on the hacienda, and you also didn't have the overseer looking over your shoulder.

That's what it was like being a tenant farmer: all you did was work for the hacienda, and there'd be no days left to work your own fields. Every day the head overseer would come by and tell us where to work on the hacienda, leaving us a hoe or ploughshare. They'd do that so we'd have to go work no matter what. And if you didn't go when the overseer left you the hoe or ploughshare, they'd deduct two or three days from the ones you'd already worked. And that's on top of the days that just disappeared off the head overseer's list. If you were supposed to work three weeks for your three tupus of land, it ended up being four or five weeks of work because everyone knew that the days you worked just disappeared off the list. That's why, year round, you'd spend month after month working there at the hacienda.

Those priests did all that—what hellish times those were! So the days we were supposed to have worked at the hacienda began to pile up, and the head overseer began insisting that we send a peon. Each time he'd come chew out my mother about sending a worker, she'd start crying, and we'd all be there at her side, crying too. There were five of us: our older brother who died of plague, and four girls. I was the third sister, and since we were all girls, none of us were able to work as peons in the hacienda.[6] Since the overseer wouldn't let women work, my mother went to the monastery and spoke with the head father, begging him to let her and my older sister work at the hacienda. So the head father accepted, saying:

"Since you're a woman and can't work as a peon, you must give up one of your tupus. Your daughter will come work as a cook in the monastery, and you'll go work at the hacienda."

So my mother came back sobbing:

"They've taken a tupu of cornfield away from us."

A week later, my older sister Justina began working as a cook at the priests' estate, while we had to go to the hacienda with my mother—so our sufferings began to weigh heavier and heavier upon us. We'd have to do our labor service there at the hacienda, as well as tend to the few fields and animals we had—there just weren't enough hands to go around. So our mother turned mean and lost her senses—she got upset with everything we did and she'd hit us. Our hair wasn't hair anymore—she'd grab us and bang our heads against the wall if we didn't do things the way she wanted. So my mother began working as a milk servant. There were two of these milk servants, and they'd have to milk more than eighty cows daily, putting the milk into large canisters. They'd leave some of the milk at the monastery, and the rest was delivered to set contracts in Cuzco; they wouldn't get home till dark. As a woman, my mother was told just to milk the cows and fill the jugs; others would take the milk to Cuzco. She'd be out early each morning, rushing around milking the cows. Milking was very tiring, and with my back bent and weary, I'd be there helping my mother. Because it was the frost season, the cows' teats were all scraped up, and some were even bleeding. I must've chafed against those sores, because the damn cow, which had been standing there nice and still, suddenly gave a jump and knocked over the milk canister, which was almost full. When my mother saw the milk all over the ground, she swung and hit me with a bucket. It only hurt a little, but when I saw the blood dripping from my head, I started shrieking as if I'd lost my mind. And a priest who no doubt heard my screams came running over, and when he saw the ground all white with milk, he told my mother:

"Oh, you damned woman—what the hell have you done, dammit!"

Then the overseer also came over, and that Christian punished my mother:

"Dammit, you're going to pay for this, bitch—nine days' labor service! Done!"

He noted it down in his record book, and just like that, my mother lost nine days' work.

I don't know why it is, but ever since I've been a little girl, whenever I cut myself, it just bleeds and bleeds without stopping. So when I kept on wailing, my mother, fuming with anger, came over and knocked me to the ground, stuffing my mouth with cow shit, saying:

"Go on, scream some more!"

I barely escaped. But when I turned around, my poor mother was still there, milking away, sobbing and sobbing. May God forgive me, but I ran away to Cuzco that day, abandoning my mother to that suffering. I must've been thinking, "Who knows what else she'll do to me when I go home." So I went straight to our field and gathered some broad beans growing to one side. I went to Cuzco by foot carrying the satchel of broad beans I'd gathered there in our field, as if I was on my way to sell them at market.

So that's how I came to Cuzco the first time, running away from that suffering, thinking I might be better off here. When I got to Cuzco, I sold the beans in the central market, but then afterward I had nothing to do and nowhere to go. When dusk was falling and I was on the verge of tears, I met a lady—the work of the blessed souls no doubt—and she took me off to be a maid in her house.[7] That lady was a schoolmistress in the community of Llullucha, which was a day's walk from Urcos. Two months after I first started living in Cuzco, we set out and traveled there; I worked for her at the school, cooking and taking care of her three children. But with this teacher, my sufferings continued.[8] The school was in the cold and snowy high reaches, where hail would be coming down almost daily; my calves began to get chapped, and they'd blister till they were bleeding. And this teacher-lady was real stingy and mean. She wasn't happy with a thing I did, and the whole blessed day she'd want me to be carrying her babies on my back. Those innocent little angels weren't troublemakers, but they'd gotten used to being carried around, and that's why I'd often pinch them so they'd scream—those were the only times the teacher-lady paid them any attention.

There at the school, that lady had everything—it was just like a store: coca leaf, sugar, salt, candles, kerosene, hot peppers, and cigarettes.[9] People came all the way from other communities, bringing potatoes, chuño, and moraya, which they'd trade for a tiny bit of salt, sugar, or coca. Everything in the store was just for bartering; she never sold a thing. That way, she'd gather together, all for herself, hundreds of sackfuls from the harvests of the communities, and then she'd load up thirty or forty llamas and have those same students of hers take the sacks to the Urcos Train Station, and from there they'd be sent on to Cuzco.[10]

Her home was like a well-stocked storehouse. That teacher-lady was a good businesswoman, but she forgot all about teaching the kids how to read—she was only interested in her business—and those very same students, together with her many godchildren, would also have to work her fields. The teacher-lady had lived for over ten years in the community, and that's why she had many community members as her godchildren.[11] She'd choose a school director from among her godchildren or other community members, and he had to be at the teacher's beck and call the whole school year. Being the school director was a lot like undertaking a cargo. Those directors were also in charge of making everyone who belonged to the community—each and every home from one end of town to the other—hand over a lamb every three weeks. For that, she'd pay them two soles and three handfuls of coca leaf. She ate just a little bit of that meat, and the rest was made into jerky and taken to Cuzco.

I saw all that while living there at the lady's school. The very day the school year ended, we went to the Urcos Train Station with the students, who were all loaded down, carrying meat, potatoes, and llama wool. We arrived in Cuzco with all that cargo. One day, two weeks after I'd been back at her house there, she sent me out to buy some wide noodles; but the lady who owned the store gave me very thin ones, and when I returned with them, the schoolmistress pulled me down by the ear, yelling:

"You no-good, stupid Indian! These ears just don't hear, do they? I told you thick noodles!"

So, crying and with my ears still ringing in pain, I went back to exchange the noodles at the store. And there in the store, a lady said to me:

"Hey, child, I bet your mistress went and hit you—if you want to, come along with me; c'mon, let's go."

It was as if I'd been in a drunken stupor, and when I heard the lady's words, I came to my senses. The teacher-lady was wicked, hitting and mistreating me, and she didn't pay me a thing. Her husband was also a real devil, and he'd already tried to rape me three different times when his wife was away. So noodles and all, I went straightaway to this other lady's home.

It was only there in that house that my life really began. This lady, whose name was María Pérez, was a kind and loving person. She lived in San Blas, in the third courtyard of a priest's house. She'd be respectful when ordering me to do the things I had to do; she'd never yell or insult me. And since she treated me well, I also worked earnestly: cooking, sweeping the house, and washing everyone's clothes, even though there were more than eleven of them. Her children were all girls, nine of them. Her eldest daughter was a schoolteacher in San Sebastián. Thanks to that sweet girl, I learned to recognize the letters of the alphabet; she'd give me lessons at night whenever I slept over at her home in San Sebastián. Even now I can spell out what my eyes are seeing, though I've never understood the letters I'm reading.

One morning, more than two years after I'd disappeared from home, my mother showed up; it was still early, and everyone was asleep. I was the only one up, and I was just getting ready to sweep the courtyard when the dog started barking; I went outside wondering, "What could that be?" And there was mother with my sister Justina. When they saw me, they broke into smiles and hugged me through their tears, saying:

"Cruel-hearted girl doesn't love her own mother!"

And I said:

"I'm doing just fine here."

My mother and sister sat there waiting for my mistress to wake up. When breakfast was starting to get cold, my mistress came out, and I told her:

"This is my mother and sister."

My mistress told mother:

"I've always wanted to meet you—your daughter has been here in my home for a year now; she's like my own daughter and has everything she needs in this house. And I also pay her."

I was pleased with what my mistress told them, because my mother and sister went away knowing I wasn't suffering in that house. And when they were just about to leave, the girls gave them lots of bread and sugar. My salary was fifteen soles a month, and I'd already saved up a hundred and thirty-five soles. So I gave my mother a hundred soles from my wages, and some months later she used it to buy a strong ox from an uncle of ours who needed money to bury his mother, our aunt. From then on, my mother and sister would always visit me whenever they came to Cuzco.

They treated me well in that house, but I worked day and night like a donkey in its prime. I'd be cooking, washing, cleaning up the house, and ironing clothes late into the night, blowing and blowing on those charcoal irons. Only the girls weren't pleased with my ironing and cooking. And though they watched over the food in that house, it was never lacking. I was also never lacking in clothes, because the girls always gave me their used ones, and I'd fix them up and wear them till they were threadbare.

FOURTEEN

EUSEBIO

After some five years working as a maid in that house, I met my husband, Eusebio Corihuamán; it was the octave of the Corpus Christi Fiesta in San Cristóbal.[1] I lived with him fourteen years and had my seven children by him: three boys and four girls. Of all those, my daughter Catalina is the only one still living, and she was born at seven months.

When I began living with my husband, Eusebio, I already knew what it was like to be with a man—ever since the Saint John's Day fiesta, back when I lived at that school in Llullucha. In the month of June, there's a big fiesta to make the sheep merry.[2] And on the vespers of Saint John's Day, the sheep owners all build fires to the sound of flutes and drums. Then, between shots of liquor, they make the sheep merry on their special night. Early the next morning, the owners, who'd still be drunk, would grab hold of the healthier male and female sheep, line them up in pairs, and make them embrace. The owners would cast spells while bathing them with the fragrant smoke of the burnt offerings, and the godchildren would fling libations to the air and make each pair of little lambs swill down liquor from shot glasses. That's how they married the sheep on Saint John's Day.

While I was a servant there at the school, the school deputy director, who was my friend, took me to the fiesta on Saint John's Vespers. And since the sheep owners are there drinking and dancing next to the sheep corral all night long, they also poured lots of liquor down my throat as well, and I don't know what kind of evil potion that shifty deputy put in my drink, but a little while later I was totally drunk and my hands and feet went dead limp, and I couldn't move—my mouth also felt like it had been fastened shut, and I couldn't speak—and then late at night, when everyone was drunk and singing, they carried me off like a sack of potatoes to a hut in another corral, and there they did their evil to me; that's how I learned what men are like.[3] That happened to me some two years after I'd started my bleeding.

The day I first started my bleeding, I got real scared and started crying. Because, as far back as I can remember, I've been like a qulla: whenever I see my blood, I go crazy and start screaming. But I hadn't hurt myself that time, and for no reason at all, blood just started streaming out of me; so I got scared and didn't know what to do. I even thought maybe I was going to give birth. Because a few months earlier when I was out in the fields, some slippery fellow had tried to take me out further into the crops, saying, "Come on."

So I thought maybe you could get pregnant that way, because when my sister came out of my mother, they'd both been covered with blood. Since I was streaming blood for three days, and my mother hadn't noticed a thing, I tearfully told her:

"It's coming out like this."

She didn't even pay attention to what I said. All she told me was, "It's your monthly bleeding." Only after asking my older sister's good friend did I learn what the monthly bleeding was all about.

I got pregnant while living in Mrs. María's house. But they didn't notice my belly till the seventh month; afraid they might throw me out, I always wore a large shawl, together with a waistband wrapped tightly around me. But since I didn't have the same appetite and my belly had changed a lot, my mistress approached me one night while I was ironing clothes and said:

"Let's have a look."

She found the waistband. So she began asking me whose it was and how it happened. And all I could do was cry. So for four days straight, she asked me:

"Whose is it? Whose is it? Speak up!"

But I wouldn't open my mouth for anything. Since I didn't say a single word for four days, my mistress began to get suspicious and started crying.

"Since you don't want to talk, it must be the wiraqucha's."[4]

Only on the fifth day did I tell her—then they had Eusebio brought in. When he came to the house, my mistress told him:

"How dare you! You've disgraced my home. She's pregnant, and you'd better marry her now—if you don't, we'll have you taken straight to jail."

And Eusebio said:

"Yes, I'll get married."

So two months went by, and I stayed on at that house. But one night when everybody had gone to a wedding and I was watching over the house all by myself, the labor pains began. Since there were always clothes to be ironed at night, I was ironing when the pains started. At first I just told myself:

"Those must be the same little aches as usual."

But it wasn't so—they kept growing and growing until they had me sprawled out on the floor, writhing in pain. There wasn't a soul in the house that night, just the house dog who'd been howling before my pains began. That was surely a bad omen. I was well on my way to the otherworld, writhing in horrible pain. But thanks to the blessed souls, the baby came out, and it felt like they'd removed a piercing needle lodged in my body. And my poor little angel was screaming, drowning in the blood between my legs. Of the seven times I've given birth, that was the ugliest. I surely paid for some of my sins that night, because the pain weighed my body down like a heavy stone, and I couldn't get up. Since there was nothing to cut the umbilical cord with, I took hold of it and tugged with all my might, pulling it out like a piece of string. While all this was happening, a village woman from the Anta region came in; she was the caretaker of the first courtyard and no doubt had heard me wailing. She helped me, giving me some herb tea.

That's how it was the first time I delivered. And two days later, my husband came by and carried me off to his room in Santa Ana, where we started living together.

He worked as a peddler, taking merchandise to the country towns—clothes, needles, buttons, thread, and knives—and he also made sandals from car tires. While he was off traveling, I stayed behind in the room. In the beginning, everything was just fine, but when our son Marianito was about a year old, he caught a bad cough that killed him.[5] I had to do the burial all by myself because he was off on one of his trips, peddling goods there in the Yanaoca area. He returned a week after our son had already been buried. From then on, he changed completely, dragged down by the women he'd meet in the towns while traveling. He started getting drunk a lot, and he'd beat me, saying, "You killed the little angel." Our life together just wasn't the same after that. He kept on traveling, and since many people knew I washed clothes, that's how I'd earn a little money for my belly, because he wouldn't give me a single centavo or even let me see the money he earned. That's the way things were the second time I got pregnant; that time I had a baby girl, but she also died before reaching a year old. She must've caught an ill wind—she just wouldn't stop crying. So I brought her to the hospital where they had her take six pills dissolved in chamomile tea, but it didn't do a thing. Instead, when she'd finished taking it, still crying, she died—it even made me think:

"Could they have given me poison?"

He wasn't with us when that baby died either. He'd gone off on a trip up around Ayaviri to buy some merchandise.

From then on, it seemed he was no longer my husband; he'd arrive as if just visiting, and then he'd be off again doing his business. Since I just stayed there all by myself while he was traveling, I took a job fixing meals at a cookhouse up on Santa Ana Street. He didn't travel alone, but had a companion who was also a peddler. Stories began coming into that cornbeer tavern, saying he and his friend were womanizers and were getting drunk at each town they came to.[6] And so, whenever he'd return from his trips, he'd get raging jealous and beat me up, just as if I was his worst enemy. One time, when he'd just arrived back from the Paucartambo area, some people passed the word:

"Your husband's all liquored up, there on the corner."

So I went straight to our room. When I got there, he and his friend were drunk and singing, but when he saw me he glared at me like I was poison; he started up with his jealous rages and began beating me. And instead of stopping him, his peddler friend egged him on:

"Give her another, dammit! Give her another, dammit!"

He beat me till he was totally exhausted. I was already five months pregnant, and the kicks he gave me made me miscarry our baby. If that peddler friend of his would've stopped him, I'd have been saved. But God is just—that wicked man came to a bad end. He was from the Limatambo region, and his name was Donato Mayta; he lived alone with just his mother in Almudena, caretaking a fenced lot. While he was off traveling, that little old lady, who was well along in years, would stay there all by herself, watching over the lot. So he traveled to the Yauri area for Carnival,[7] just he and his merchandise, something he'd never done before. Well, we don't know if it was the rains or because he'd been getting drunk, but he didn't return for close to a month. They say that a month or so later, when the poor man returned from his trip hauling merchandise all over, his mother was no longer alive, and the house reeked heavily—even before he entered, there was the rank stench of rotten flesh. When he opened the door to his room, his mother was strewn out on the floor, dead and worm-ridden, and some mice were nibbling on her feet. When he saw that, Donato was scared stiff from head to toe, and he began screaming and shrieking with laughter. So he went mad. While he was out walking the streets raving mad, a sister of his from the Limatambo region arrived. Who knows what has become of him since then; maybe he died crazy or maybe they cured him. Because I've heard you can cure crazy people by having them drink the unsalted stew made with the head of a black dog.

After that tragedy befell Donato, my husband Eusebio didn't have anyone to travel with, and he didn't take any trips for about a month. But now he'd bully me:

"What good are you, dammit?! I don't need some yapping bitch in my house. At least be good for something, dammit!"

And saying that, he'd grab me and pull me down by my hair. But what a fool I was: right then I'd remember what my mistress, Mrs. María Pérez, used to tell me:

"Now that you've gotten involved with this man, you must live and die at his side like a good Christian woman."

So I left my job up on Santa Ana Street, and we traveled to Ocongate carrying goods, and from there we went on to Paucartambo. From Paucartambo we went on to Urcos, and from there we began walking from one town to the next, offering our merchandise all the way to Sicuani. And we arrived there about a month later without any merchandise left. Then we went by train from Sicuani to Santa Rosa and to some people he knew; we bought some goods from them: powdered dyes, woven bands, and hankies. Those goods were all Bolivian—the person he knew was a smuggler. When we got all the goods together, we traveled by foot over the hills of Ayaviri with another peddler. Less than a week later, right when we'd finished selling almost all the merchandise, my husband began to drink and drink, spending our money as if there was no tomorrow. And I was staying at the house of the people he knew, going hungry. One day, after he'd been drinking for about two weeks straight, he met a road worker from Ayaviri in the house where we were staying. He'd been an overseer in the construction of the road going from Puno to Arequipa. So he told him:

"I'll give you work; you'll be my assistant."

He accepted. We got ready to leave for that job, and then we set out from Ayaviri with no merchandise at all and went to Santa Rosa. But I began to suffer on the long walks. I was already five months pregnant, and my belly had begun to round out. We caught a train in Santa Rosa and took it past Juliaca. The train left us at a station, and we walked from there to a camp near a lake. A lot of workers were living there with their wives and kids; but it was much too cold there, and the wind would slice through like a knife. That's why the houses there in camp were just holes in the ground covered with sheet metal. They also gave us one of those holes to live in, and he began working, but not as assistant overseer, only as a workhand in the construction of a bridge. After finishing the bridge, they went further away from camp to build ditches and another small bridge; we women all had to carry lunch to our husbands way out there, paying no mind to the strong wind that was always blowing.

One day, after having worked in that camp more than three months, our work unit received an order to move a long ways away, to a place fairly near Arequipa. Dear God! What sins had I done to deserve that? It was right when my belly was about to burst with child. But we still went, going by train with the whole work unit, about fifty people. The train left us on a hillside, and from there we went to another hill where the camp was going to be. You could even see the croplands of Arequipa from there. It was a new camp, and there wasn't even a single hut there yet; the overseer handed out sheet metal, and the workers all began building stone walls for their little huts. We too built our hut. Work began two days after we arrived. And two weeks later, my daughter Martina was born; that delivery was easy, and I didn't suffer too much, probably because of all those long walks.

The whole time he worked there, I never knew just how much he earned. But in those camps, there was always a store that had everything: clothes and provisions. You could take out anything you needed against your wages, and there were also merchants and other old fellows who brought all kinds of things to camp—meat, corn, potatoes—which they sold real cheap. So you had everything you needed for cooking.

When I'd recovered from the delivery, I began cooking daily meals, lunch and dinner, for five workers. Things were different now. I could meet my expenses with the few centavos I was making and didn't have to depend on his pockets anymore. So everything was going as well as could be: I was doing my little food business, and he was also doing his job just fine. I was pleased with that, because between the two of us we were saving up a little money. But then, as if bewitched, my husband changed overnight and began drinking. At first, even when he was drunk, he'd still go to work, but after a while, when he was in the grip of his drinking binges, he began missing work. Finally, he stopped showing up at all—he'd just get drunk all day long, spending away the little bit of money we'd saved. And on top of that, a few months later the encampment turned into a much larger camp where liquor was never lacking.

We'd now been there over a year, and months had passed since he last worked; I was just doing my little food business all by myself, cooking meals for my steady customers, and toward the end, more and more of them were coming. But once again the order came to move camp, and we had just three days to do so—this time we were going to be even closer to Arequipa. But because he'd stopped working long before, and everybody knew he was a drunkard, no one told him a thing. That's because when he was all liquored up, he'd see blue devils, and on top of that he was a roughneck who'd pick fights.[8] We left camp only after it was completely deserted—we were the very last ones to leave. And with just our one little bundle of pots and pans, we caught the train and set out toward Juliaca. Now that many years have passed since the things I lived through there in that camp, I say to myself, "What a good-for-nothing I was!" I was right there near the city of Arequipa, and I didn't even go in and see the town. That's being a good-for-nothing. If I'd have gone in and seen Arequipa back then, at least now I'd be able to tell my daughter Catalina's children that I've been to Arequipa.

FIFTEEN

"I STOPPED BEARING THAT CROSS"

B ut so it is—with all the sin that exists in the world, to live this life is to suffer.[1] Yet, everybody, from the tiniest moth to the mountain lord's fearsome puma, from the largest tree to the smallest blade of grass spreading without a thought, all of us here since those distant times of our ancient ancestors, we're all just passing through this life.[2] But our soul, our spirit, doesn't disappear. It's the same with the souls of the ancient ones and with those of our family members and friends—they haven't disappeared; they're living in the other life, in either the underworld or upperworld. There you have everything you need, and you can rest from these sufferings and this life of tears. It's only in death that all of us who've lived in this world pass into the otherworld, and it's only on Judgment Day that our souls will set out from the otherworld in search of our bodies. And on Judgment Day, all of us, every single soul from this world, will have to appear in body and spirit before our Lord of the upperworld and be judged. And when we're being judged, we'll be just like those found guilty at a court hearing: there before our Lord, our bodies will appear transparent as a pane of glass, that is, if we've been good-hearted people in this life. If our hearts are full of wickedness, our bodies won't be transparent, but murky and full of stains like dirty glass. That's how our Lord will judge us on that day: for our good deeds in this life and for our bad deeds as well—that's why the damned are also found there in the otherworld.

When we leave this life, our soul presents itself before the Lord, and he decides where our soul should go till Judgment. If a person has offended our Lord, tarnishing themselves with sin in this life, then they're destined to return to this life as one of the damned. Those souls who've soiled their bodies while alive—sinning with their mothers or daughters, or hitting their parents—are all damned; they can't even approach our Lord. That's why there's even sayings: "Those who've sinned with their mother or daughter have no place to rest in

121

their wanderings, not even hell." That's why, when those souls come back from the otherworld, they go and raise their bodies up from where they're buried. And that's why, when the dead soul's kinfolk know about his dirty deeds, before they bury him they shave his eyelashes and eyebrows, and they yank his toenails out by the roots and then sear his hands and feet with burning straw.[3] Then they bury him face down like that, his back to Sun Father, and they place a large stone on his back so he stays put. That's how they stop the damned one from taking back his body when he returns to the grave. And that's why, from the moment of the burial, they watch over the person, be it the mother or sister, who the dead soul soiled his body with—they're shut away inside a room full of crosses till the octave passes, because it's during those days that the damned can still return to their partner in sin and try to carry them off alive.

When we arrived in Juliaca, I was all by myself for three days, carrying my baby and going hungry, my pots and pans all in a pile. Because the day after we'd arrived in Juliaca, Eusebio ran into a friend of his who'd been a road worker at the first camp and who'd also been let go. He disappeared with his friend, no doubt to go get drunk. He showed up three days later, still drunk, and said:

"We're going to the mines."

It was really true. The next day he began to prepare for the trip and bought a Coleman brand kerosene stove for sixty soles, using the capital we still had left over from peddling goods. I also sold three of my four used pots there at the Juliaca market, and with that we bought twelve pounds of rice, a gallon of cooking oil, and a gallon of kerosene; that's all we took with us on the trip. So just like that, we traveled by train past Ayaviri, and from there we spent three days walking along the mountain ridges until we arrived at the mine, which was way up in the high mountains near Santo Tomás. It was a tiny encampment, with some forty or fifty families living there. Once we'd arrived, they also gave us a little hut to live in.[4]

So my husband Eusebio went off to work; he came back two days later, saying that they'd sent him deep down the mine shaft to pick and shovel. Before then he'd been happy, but from that day on he'd always come and go to work raging mad. So he began mistreating me again, chewing me out for the food I cooked—he'd dump it on the ground or even throw it in my face:

"Damn bitch! You cook as if I was your dog! Here dammit, take some! Chow it down!"

And with that, he'd throw it in my face.

No doubt, for him to be so angry, his job must've been real tough—the poor man would come back dripping wet, dragging along his little carbon lantern behind him. Some months later, they transferred him to wheelbarrow duty, carting rubble out of the mine shaft. He was down in the mine working behind the wheelbarrow when my baby Ubaldito was born, but two weeks later my baby caught an ill wind and died. Since my husband kept on mistreating me, and I saw that many women were working as gleaners there in the mine, I also went to get work doing that. The workers there would haul out buckets and wheelbarrows full of rocks that had copper in them. Once outside, those rocks and boulders were pounded to bits by other workers using big sledgehammers. Then the women called gleaners would sort through the copper, making piles of first and second grade copper. When I went to ask about that job, the overseer accepted me as a gleaner. So I began working, sorting out the ore. The job was real easy; we just sat there sorting through it, but we'd also have to be fighting off the coldness, rain, or snow the whole blessed day. With that alone, you'd suffer. The life I led in that mine was one big lie—you'd work month after month, but your full wages never showed up. If you worked two months, they'd just pay you for one. So when people wanted to quit and leave the mine, they'd always have to wait around for their wages. They'd keep on working, but they'd still never receive their full pay and would have to leave behind two or three months of unpaid work. The daily wage for a worker was three soles and twenty centavos with no Sunday allowance. Women would get one sol and fifty centavos a day, also without any Sunday allowance. Muleteers would take the ore we'd worked over, put it in sacks, and load up some fifty or sixty horses and mules, packing it all the way out to the roadhead. I have no idea where that was, but they said it was a two-day journey from the mine.

Life in the mine was pure suffering. Though you'd work, there'd be no money. But there were always plenty of cooking provisions from communities near the mine. We ate llama meat the whole time we lived there at the mine; it was never lacking. That's why, to my way of thinking, it's un-Christian of the mistis here in the city to look down on and sneer at such delicious meat.[5] There was also a tiny store there at the mine that let you take out supplies—sugar, salt, and rice—against your wages. And others sold liquor, which was never lacking.

I think I stayed at that mine close to three years because my two baby boys were born there; the first was named Ubaldito and the other little one was stillborn. There in the mine, they'd hire us women as gleaners whenever they needed us, and they'd fire us whenever the overseer wanted to. And when you weren't working, there were no other jobs, nor even any customers to sell food to, because everyone had their families there with them. Such was life in the mine.

From the very day I'd gotten involved with that man, all I'd ever done was cry and suffer. I lived like an accursed bastard daughter, that very same husband of mine the cross I had to bear. When he wasn't getting jealous, he'd be treating me worse than his mortal enemy. He also never let me know how much he earned, and he'd forgotten all about my belly, not to mention my clothes. Our daughter Martinacha was a bit more grown up by then, but he never gave her a thought—she was like a little unbaptized orphan-child. She never had any good clothes; they were always ragged and threadbare. That's how he was with me and my children, like an apparition that came and went. If he would've looked after me each time I got pregnant, my little ones wouldn't have died—they wouldn't have died the bad deaths they did. They'd be grown-ups now and they'd surely be working and looking after us. Since life there at my husband's side was truly miserable, and since the only thing he was good for was his raging jealousy and mistreating my body, I beseeched my father's and brother's blessed souls to take me away from that no-good Christian:

"What kind of life is this that I can't separate from this man, if I have hands and feet, a mouth to talk with, and eyes to see? What am I, a cripple? These hands here make all the meals!"

And so, with those thoughts in mind, I walked out on my husband, leaving behind both him and the mine.

It was close to Christmas when I stopped bearing that cross, a day when the muleteers were loading ore. I only had twenty soles hidden away to leave with, and I got another twenty pawning the kerosene stove at the store. I packed myself a meal to take on the trip: some steamed moraya and boiled llama meat. So, while he was picking away down in the mine shaft, I followed after the muleteers, carrying just my baby Martina and the small meal I'd packed. I trailed after those muleteers only part of the way, because they took a turn toward Yauri, together with the whole shipment of ore. I went with some other travelers to Santa Rosa, and from there I took a train straight to Cuzco—that's how I saved myself from that husband of mine.

When I arrived in Cuzco, I got a job in Huánchac cooking in a cornbeer tavern, one that was owned by Mrs. Chihuantito. Just as I was beginning to feel more at peace and was happily working away there at the tavern, my daughter Catalina was born at seven months. She's the only daughter, the only one of all my children, who's still living. I must've already been three or four months pregnant when I left the mine, and that's why I gave birth to Catalina a few months later. The night she came into this world, I was cooking over the hearth in Mrs. Chihuantito's cornbeer tavern, boiling water in the big pots to make the cornbeer. Right about the rooster's first crow, the labor pains began, pains I knew all too well. As the pains got worse, I leaned and braced myself against the hearth, parting my legs and squatting down. In the midst of my agony, while pushing and moaning, the baby came out without my realizing it—there she was, wailing away between my legs. So I put her on top of a small wool pelt and collapsed next to her. But the pains continued, and then around daybreak they grew worse and the placenta came out. When day had fully dawned, the owner of the cornbeer tavern came in, and when she saw me there with my baby, she got alarmed:

"What, you mean you haven't made the cornbeer!"

But she gave me some herb tea and bathed the baby. The baby was so tiny it was really startling; it looked like a small pile of silk that would come apart if you touched it. Her little head was softer than a ripe papaya. They bathed her and wrapped her all up in some rags, because there weren't any diapers; then they laid her down next to the big hearth, saying:

"She won't get cold here."

The little angel slept there one day, two days, for three whole days she slept; she just slept and slept, and since she wasn't crying or nursing, I'd look at her from time to time, wondering:

"Could she have died?"

But she kept on breathing, though not without difficulty; that's the way she was for some months till she filled out. Yet fate is a strange thing! The people who saw my poor baby would say:

"That baby's going to die."

But it was our Lord's will that, though she was right there being dished up onto death's plate, she escaped the jaws of death. And now she's the only child who looks after us and eases our woes.

Three years then passed by while I lived there with my two daughters. Martina was bigger by that time and was even doing some chores for me; Catalina was already able to talk pretty well. But then around came that goddamned, accursed man—if I've dirtied my mouth by saying this, may our Lord forgive me—and he must've been spying on my little one, because while I was there in the kitchen and she went out in the street, he led her away with who knows what lies, and then he left her as a maid servant in the home of his comadre, a mestiza from his hometown who now lived in Santiago. So it happened—one morning, when my baby Martina went outside, her father stole her away from me.[6] And it was only later that afternoon that I realized she was gone; when night fell and she still hadn't shown up, I began to get scared, wondering, "What could've happened to her?" And that night, sobbing, I went all over asking for her: to the police station, to the hospital. I must've asked at every home in Huánchac; back then there weren't as many houses as there are now. So she'd just vanished into thin air, and I had no word of her for three days. Since I'd had no word of her, I was walking around as if I'd lost my mind, but on the fourth day I got a message from her father, Eusebio, saying that my daughter Martina was with him. That damned wretch must've been watching me search for my child, and he'd sent me the message when he saw me in such bad shape.

I didn't hear a thing about my baby after that day. Some two years after she disappeared, I received news that my child had traveled to the jungle with that lady, to a gold mine in Quincemil where her husband was a contractor. Once there, she'd come down with anemia, from the heat no doubt, and right after they came back, they had her put away in Lorena Hospital. And since they just dumped her there, and no one ever went to visit, a couple of weeks later she contracted smallpox from some other people at the place. That's how Martina died, from anemia and smallpox, with no one caring for her. Never again, not once after she had Martina put away in the hospital, did her mistress go there and see how she was doing. So she died there all by herself, all alone, with no one looking after her. Nor did anyone go to her burial, and no doubt the morgue workers just dumped her in the common grave. That's the ugly death my Martina died, all because of her father. If he hadn't gone and stolen her from me, she'd still be here at my side, keeping me company even now.

After this happened to my Martina, that husband of mine still had the nerve to show his face in San Jerónimo and say to my mother:

"I want to make up with Asunta, dear mother-in-law, if for nothing else, for the good of Catalina, who's still living."

Who knows what else he said, feeding her liquor to convince her, but my mother came to Cuzco and told me that I shouldn't have to suffer all by myself, that I should keep on living at my husband's side.[7] So I told my mother:

"Look here, Mama. You have no idea of the way that man would get raging jealous and beat me, do you? As for me, I'm not going to patch things up with him, even if they pay me an hacienda, because he's the cross I've had to bear in this life."

I think my mother went back home after we talked that time. After some years—it must've been four or six years later, when I'd already been living several years with Gregorio—some friends of mine told me that my daughter Catalina's father was doing nothing but going around the streets of Sicuani a drunkard, day in and day out, looking for handouts like a beggar. So one day, while walking around drunk like that, they say he turned up dead beneath the Sicuani Bridge. That's how he died. Since he was so horribly wicked to me in this life, who knows what became of his poor soul. He died unforgiven, burdened down with sin.

SIXTEEN

LIFE WITH GREGORIO

My daughter Catalina was a very sickly baby, and I was always having to take care of her. The owner of the cornbeer tavern in Huánchac got fed up with that and started acting sullen with me. So I had to find another cornbeer tavern to work at. That's how I went on to the Fly Jail Cookhouse in Puente Rosario, owned by Mrs. Mercedes. I was there a good while—it must've been about two years—making cornbeer and cooking side dishes. Gregorio's home was near the cookhouse, and he says that he'd already been going there regularly to drink cornbeer. So, from the moment I'd arrived, he was checking me out because he'd noticed I didn't have a husband.[1] One day, the owner of the cookhouse got sick and didn't come in for several days, and I stayed there all by myself serving the usual customers. On one of those days when I was there all alone, Gregorio came by and treated me to a glass of cornbeer, and that loosened up my tongue—who knows what I talked about. But that's how we began our friendship, and from that day on, he kept on coming by—he'd always offer to treat me to some cornbeer. So our friendship grew. We began to trust each other, and sometimes we'd tease and kid around with each other. And back then, Gregorio used to bring gifts— pastries and pork rinds—for me and my daughter Catalina. But ever since the day we started living together, no more pastries or pork rinds. One day when we'd gotten to know each other better, he told me:

"Ask for the day off. We'll go to the Corpus Christi Fiesta in San Sebastián."

So I asked the owner to give me the day off so I could go to San Jerónimo. But we didn't go to either San Jerónimo or San Sebastián's Corpus Christi that day because he took me off to a cookhouse in Almudena,[2] where I think we ate two, maybe three, different dishes. Those dishes weren't well cooked or properly seasoned, but the pork rinds were good—that's why from time to time I still tease him:

"You tricked me, making me eat those two poorly cooked dishes."

Back then and still today, Gregorio loves pork rinds. That's why I've always wanted to raise a little pig, even though you can't do it here because you need more space for that. But one time I brought home a little pig I'd bought at the Saturday flea market, and I tied it up real tight to the kitchen door. But when that uppity, hot-headed pig grew a bit bigger, it got loose, and a car ran over it.[3]

Well, the time Gregorio took me out to the cookhouse, after we'd eaten, he made me drink two or three large glasses of strawberry beer,[4] and then some cornbeer mixed with regular beer. With just that, I got stumbling drunk. I'm not the kind of woman who gets stumbling drunk, like those who drink with their husbands till they can't drink another drop and then start hitting each other. Each time I drink, my body goes limp like a corpse, and I feel like a heap of stones. I'm sure that's how I must've been that night, because he hauled me straight off to his home to sleep with him till the next day. So that's how I first stepped foot into my husband's house. After that, I still kept going to Mrs. Mercedes' cookhouse, but for just a few more days, because Gregorio told me:

"Go ask for leave and come move in with me. We'll live here together—that's why you're my woman now."

Well, I went and did the things he said, and like a fool I put myself in this man's hands! So again I went and asked for three days' leave. I think I came over that very same day, dragging my child along—by that time she was somewhat older—together with my bedding and everything else. That's all I really had, my bed and my daughter.

Why should I speak falsely and anger the good Lord? You shouldn't do that. Why, even though Gregorio has hit me and my daughter many times, even kicking us out of bed and into the rain all night long wearing just our underskirts, and even though we sometimes fight and insult each other, we're doing fine together. And from the very first day, he has been concerned for my daughter and looked after her. Even now he calls her "my baby." And everything he earns working has always been for all of us. He was already working as a sweeper at Huáscar factory when we started living together. That's why sometimes he'd proudly declare:

"I'm a Huascaran, dammit—I may not make much, but it's a sure thing."

He kept working at that factory a few more years, until people began saying, "The factory's going to close." So, when word spread that the factory was closing, Gregorio got worried. They finally did shut it down a short while later. After they closed down the factory, we kept on living in Puente Rosario. All during the time he worked there at the factory, I used to just stay home and cook, though I'd still go help out at Mrs. Mercedes' cornbeer tavern so they'd give me some cornbeer slag for the chickens and guinea pigs I'd begun raising. Ever since the day I first started living with Gregorio, I've always had chickens and guinea pigs. When he left the factory, he worked in construction from time to time, but since that kind of work building houses always comes to an end, he began spending his days looking around for work. So from then on, he was left without a steady job, and when he'd go around offering himself as a workhand, they'd turn him away or say, "Come back next week" or "Come back in a couple weeks." So at one point during that time, I told some friends of mine, "This is the situation my husband's in." They were Mrs. Mercedes' clients, and they worked as food vendors at central market.[5] I told them:

"And me, I'm not earning a thing here either; she just pays me slag for my animals."

So they told me:

"But you know how to cook real well. Starting tomorrow, why don't you cook a little something? We'll make a bit of space for you next to us so you can sell your food."

I stopped going to the cookhouse the very next day, and I'd just send my daughter Catalina, who'd grown up a bit by then, to help out a little with things. But the slag they paid her wasn't even half of what they used to give me. That same morning, I went to have a look at the meal section of Cascaparo Market, just to see how they were cooking. I ate a plate of spicy *tarwi* and *soltero*. And when I saw how the food business worked, I returned home all excited, thinking about how I might change from cooking for a cookhouse to having my own food business. So then, over the next three days, I began getting everything ready to take a pot of food to market. I didn't have any good plates; mine were all chipped and full of holes that'd been welded shut. So I went to my comadre, Rosa Salas, and borrowed three metal plates and two spoons. I don't know what else I did, but on the fourth day I went on my way, lugging my pot along. When I showed up at the market, my friends called me over, and, making a little room for me between the two of them, they set me up with my pot.

The marketplace was the street itself; there weren't even any vending stalls or tables. Everything being sold there was just laid right out on the ground, and the market was full of people until well past noon. That first day I didn't sell a single serving till well past noon when two runas, who looked like workers, came by and ate four servings. Then about five or six people who looked like travelers came by, but there weren't enough plates to serve them on, so I had to borrow some from my friends. Each traveler had a serving, but when they asked for more, there wasn't enough to go around for everybody. A serving of stew cost eighty centavos back then. The food I'd brought with me that time was only enough for two sales; so my friends told me:

"You see! You've started with good luck! You should cook in a much bigger pot for tomorrow."

So I began cooking in a pot that could hold much more. And the workhands who'd eaten lunch that first day began coming every day, and they became my steady customers. They brought over some other workers, and in the end they all approached me formally, saying:

"Please cook just for us."

From that day on, I'd no longer go to market in the morning; I'd wait until twelve or so, timing it with their midday break. But ever since Christians first appeared in the world, there's been envy, and it's growing everywhere, day and night, right under God's nose. My friends saw that I had steady customers for the food I carried to market each day, and envy began to well up inside them. And since I was right there next to them, they became sullen, and the times when I didn't have enough plates or spoons, they'd no longer want to lend me theirs. So that same day, I told all my steady customers, those I was now feeding daily:

"I'm leaving here—they're getting envious of me."

Then I pointed them over to a spot near the end of the food section.

Those are the things I went through when I began selling food, but thanks to the blessed souls, that business of mine was helping to lighten my burden. Since Gregorio didn't have a steady job, he also began working, hauling people's goods.

"Working the street's a sure thing," Gregorio would say.

But ever since the day I began my business, Gregorio's back isn't the only thing we have to depend on. Because I also squeeze out a few centavos for our bellies.

One day, just when my little food business was going along well, the City Hall employees, all dressed up in uniforms like policemen, came around asking for our municipal licenses. I didn't know what a municipal license was all about, and I kept on going there to sell, till one day those same municipal police began confiscating our pots and plates. The people who had their papers were able to get back their things by paying a fine at City Hall, but since I didn't have any papers at the time, I was never able to get my plates and pots back; I still haven't, not even now. I'm still sad about my six metal plates—they cost a lot. I kept on going there after that happened, quietly selling my food where those municipal dogs wouldn't see me. But the souls must've sent down a punishment, because one day I let myself get caught. I'd just gotten there that day and was waiting around for my steady customers to arrive, when suddenly a municipal policeman came around the corner, and there just wasn't enough time to get away with my pot. Then he told me:

"Dammit! What are you, deaf? No-good, fucking Indian!"

Boom! Boom! He kicked my pot over and stomped up and down on my plates, which were all made of red pottery. Seeing the plates smashed to bits and my food all over the ground, I began screaming for help, feeling a raging anger for the municipal policeman. And some mestiza women passing by called over:

"Bully!"

May God forgive me, but right then my blood was boiling over with rage, and I even wanted to kill that municipal policeman. What had those pots done to that Christian to make him kick them? Nothing! Why didn't he kick me instead? When I got over my anger, I didn't go back to that market again. Instead, I'd go to the fields to gather forage for guinea pigs.[6] And I'd sell it on a corner in Limaqpampa in the late afternoon, right when night was falling. A lot of women would come sell forage for guinea pigs at that hour, and nobody stopped you from doing it.

Ever since the day I'd moved to Puente Rosario with Gregorio, we'd lived there peacefully. It was a little house that Gregorio had built when his wife was still living; it was in a fenced lot and we lived there by ourselves, though there was a soldier living in the lot next to ours. That soldier's wife was a raving bitch who liked to pick fights.[7] From the day she first laid eyes on me, she treated me as if I was trying to steal her soldier away from her—she became my enemy. And so began the never-ending days of fights and insults. That woman would fight over any old thing. She'd always be saying little things for me to overhear, any old thing, and I'd come back with even ruder insults, and then we'd end up fighting, sinking our fingernails into each other and pulling each other's hair. But I'll tell you, when it comes to being a raving bitch, I can be even more of a bitch. That poor little mestiza was like a big moth: all bulk, no strength. And so, I'd often get raging mad and grab her by the hair, dragging her around on the ground.

"This'll surely teach her a lesson," I'd say to myself.

But no way—like a rabid dog, she'd get even worse. So we'd often end up at the police station filing a complaint. I didn't want to give up that house, but one day that anger of mine made me ill, and Gregorio got scared. My tongue was so swollen that it filled my mouth until I couldn't talk or even swallow. So while I was still sick like that, Gregorio took me away to a different house in Coripata, and there I recovered from that illness, which they said was poisoning from anger spells. That house was also in a fenced lot, there where the army officers' housing is now. It was a little hut that Gregorio had fixed up, and in exchange for it, he'd have to go work and do chores for the owner each Sunday; that lady had a deep, manly voice. But when Gregorio didn't go one Sunday, the lady evicted us from her hut, and we had to move to a shack that Gregorio went and found in Dolorespata.

Gregorio and I got married while living in Dolorespata. He'd already lived with two women, but both of them had died. That's why, when I came down with anger spells, he got scared, and his compadre Leocadio had said:

"Compadre, if your woman lives at your side with God's blessing, she won't die—so get married by the Church."

So, since I hadn't been lawfully married to Eusebio and neither had Gregorio with either of the two women he'd lived with, we said:

"Might we be better off if we got lawfully married? Well then, let's receive this blessing."

That was the thinking behind our getting married. Everything went just fine for my wedding. One of the things I most remember about that time was Gregorio calling me:

"Mud-brained woman."

When we found godparents for our wedding, we set the date of the ceremony, but it was postponed three or four months because I just wasn't able to get the prayers into my head, even though they were teaching me them daily.

After we got married, I went back to doing my food business at Huánchac Market, where I'm still working. I still have my steady customers, the stove mechanics and market sweepers. I started going to that market after they kicked us out of our shack in Dolorespata. The time that they evicted us, they threw our things all over, and a wiraqucha gringo, who must've taken pity on me when he saw me there sobbing,[8] told me:

"Go live in shed."[9]

That open shed was in the middle of a potato field. We stayed there a few days. Sometime later we fixed up this house we're living in now; back then it was all falling apart. Coripata was just fields at the time.

The Huánchac Market was still very small back then, and only later did they make it bigger. It was when they were expanding the marketplace that I began going there to do business. That's why I'm an old-timer there now, and everyone knows me. After I'd been there a while, they also began asking everyone doing business for their licenses. So, when they asked me for my license, I had to get hold of my marriage certificate, but when I tried to obtain the certificate, the priests at the monastery couldn't find our names in the book. And so I'd go there every single day asking for it, and they'd tell me, "It's not here; it doesn't appear here." I went there asking day after day for about two months, until I wore out the priests' patience—they must've gotten tired of seeing me there every day, because they finally gave me my marriage certificate. With that I took out my vendor's license, and they also gave me a sanitation

card. And every single day, I have to pay City Hall two soles and fifty centavos—that's their cut for the things I sell there in the market.

In the old days, I used to take my food business to market every day, but four years ago I started going only on Tuesdays and Fridays. The business just doesn't pay nowadays: the cost of cooking supplies is sky-high, and there's no profit anymore. When I'm not taking my food business to market, I spend my time buying bottles from the stores of people I know, here in Coripata and in Santiago. I also go to the dump, sometimes with Gregorio, other times by myself, combing it for bottles and scrap metal. It's hard work, and there's also lots of other people tripping over each other looking for stuff—fights even break out when the garbage trucks arrive with their loads. But if you're lucky, you can still find lots of things. We use detergent and brushes to wash and scrub out the bottles I've bought or those that Gregorio and I find while gleaning together, and then I sell them all at the Saturday flea market. Sometimes you can sell a single bottle for as much as four soles. If I had some capital, I'd be in the clothes business, buying used clothes from wealthy professionals and selling them at the Saturday flea market.[10] I've seen that it sells well, and you can make money at it, though it's too late for me to do that now, since I have no education and my strength is failing me—I'm all huddled in a corner of my house these days, and I don't get around much anymore.

And lately, after having slept well all night long, I wake up exhausted: the calves in my legs are all tired out, as if I'd been walking for miles and miles throughout the night. No doubt my soul's spirit has already begun walking, because it's said that eight years before we die, our souls begin their journey, tracking our footsteps back to all the places we've gone while living in this world. So our poor souls must stop time and time again, suffering at each and every place we were careless, even the places where we let a sewing needle drop to the floor. That's why, when sewing or mending clothes, one must work the needle carefully.[11] So my soul must've already begun its journey, and that's why at daybreak my legs are all tired out.

POSTSCRIPT

Asunta and Gregorio have since passed away. Gregorio, in 1979, met the fate he had anticipated: he was run over by a car. Gravely injured, he was taken to Lorena Hospital. Asunta was not notified, and four days later, after searching the hospitals, she found him at the morgue. He was given a Christian burial in Almudena Cemetery. Just four people attended. Ricardo and Carmen, the original editors, had moved away from Coripata by that time and were living in another part of the Andes. They were able, however, to sponsor a mass for Gregorio a month later. They and their families helped Asunta during her remaining years, giving her food and money. She died of her maladies in 1983.

Ricardo and Carmen returned to Coripata in 1985. Steps had been built over the site of Gregorio and Asunta's home, and no signs remained that it had ever existed. The steps were later torn down to provide space for a road. Today the spot is marked by a curve in the highway between Cuzco and Huancaro. Time has erased their tracks, and if Ricardo and Carmen had not retained their words on paper, the wind would have taken them, like it has those of so many other Gregorios and Asuntas.

Their words have traveled far. Their narratives have received many editions and translations (see Introduction), raising consciousness about the poverty and brutal living conditions in the Andes. In 1987, a nongovernmental organization called the Gregorio Condori Mamani Association was started by a group of Germans and local Cuzqueños who were moved by the narratives and who realized that there was a complete dearth of social services for strappers.

This led to the establishment of The Strappers' Association and The Strappers' House. The latter is a place where these marginalized workers are given housing, food, health services, and legal advice.[1] In the case of Asunta's narrative, a bilingual Quechua-Spanish edition was released in 1994 by a nongovernmental organization in Cuzco as part of a literacy campaign for women in southern Peru. Asunta's life and words are thus helping to create and bolster women's groups in the highlands.[2] The published narratives, then, have indeed fulfilled Asunta's and Gregorio's wishes "that the sufferings of our people be made known."

P.H.G. and G.M.E. 1995

NOTES

The origin of foreign words is marked by either "Q." for Quechua or "Sp." for Spanish. Terms italicized in the narrative texts are explained in the Glossary that follows. Some glossary definitions from the original bilingual edition are incorporated in our notes and are cited as "Valderrama and Escalante 1977."

INTRODUCTION

1. The friendship between the two couples is described below and in Valderrama and Escalante's Preliminary Note to the original edition, which follows this Introduction. Asunta is a pseudonym, as she desired (see the Preliminary Note). When they originally created her pseudonym, the original editors limited it to her first name; they have supplied us with a complete pseudonym for this English translation. Gabriela Martínez and I have changed the title of the book to include Asunta's name.

"Strappers" is our translation of *cargadores* (Sp.); another term is *cargadores de soga* (Sp.), or "rope strappers," because of the rope they carry around with them and use to strap on and haul packages and bundles. Other terms used in the Andean countries include *wasa q'ipis* and *q'ipiris* (Q.), as well as *changeadores* (Sp.). A common figure in imperial travel literature, in Latin America and elsewhere (see, e.g., Pratt 1992), this kind of worker is also referred to in translation as "cargo-bearer" (Muratorio 1991), and as "carrier" and "street porter." In the Andes, and indeed in many societies around the world, this kind of work is considered to be menial labor of the lowest sort. Until fairly recently, the term for this occupation in the United States was "lumper." The rope used to secure the goods to one's "hump"—one's back, that is—was called a "humpstrap" (Richard Carter of Searles Van and Storage, personal communication, 1992). In an early survey of this type of work, Mason (1887) differentiates between types of carriers and makes the point that humans were the first beasts of burden. Today the image of the strapper is iconic of the marginality, poverty, and domination of indigenous peoples in the Andes and is found on the covers of several publications concerning highland society.

2. These are the Andean countries where a large percentage of the population is Quechua-speaking. To a lesser degree, Gregorio's and Asunta's narratives also speak to the life experiences of many indigenous people in the highlands of Argentina, Chile, and Colombia.

3. Before, during, and after the Inka Empire, the Andes has been characterized by many distinct indigenous polities and ethnic groups. Of the different indigenous languages in the Andes, Quechua became the most widely spoken. As Mannheim puts it, "Prior to the European invasion, Quechua served as the administrative language of Tawantinsuyu, the Inka state, and was the medium of communication among the diverse peoples who were incorporated into the state. . . . After the European invasion, the Spaniards recognized Quechua's potential as a *lengua general* (lingua franca) for administrative purposes . . . and consciously promoted it as a vehicle of linguistic homogenization" (1991:64). Different figures are given for the current number of Quechua speakers. Cerrón-Palomino (1987:76) estimates that, in Ecuador, Peru, Bolivia, and Argentina, there are more than eight million Quechua speakers; he also estimates there to be some five thousand in Colombia and Brazil. These figures are based on old censuses, and the total population of these countries (and therefore the number of Quechua speakers) has risen dramatically in the last twenty years. There has also been a tendency to shift "bilinguals from the Andean to 'national' columns" (Murra 1982:31) in these censuses; the figure of ten million is therefore, if anything, conservative.

4. See, among others, Albó (1973), Cerrón-Palomino (1987), Godenzzi (1992), Harrison (1989), Mannheim (1985, 1991), Montoya (1987), and Murra (1982). As Mannheim's rich study of the Quechua language reveals, there are two major dialects in Southern Peruvian Quechua (1991:113): "Ayacucho-Chanka" and "Cuzco-Collao." Gregorio and Asunta speak the latter. It is worth noting that their speech is sprinkled with a tremendous quantity of Spanish loanwords, some of which are archaic. The English word "supermarket" even finds its way into their narratives.

5. The original publisher of these narratives, the Centro de Estudios Rurales Andinos "Bartolomé de las Casas," has produced a number of works in Quechua and is actively promoting indigenous literacy in the native language (e.g., Beyersdorff 1984, Condori and Gow 1982, Payne 1984, Valderrama and Escalante 1992). The same is true of the Bilingual Education Project of the Centro Andino de Educación y Promoción "José María Arguedas" (e.g., Chirinos 1994a), also of Cuzco.

6. Other texts published in Quechua (see note 5) have not been as widely diffused or have not received the number of editions and translations that the present narratives have. One Quechua text that has been widely published and translated is the Huarochirí Manuscript (see Salomon and Urioste 1991); however, this text has not been made readily accessible to Quechua speakers.

7. I mean "voices" here in two ways: in the sense of Gregorio's and Asunta's life histories and their perspectives on highland life, on the one hand, and, on the other, the vernacular Spanish of the translation. This type of Spanish, spoken by millions of people in the highlands (though not by Gregorio and Asunta, who are monolingual Quechua speakers), finds relatively little literary expression. For important exceptions, see the novels of Arguedas (e.g., 1978, 1985, 1986), as well as Valderrama and Escalante (1992) and Sindicato de Trabajadoras del Hogar de Cuzco (1982).

8. As Kaplan puts it, "The ideal vision of the 'subaltern' brought to the realm of public discourse via the efforts of a transparent medium cannot be maintained" (1992:

123). This problem has to do not only with the nature of authorship but also with the transfer of an oral text to a written one. Indeed, "oral theorists have been almost unanimous in holding that there is no way to transfer an oral text to written form and maintain its integrity" (Davies 1992:16). Yet testimonial accounts such as the present one imply "a challenge to the loss of the authority of orality in the context of processes of cultural modernization that privilege literacy and literature as norms of expression" (Beverley 1992:106). See Beyersdorff (1986), Adorno (1986), and Classen (1993) for insightful discussions of spoken Quechua and the written word. For critical discussions of, and experiments with, the transfer of oral to written texts, see Tedlock (1983, 1985, and 1993). For other important issues concerning the transcription and translation of native Latin American discourses, see, among others, Basso (1990), Brody (1994), Hendricks (1993), Preuss (1989, 1990), and Sherzer and Urban (1986). For discussions of authenticity, writing, and the anthropological subject, see, among others, Marcus and Fischer (1986) and Clifford and Marcus (1986). And for the politics of representation in Andean studies, see, among others, de la Cadena (1991), Kristal (1987), Mayer (1991), Montoya (1987), Poole (1990), Starn (1991) and Urbano (1991).

9.   There may be some kind of precedent for testimonials in church confessions or judicial testimonials (Beverley 1992:92), instances that present themselves in the narratives here. Perhaps the notion of Judgment Day and all that it presumes in terms of the good and bad deeds that one has done in life (see Asunta's narrative) is another example of what could be called a "testimonial situation," one that prefigures life history and testimonial narratives in highland culture. Yet, even though Quechua culture has an extremely rich repertoire of oral, and increasingly written, genres and narrative devices (see, among many others, Ackerman 1988, Beyersdorff 1986, 1988, Bolton 1980, Godenzzi 1992, Harrison 1989, Mannheim 1991, Montoya, Montoya, and Montoya 1987, Morote 1988, Salomon and Urioste 1991), the development of testimonial narratives in the Andes is clearly linked to larger liberation struggles in Latin America. Other testimonies from the Andes include those of Domitila Barrios de Chúngara (Barrios de Chúngara with Viezzer 1979), Juan Rojas (Nash 1992), Victoriano Tarapaki and Lusiku Ankalli (Valderrama and Escalante 1992), as well as the testimonies of women belonging to a Bolivian savings and loan cooperative (Wasserstrom 1985), and those of women who have worked as domestic servants in Cuzco (Sindicato de Trabajadoras del Hogar de Cuzco 1982). Testimonial narratives from the Peruvian coast include those of Erasmo Muñoz (Matos Mar and Carbajal 1974) and Juan H. Pévez (Oré 1983).

10.   The original bilingual edition of Gregorio's and Asunta's narratives has been cited in different ways: some list it under the name of the principal narrator ("Condori Mamani, Gregorio"), and others under the name of the original editors. For several reasons, we have taken the latter route and have listed the different editions of this text under Valderrama and Escalante (1977) in our Bibliography. First, one problem with listing the book under Condori Mamani is that it excludes the second narrator, Asunta. In creating Asunta's pseudonym, the original editors limited it to the first name (see Introduction, note 1), listing her only as "Asunta: Gregorio's wife" ("Asunta: Gregorioq warmin") and only in the text itself (not in the title). We have changed the title to include Asunta's name. Second, while we agree with current analyses that assert the need to privilege the narrators of *testimonio* and to "decolonize the subject," in this case at least, to do so in our citations would be to effect a different kind of erasure and colonialism. The original editors are rural ethnographers and low-paid university teachers in

a peripheral area of an impoverished country and were poorly compensated for the huge amount of work that went into taping, transcribing, editing, and translating these narratives. And as discussed below, we should not downplay the authorial role of the interlocutors; making a passing reference to them as "editors" does not do justice to the way in which the questions they posed to the narrators, and the decisions that they made about which materials to transcribe and edit, helped author the present narratives. Indeed, to cite this work under the narrators' names would support the illusion that these accounts are authentic and unmediated. For further discussions on the problems and prospects that *testimonio* presents, see Beverley (1993), Gugelberger (forthcoming), Gugelberger and Kearney (1991), and the collected articles in issues 70–71 (1991) of *Latin American Perspectives* 18(3–4).

11.   As Beverley says, one must consider the ways in which "the contradictions of sex, class, race, and age that frame the narrative's production can also reproduce themselves in the relation of the narrator to this direct interlocutor" (1992:98). I would argue that there was a cultural complicity between the editors and the narrators (see below and Preliminary Note) that is unusual in the life history or testimonial format. Ricardo is completely bilingual, Quechua being his mother tongue, and Carmen understands Quechua well. Both grew up in the Cuzco area and are part of the social world that Gregorio and Asunta describe in their accounts; they also developed a close relationship with the narrators over more than a decade. Thus, even though the original editors were not part of the narrators' ethnic group or class, there was a somewhat-shared cultural and social experience. There certainly were not the kinds of resistance and cultural, class, and ethnic differences found in the production of most other *testimonios,* such as that of Rigoberta Menchú (Menchú with Burgos-Debray 1984). Among the foremost ethnographers working in the Andes today, Valderrama and Escalante have published extensively on many aspects of Andean culture (e.g., Valderrama and Escalante 1976, 1988, 1992).

12.   This passage, and the supplemental information regarding the history of the text, has been excerpted from a personal communication (Valderrama and Escalante 1993). See the Preliminary Note for more information on the editors' relationship with the narrators. Phrases in parentheses are from the original.

13.   San Jerónimo is a town that lies about ten kilometers outside the city of Cuzco.

14.   These fascinating accounts were recently published in a bilingual Quechua-Spanish edition (Valderrama and Escalante 1992).

15.   Our ability to render a more fully ethnopoetic translation was also limited by the fact that we were working from the Quechua transcription and not from the original tape recordings. Scholars interested in the intricacies of Quechua verbal art are encouraged to consult the original bilingual Quechua-Spanish version, which is readily available: a new edition was recently published by the Municipality of Cuzco (1992) as part of its quincentennial remembrance (see the 1992 edition listed under Valderrama and Escalante 1977). Regarding the translation, it is worth mentioning that Gabriela is from Cuzco, and while Quechua is not her mother tongue, she has heard and spoken Quechua since she was a child. I have lived in Peru for several years and have studied Quechua and translation theory. We have both done extensive ethnographic research in the highlands, and this has informed many of our translation decisions. The translation has benefited greatly from our ongoing discussions with the original editors, who clarified some of the ambiguities and errors in the Quechua transcription. I would like to add

that our translation decisions should be read in the context of the translation as a whole and not in terms of a particular sentence or passage. There are many ways of translating this difficult text, and ours is just one of them.

16. Several of our notes are informed by Allen's *The Hold Life Has* (1988), which details many of the concepts and institutions described in Gregorio's and Asunta's narratives. I warmly recommend it as a companion piece to the present work.

17. Another definition that Allen provides for *ayllu* is "the collection of several individuals into a group that is distinct from (and thus potentially opposed to) other groups that might be formed in the same context" (1988:109). For different instances and uses of the term *ayllu*, see, among many others, Arguedas (1985), Bastien (1978), Bolton and Mayer (1977), Dover, Seibold, and McDowell (1992), Flores Ochoa and Nuñez del Prado (1983), Isbell (1974, 1978), Ossio (1980, 1992), Pease (1981), Platt (1982), Sallnow (1987), and Zuidema (1977).

18. In fact, the terms *qhari* and *qusan* (the latter a specific term for "husband") become unavoidably conflated in our translation. It is much easier to translate the few instances of legally sanctioned marriage by the Church—the context of which is signaled in both narratives by the Spanish loanword *casarse* or *casado* ("to marry" and "married," respectively)—as "lawfully married by the church," rather than have to provide the unnatural and cumbersome glosses of "spouse," "my common-law husband," or "the woman I lived with" each time that *qhari* and *warmi* are used in the text. SeeBolton and Mayer (1977) for discussions of different kinds of cohabitation and marriage in the Andes.

19. Not all instances of reportative validation are marked; the context often makes clear that the narrators are relating something told to them or that they are unsure of its veracity. In a similar vein, we have often suppressed the Quechua marker for a direct quote (*nispa*), as quotation marks fulfill this function in English.

20. The section breaks in the original bilingual edition were used in large part to align the Quechua version on the left page with the Spanish on the right.

21. The officially approved and standardized Quechua alphabet, established in Peru in 1975, was amended in 1985 with several important changes, such as establishing it as trivocal (*a, i, u*). Much has been written about this new alphabet, and the reader can consult any number of sources (e.g., Cerrón-Palomino 1987:380, Chirinos 1994b: 58–60, Godenzzi 1992, Mannheim 1991:235–238, and Valderrama and Escalante 1992: 241–245).

22. It is worth noting that such utterances by superiors are not always marked by language shifts in the narratives.

GREGORIO CONDORI MAMANI

1. Beginnings

1. *I'm from Acopía, and it's now forty years since I came here from my town—my name is Gregorio Condori Mamani:* Andean peasant villagers have a distinct sense of place (see Introduction), and it is significant that Gregorio mentions his town before telling us his name.

2. *a dirt poor orphan:* The Quechua word for orphan, *wakcha,* is synonymous with poor, and this phrase indicates that Gregorio is doubly poor, having neither money nor social ties. In the Andes, having a large family is equated with wealth (see Gregorio's discussion of this in Chapter 4), and it is being an orphan that determines much of Gregorio's fate.

3. *It was she who first cut my hair:* The first haircut is an important ritual in many regions of the Andes and is generally carried out by the godparents of the child (sometimes by the baptismal godparents, and other times by godparents especially selected for the hair cutting), who are accompanied by other relatives, at about the age the child begins to walk. See Bastien (1978:103–114) for a good description of this ritual.

4. *salt in your soup:* The word "soup" is our translation of *lawa* (Q.): "Soup made of maize or *chuño* that is consumed daily. An indispensable meal prepared by indigenous peasants as part of their daily diet" (Valderrama and Escalante 1977).

5. *Your bones are sturdy now, you've got the strength:* The virtual repetition of this line in this passage is one of the clearest "parallelisms" in the narratives, and it is significant that it comes in Gregorio's rendering of the fateful words spoken by his godmother long ago. Mannheim (1985, 1991) has pointed to the importance of parallelism in Quechua verbal art (see also Harrison 1989:159, Salomon 1991:35). One instance of this is the use of semantic couplets, which are "a peculiarly Quechua poetic device" (Mannheim 1991:133) that can be defined as a "pair of sentences that express closely related ideas phrased in related (sometimes syntactically parallel) fashion" (Salomon 1991:35) and that are commonly used in contemporary song and folk poetry.

6. *Tomorrow you'll have a wife and child, and you may just get a woman who doesn't help you with anything:* See the Introduction for a discussion of how we have translated the word *warmi* (Q.) as "wife." In this sentence, we have translated it as both "wife" and "woman."

7. *because I might just be punished and turned into a lost soul, made to wander and suffer:* This is our translation of *penantemanpas tukuyman* (Sp. & Q.): *Penante* (Sp.) refers to a "malignant spirit that represents a human being which, after death, continues wandering and is condemned to suffer punishments in the other world" (Valderrama and Escalante 1977). If one commits sins in this life, one must suffer (*penar*) for these after death; the person who commits certain horrible sins, such as incest (see Asunta's narrative, Chapter 15), turns into a *condenado,* or as we have translated it, "one of the damned" (see Chapter 6, note 2).

8. *wiraqucha Jacinto looked me over head to toe:* As mentioned in the Introduction and Glossary, *wiraqucha* can be translated in different ways. In this instance, it could be translated as "mister" or "master," again with the caveat that this master be thought of as "whiter" in the sense of wealthier, more urbane, using Western clothes (e.g., shoes rather than sandals made from tires), speaking Spanish (in addition to Quechua), and tied to the *misti* world of Cuzco. Other terms of address and deference used in the text include "master" (*patrón,* Sp.), "mister" (*señor* or *don,* Sp.), "father," "papa," or "good sir" (*tayta,* Q., and papa, papay, and papacito, Sp.), "uncle" (*tío,* Sp.), "mama" (*mama,* Q. and Sp.), and "ma'am" (*mamitay,* Q. and Sp.). Other social categories referred to as *wiraqucha* by Gregorio and Asunta in their narratives include *mestizo, gringo,* and "Spaniards" (*españas*)—all of these can be subsumed within the category "*misti.*" When quoting members of the dominant society in their accounts, certain racialized terms used to denigrate *runa* appear, such as "Indian" (*indio,* Sp.) and *cholo* (see chap-

ter 6, note 1 and Glossary). Gregorio's and Asunta's different classifications for themselves or other *runas* in the text include "native people" (*indígena,* Sp.), "Indian" (*indio,*
Sp.), "villager" (*paisano,* Sp.), "peasant" (*chacarero,* Sp.), "tenant farmer" (*arrendíre,*
Sp.), and "children of the Inka" ("Inka runa . . . churinkuna kanchis"). Thus, as with
the ethnic categories of *runa* and *misti,* use of the word *wiraqucha* signals the class,
perceived race, and ethnicity of the speaker and the person being addressed. The term
wiraqucha often also connotes a certain compassion and benevolence in the power
holder—indeed, this is part of their power. See also Chapter 5, note 4; Chapter 16,
note 8.

9.   *working shoulder to shoulder at a work party there in the community:* This is our
translation of *faena* (Sp.), a word that can be used to designate almost any kind of labor.
In the Andes, it is generally used to designate communal work parties, that is, a type of
labor tax levied by rural communities on their members. This institution is found in
peasant villages and towns throughout the Andean highlands. See also Chapter 4, note
1; Chapter 9, note 17.

10.   *one of the town elders, Laureano Cutipa, talking about Cuzco. Papa Laureano was
Staffholder at the time:* In these sentences, we have used the words "town father" and
"papa" to gloss *tayta* (Q.): "Literally, father, a term that is also extended to any elder
man that is loved and respected" (Valderrama and Escalante 1977). Depending on the
context, we have translated *tayta* as "papa," "elder," "father," and "parent." When used
in a religious sense, we have translated it as "Father" or "Lord"; the term can refer to
both Andean and Christian deities, as in "Sun Father" (see Chapter 1, note 12) and "the
Lord" (*Inti Tayta* and *Taytacha,* respectively). *Taytacha* "refers to the Christian god"
(ibid.), and we gloss this as "the good Lord" when used as a noun and as "divine" when
used as an adjective (see Chapter 2, note 4). In the above sentence, we have used the
word "Staffholder" to gloss *alcalde* (Sp.) *varayuq* (Sp. and Q.): "Traditional authority
of an indigenous community" (Valderrama and Escalante 1977). This office, represented
by a long staff of authority, replaced other forms of traditional authority in highland
communities in the late eighteenth century (see Spalding 1984), and today is the principal post within the civic *cargo* system of *Varayuq* or Staffholders, found in communities in Colombia, Ecuador, Peru, and Bolivia. See, among others, Allen (1988), Arguedas (1985), Fuenzalida (1970), Isbell (1978), Núñez del Prado (1973), Rasnake (1988), and
Rappaport (1994).

11.   *when Inka was building Cuzco:* As mentioned in the Glossary, the term *Inka* is
used in different ways in the text. Often, as in this instance, it refers to a mythical figure,
a creator god and first class of ruler in a foundational sense. Here Inka is the same as
Inkaríy (see Glossary), to whom Gregorio refers later in his narrative; Arguedas (1985
[1964]) and Ortiz (1973) have shown that these names are used interchangeably to refer
to the same mythic complex. Building Cuzco is just one of the foundational acts of this
culture hero, and many communities peripheral to Cuzco also have stories about Inka/
Inkaríy founding their towns. Inka Qulla, on the other hand, is a foundational deity
from the high plateau. Some have taken the mythic battles between Inka and Inka Qulla
(or Inkaríy and Qullaríy) to represent an historical confrontation between two pre-
Columbian polities (see, e.g., Ortiz 1973:160). In any case, the battle between these culture heroes of an ancient, primordial time is part of a widespread mythic tradition in
the Andes (see, e.g., Getzels 1983, Ossio 1973, Pease 1982). For an incisive discussion of
myth and history and the foundation and social organization of Cuzco, see Urton

(1990). The Inka was the largest indigenous polity to develop in the New World and there are many detailed studies of this empire (e.g., Bauer 1992, Julien 1982, Murra 1980, Patterson 1991, Rostworowski 1988, Rowe 1982, Sherbondy 1986, Mosely 1992, Zuidema 1990).

12. *when Sun Father was on his way down:* "Sun Father" is our translation of *Inti Tayta* (Q.). The sun was one of the supreme deities of the Inka Empire and is still revered in many highland communities today. Sun Father is conceptually opposed to Mother Moon (*Mama Killa*), and it should be noted that there are other kinds of mothers (*mamas*) and fathers (*taytas*) as well (see, e.g., Chapter 1, notes 10, 22, 30; Chapter 4, note 14). We have followed word order here in glossing these terms, and as stated in the Introduction, we have capitalized them to accord them the same status as the Christian God and saints. To a certain degree, capitalizing these is something of an "exuberance," in that doing so gives "the English a poetic or at least a euphemistic sense that does not reflect the ordinariness of the original" (Mannheim 1991:129). Yet, other glosses tend to be "deficient" in translating the important meanings that these terms have for highlanders. The conceptual opposition and symbolic importance of the sun and moon, and their relationship to sexual symbolism and gender ideologies, is well documented in the literature (e.g., Isbell 1978, Ossio 1973, Silverblatt 1987, Urton 1981, Zuidema 1977).

13. *wasn't in the stars for me to reach Cuzco:* We have used "in the stars" as a gloss for *estrella* (Sp.) in this instance: "Spanish word used in Quechua to refer to the destiny of a person" (Valderrama and Escalante 1977). The use of this Spanish loanword apparently reflects a mix of European and Andean notions of fate and destiny (in Chapter 9 Gregorio uses the Spanish loanword *suerte* in this sense). In Chapter 8, we have glossed it as "the star one is born with." This reference to "star" probably also encompasses an Andean astrological tradition and conception of "fate." In Chapter 4, while not referring directly to such a notion, Gregorio mentions stellar divination. Urton, who has documented different forms of this practice among Andean peasants in the Cuzco region, makes it clear that stellar divination depends on distinctly Andean constellations and criteria and requires "the ability to interpret the specific meanings of various types of starlight, its color and degree of scintillation" (1981:93). Allen (1988) reports that in the Cuzco region where she worked, the word *estrella*—which she writes *istrilla* to signal its appropriation by Quechua speakers—means "power object," one that can impact the destiny and well-being of a person. In any case, Gregorio's notion of fate is quite different from that of Asunta (see Chapter 13, note 7).

14. *leave me with some money at a herd stead:* "Herd stead" is our translation of *estancia* (Sp.). In the Andes, this term often refers to small, isolated herding stations in the high mountain pastures, in which alpaca and llama, as well as sheep and other livestock (bovine, etc.), are kept. These remote stations often consist of just a small compound, made up of a shepherd's hut and stone-walled corrals. They are often one-family satellite colonies of a parent community, be this a free community or one subject to an hacienda. The stead keeper often watches over the herds or individual animals of other peasants, as well as a personal herd. For herding culture, see, among others, Flores Ochoa (1977, 1985), Orlove (1980), and Webster (1983). See also the film *Ch'ullacuy* (Martínez 1993), which documents the ritual life of herders.

15. *ready to pass into the otherworld:* "The otherworld" is our translation of *huk kaq vida*, "the other life." See Chapter 1, note 16.

16. *climbing toward heaven or entering the underworld:* We have used the word

"heaven" as a gloss for *cielo*, a Spanish loanword that appears to be a clear reference to the Christian concept of "Heaven." However, the reader must remember that here and elsewhere, this and other Christian concepts and images are entirely fused and inter-penetrated with Andean religious concepts and images. This is evident, for example, in the concept of "underworld," also found in this sentence, which is our translation of *uku pacha* (Q.): "The lower world, inhabited by tiny little beings and local protective spirits. A deity of Christian origin, the devil, also resides in this world" (Valderrama and Escalante 1977). In the rest of the two narratives, rather than use *cielo*, the narrators employ the Quechua *hanaq pacha* (which we gloss as "upperworld") as a complemen-tary opposite to "underworld." Much has been written on the word *pacha*, which en-compasses notions of time and space (see especially Allen 1988:64–66) and which we gloss above as "world" (see also Chapter 3, note 6); the same is true of the concepts of *uku pacha, kay pacha,* and *hanaq pacha,* which we gloss as "underworld," "this world," and "upperworld." In this scheme of things, humans are viewed as inhabiting the inter-face ("this world" or "this life") between two opposed worlds and as having to negotiate and balance the forces of the upper and lower worlds to achieve equilibrium (e.g., Allen 1988, Earls 1971, Maybury-Lewis 1989, Ossio 1973, Palomino 1984, Platt 1986, Silverblatt 1987). Dualism, as expressed in the polarity between upper and lower worlds, is "a fundamental tenet of native Andean cosmology" (Sallnow 1987:217) and is an ancient cultural phenomenon in the Andes. Today, dualism encodes a variety of activities in a multitude of Quechua-, Aymara-, and Spanish-speaking villages and towns throughout the highlands of Ecuador, Bolivia, and Peru, ranging from symbolic classification in the aesthetics of weaving (see, e.g., Cereceda 1987, Harris 1985, Silverman-Proust 1983, Zorn 1987) to the rigid institutionalization of duality in spatially localized social groups and natural resources (Gelles 1995). As regards *kay pacha*, "this world, the terrestrial sphere between *hanan pacha* and *ukhu pacha*" (Allen 1988:259), Gregorio and Asunta often refer to it as "this life" (*kay vida*), which they oppose to the generic "other life" (*huk kaq vida*), that is, the "world of the dead" or the "afterlife" (MacCormack 1991). Because the narrators in many cases use the Quechua *pacha* and the Spanish *vida* to refer to the same concept, and because "this world" and "the otherworld" are more idiomatic and evocative in English, we have, with few exceptions (see Chapter 15, note 1), translated both *kay pacha* and *kay vida* as "this world" and *huk kaq vida* as "the otherworld" throughout the text. We have refrained from using "afterlife" for the latter concept because "afterlife" implies a temporal separation between this world and the other-world. As Allen has explained, "When *Runakuna* die . . . they do not cease to exist but exist in a less immediate state than the living—a parallel world from which they directly influence this one" (1988:63). Indeed, "*Runakuna* are convinced that they can and sometimes do encounter both saints and *condenados* in their own lives" (1988:65). Both Allen (1988) and Weismantel (1988) have translated *uku pacha* as "inner world," and while the term certainly does convey this notion of interiority (see especially Weisman-tel 1988:197–201), we feel that this quality is also conveyed in English by the term "un-derworld." The latter is a better gloss because of possible aberrant readings of "inner world." In sum, in the above phrase and throughout the text, we attempt to evoke the distinct religious synthesis found in the Andes by using concepts from both Roman Catholic and Andean traditions. As Allen (1988:61) says, "*Runakuna* hold contradictory beliefs simultaneously and employ them in different contexts." For studies of Andean religion, see, among many others, Dillon and Abercrombie (1988), MacCormack (1991),

Marzal (1977, 1985), Sallnow 1987, Silverblatt (1987), and the collected articles in Dover, Seibold, and McDowell (1992).

17.   *Benavides*: Oscar Raimundo Benavides took power in August 1933 and was president of Peru from 1933 to 1939.

18.   *That's what this Christian did to me:* The word "Christian" is applied to diverse things by Gregorio and Asunta, including humans, animals, and airplanes; in this colloquial usage of the word, it simply means "person or living soul" (*Diccionario de la Lengua Española* 1984:398). In the sentence above and in some other passages, the word appears to be used in a somewhat ironic way. In other contexts, it is clear that the narrators are using the term in the accepted religious sense (e.g., Christian burial).

19.   *I forgot to feed the guinea pigs:* "Guinea pigs" is our translation of *quwikuna* (Q.). See Chapter 16, note 6.

20.   *to the village of Arisa, his wife's people:* This is our translation of *warminpa llaqtanta Arisa ayllu:* We have generally translated *llaqta* as "town" and *ayllu* as "village" (see Introduction), but because we are trying to maintain a separation between these terms, and since *llaqta* can equally well be glossed as a "people," we have chosen the latter for this particular instance.

21.   *As if they were horse cankers!:* "Horse cankers" is our translation of *mata caballo* (Sp.): "Horse with ulcerations on its back" (Valderrama and Escalante 1977).

22.   *foreigners have gone to Mother Moon:* We use "Mother Moon" as a translation of *Mama Killa* (Q.): Together with the sun, the moon was considered a supreme deity of the Inka Empire, and its symbolic importance continued through the colonial period (see Silverblatt 1987). Today the moon continues to be revered, conceptually opposed to the sun, and tied to sexual symbolism and gender ideologies in highland culture. See Chapter 1, note 12.

23.   *At that time, I still wasn't drinking cornbeer or liquor:* "Cornbeer" and "liquor" are our glosses for *aqha* (Q.) and *trago* (Sp.), respectively. Cornbeer, also referred to as *chicha* (Sp.) in the original text, has been an important part of the diet, as well as of the ritual and social life, of highland peoples since pre-Columbian times (see, among others, Allen 1988 and Murra 1980). It should be noted that while *aqha* and *chicha* are used in the text to mean beer made out of maize and this is the most frequent usage of these terms, they can also refer to fermented beverages made of other crops, such as barley or potato. *Trago* is a low-grade rum of the "rotgut" variety, and, like cornbeer and coca leaf (see Chapter 13, note 9), hard liquor is an essential ingredient in many social gatherings and ritual occasions. See Allen (1988) for the role of *trago* in Andean social life and ritual celebration.

24.   *rich pasturelands:* "Rich pasturelands" is our translation of *wayllar:* "A grazing reserve for cattle" (Valderrama and Escalante 1977). Zimmerer (1994:122–123) defines *wayllar* as a saturated bog that, among other things, provides well-watered forage for cattle.

25.   *He was one of us—a villager, not a misti:* "Villager" is our translation of *paisano* (see Introduction). This is one of the clearest statements of the *paisano-misti* divide found in the text and shows the clear correspondence between *paisano* and *runa*. We have supplied "one of us" to capture some of the affect and affinity lost when translating *paisano* solely as "villager." See Chapter 1, note 8 for other ways in which Gregorio and Asunta self-identify in the text.

26. *this was done by the stewards, those runas who were just beginning their religious cargo obligations:* "Stewards" is our translation of *priostekuna* (from the Spanish *prioste, kuna* being the pluralizer in Quechua). As this passage indicates, in addition to the financial and social burdens of undertaking a *cargo* (see Glossary), sponsors were also required to provide unpaid labor service to town priests. Gregorio refers to himself here as a "manor servant"—our translation of *pongo* (see Chapter 8, note 5; Chapter 13, note 5)—that was just one of many forms of servitude supplied by *runas* to religious and civil power holders in the countryside. Reforms instituted during the late 1960s and early 1970s did away with most of these practices; some of these, however, still continue today.

27. *I'm going to go sell pots at the Lord of Huanca's shrine:* See Sallnow (1987:243– 258) for a detailed description of the Lord of Huanca. Gregorio describes the foundational miracle for this shrine in Chapter 9. See also Chapter 9, note 18 for background on the religious beliefs embodied in this kind of sacred place.

28. *as far away as Puno Lake:* Gregorio is referring to Lake Titicaca, located on the high plateau bordering Bolivia, hundreds of miles away from the shrine. Puno is a large city on the Peruvian side of the lake.

29. *the cars and trucks swarm there like ants:* "Trucks" supplied here. Although Gregorio uses just the word *carros* (Sp.), he is referring to "cars" in the generic sense of "vehicle" or "motorcar," one that includes trucks and buses as well. A good part of peasant transportation in the highlands is in the back of large trucks.

30. *springs come gushing out of Earth Mother:* "Earth Mother" is our translation of *pachamama* (Q.): "Mother earth, deity of pre-Columbian origin which represents fertility and which resides in the earth" (Valderrama and Escalante 1977). As Allen mentions in passing, "World" may be a more appropriate translation than "Earth" for *pacha* because *pacha* is simultaneously temporal and spatial (1988:45). Yet, while "World Mother" or even "Life Mother" are other potential glosses for *pachamama,* the fact that the "mother" spirit is viewed as dwelling in the earth and in its different manifestations—houses made of earth, cultivated fields, mountains—makes Earth Mother a better gloss in our opinion. Like "Sun Father" and "Earth Shade," we have chosen to gloss *pachamama* (which appears as both one and two words in the original transcription) as two words and in the order in which they appear (see Chapter 1, note 12). Many authors have translated it in Spanish as "Madre Tierra," and in English as "Mother Earth," rather than Earth Mother. Besides being a closer rendition of the original (i.e., maintaining word order), Earth Mother also implicitly suggests that there are other "mamas." See Allen for a rich discussion of Earth Mother and her different manifestations (1988:37–67). See also Chapter 3, note 6 for the related concept of "Earth Shade" (*pachatierra*).

31. *Saint Isidore the Farmhand:* This is our translation of "San Isidro Labrador" (Sp.), the patron saint of farmworkers, peasants, and field laborers.

32. *the same amount keeps flowing to the fields, even during a drought:* We have supplied "to the fields." While this spring water is also used for domestic purposes and cattle, water ritual primarily concerns irrigation activities. Indeed, irrigation rituals such as the one alluded to in this passage are common in the Andes.

33. *belongs to the devilish demon:* "Devilish demon" is our translation of *saqhra* (Q.) *demonio* (S.): The original editors define *saqhra* as "devil" or "demon" (Valderrama and Escalante 1977); it is also used as an adjective.

34. *only witches drink from it:* "Witch" is our translation of *layqa* (Q.), which can also be glossed as "sorcerer" or "wizard." *Layqa* is gender neutral, and our use of "witch" here and elsewhere in the text includes both male and female practitioners.

35. *they got caught red-handed near the earth shrine there at Wamani Pass:* We use "red-handed" as a translation of *pilu* (from *pelo*, Sp.): "The act of surprising a cattle rustler at the scene of the crime" (Valderrama and Escalante 1977). We use "earth shrine" and "pass" as a gloss for *apachita* (Q.): "Place situated on ridges and mountain tops where a trail passes by, and where each traveler places a rock that has been especially brought for this magical ceremony, in which the energy lost on the trail is restored" (Valderrama and Escalante 1977). We take our gloss "earth shrine" from Bastien, who states, "throughout the Andes, the *apacheta* [sic] is the highest place on a road, where the Indian rests from his ascending journey, discards his coca quid, and throws several stones in a large pile, consciously symbolizing the removal of his load and the restoration of strength" (1978:69). Bastien notes that these sacred cairns are one manifestation of a widespread and ancient tradition of telluric symbolism in Andean religion (see Chapter 8, note 2), and at the same time notes that crosses are often carried to and placed on top of these rock piles. Thus, as with most forms of religious belief and practice in the Andes, "the multivocality of the cross and the apacheta allows the possibility of many meanings . . . yet to them it is one whole system of religious beliefs and practices" (ibid.). Lira (1982) provides a more general definition of *apachita*: "mound of rocks over provisional burials which are made for those who die while traveling. Rustic tomb. Holy earth." *Apachita* derives from the Quechua verb *apachiy*, "to send" or "to ship"—or as Bastien puts it, "to have something or someone carry the load away" (1978:69). What is important, then, is that mountain passes are marked by earth shrines and conceptually linked to powerful spiritual forces. Thus, while Gregorio sometimes uses the word *apachita* simply to mean "mountain pass," the sacred nature of these areas is naturalized in this usage. Where we think it relevant, we include the words "earth shrine," and where it is clear that *apachita* is being used only as a metonym for the physical place itself, we simply gloss it as "pass." See also Chapter 9, note 13.

36. *I'd have to go half a league to get water:* A league is about three or four miles; it is not a fixed measurement, as there are different standard leagues. In the text, we have occasionally glossed "leagues" as "miles."

37. *after my master had forgot all about me, one of his own people:* "One of his own people" is our gloss for *patroniypa huk partidon* (Sp. and Q.); *Partido:* "Spanish word used in Quechua to refer to a person with whom one is close, that is, friends or kinfolk who belong to the same coalition" (Valderrama and Escalante 1977).

2. Aeroplanes and Other Beasts

1. *an aeroplane—those they now call plane:* Gregorio often uses the outdated Spanish loanword *aeroplano* (rather than *avión*) when he speaks of an airplane. We therefore use the outdated term "aeroplane" when he uses *aeroplano* and "plane" when he uses *avión*. Gregorio was about thirteen years old when this event occurred (Deeds, n.d.)

2. *Humans are going to travel by trotting on the wind:* "Humans" is our gloss here

for *runas,* as it is elsewhere in the text when it is clear that the narrators are using the word generically to mean "humans" or "all of humanity" rather than identifying their specific people (see the Introduction and Glossary for *runa* and "villager"). This is a clear instance of Gregorio's using the term *runa* in a way that excludes his own group. As he makes clear in Chapter 7, *runas* do not know how to work machines such as airplanes.

3. *a messenger eagle with a condor's head and llama feet:* "Messenger eagle" is our translation of *alqamari* (Q.): "Atahorm: In Andean lore, it is the messenger between humans and mythic deities" (Valderrama and Escalante 1977). Lira (1982) also defines *alqamari* as *atahorm* but describes it as "a large eaglet with white and black speckled wings." The *Diccionario de la Lengua Española* (1984) defines *alcamar* [*sic*] as a bird of prey from Peru (and *atahorm* as a white-tailed, red-and-gray-breasted, ash-colored bird of prey, but of African origin). Hughes (1987) identifies the *alcamari* [*sic*] as *Phalcoboenus megaloptererus* and gives an English translation of "mountain caracara." Like the beasts of other mythic traditions (e.g., the unicorn, dragon), the *alqamari* joins the features of different animals into a composite whole.

4. *It's a divine miracle:* "Divine" is our gloss for *taytacha* (Q.): "Refers to the Christian God" (Valderrama and Escalante 1977). Throughout the next several lines, we continue to gloss *taytacha* as "divine" and use the word "Lord" for *tayta* (see Chapter 1, notes 10, 12). Gregorio appears to be speaking ironically when he talks of them all "praying to the divine airplane."

5. *Then the diviner, Machaca, said:* "Diviner" is our translation of *paqu* (Q.): "Sorcerer. This role has a higher standing than witch and communicates with the deities" (Valderrama and Escalante 1977). *Paqus* are ritual specialists and spiritists who mediate between the human and spirit worlds, who can communicate with mountain and earth deities, and who carry out agricultural, pastoral, and healing rituals on behalf of individuals, families, and entire villages and towns. Some *paqus* also practice witchcraft, and in some communities the same individual fulfills the roles of *paqu* (diviner), *hanpiq* (healer, see Chapter 6, note 5), and *layqa* (witch, see Chapter 1, note 34).

6. *Enrique Rondán is the driver:* As mentioned in the Preliminary Note, the pilot's true name was Enrique Rolandi; he was an Italian pilot who landed in Sicuani on June 7, 1921. This is one of the few fairly concrete historical dates that we have to situate Gregorio's narrative about his early life. If the birthdate on his conscription card was correct (July 6, 1908), then Gregorio was just shy of thirteen years old when he saw the airplane (Deeds n.d.). This means that Gregorio probably left home when he was about ten or eleven years of age, though he may have been younger.

7. *there were also songs like this one:* In translating this song, we have used "old smoky" as a gloss for *yana machu* (Q.): "Literally: old black one. It refers to the train" (Valderrama and Escalante 1977). This poem is a clear instance of "semantic coupling" (see Chapter 1, note 5), and we have chosen to translate it in a way that mimics the cadence of the song. The combination of *yana* and *machu* can be read in different ways: *yana,* besides meaning "black," also has the connotation of "sweetheart," "beloved," or "spouse"; *machu,* besides meaning "old one," can mean "ancestor, deity of evil" (Cusihuaman 1976). See Allen (1988), Beyersdorff (1986), Harrison (1989), Mannheim (1991), and Salomon (1991) for their renderings and insightful analyses of Quechua poetry and song. The original song reads as follows:

Maypiñan yana machu?
ña Santa Rosapiña
carritay
ña kisa kisapiña.

Sichus Rosalina
mana waylluwanki
sichus Rosalina
mana munawanki
yana machu rakrawachun.

3. Military Tricks

1. *Auntie, with a little luck:* We have used "auntie" for *ipay:* "Quechua kinship term that designates the father's sister or paternal aunt" (Valderrama and Escalante 1977). For discussions of Quechua kin terminology, see Bolton and Mayer (1977), Isbell (1974, 1978), and Allen (1988), among others.

2. *Stay in the village, together with us here in the family:* This is our translation of *Nuqaykuwan kuska ayllunchispi quedakuy.* We gloss *ayllu* as both village and family here, since it is apparent in this chapter that Gregorio is referring to the *ayllu* as being part of a multi-*ayllu* settlement and as engaging in social relations with other families within the town of Acopía. Thus, while somewhat ambiguous, *ayllu* probably refers here to a localized, neighborhood-focused or to a kin-based group (probably a bilateral kindred), or quite probably a combination of both. We have used "the family" rather than "our family," because in English, the former implies an inclusiveness (i.e., an inclusion of the person being addressed, in this case Gregorio) that is ambiguous in the latter. This inclusion of Gregorio as part of the family is clearly expressed by his aunt's use of - *nchis* (*ayllunchispi*), the suffix for the inclusive first-person plural in Quechua (as opposed to the exclusive first-person plural-*yku,* found above in the word *nuqaykuwan*). See the Introduction and Chapter 1, note 20, for discussions of *ayllu*.

3. *we saw some policemen coming from Combapata:* "Policemen" and "police" is our translation of *guardia* and *guardia civil* throughout the text. What this gloss does not convey is that the *guardia civil* is a national police force, one that is foreign to most communities in the Andes.

4. *I was drafted during the time of Sánchez Cerro:* Luis M. Sánchez Cerro led a military junta that took over the government in 1930. He was elected president in 1931 and held office until his assassination in 1933.

5. *Recapture Tacna-Arica:* Our gloss for *Rescataremos Tacna-Arica.* Here Gregorio uses a Spanish phrase in the midst of his Quechua narrative to signal the language being used by his superiors. As discussed in the Introduction, we use italics to signal such language shifts. The cities of Tacna (Peru) and Arica (Chile) are currently border cities. The Peruvian border used to lie much further southward, but this territory was lost to Chile during the War of the Pacific (1879–1884). Gregorio's narrative here "telescopes" three historical events—the coming of Columbus (1492) and implicitly the Spanish invasion of Peru (1532), the War of Independence (achieved in 1824) embodied in the figure of a hero of that war, San Martín, and the War of the Pacific (1879–1884)—into

one. He thus collapses three invasion episodes, framed in an "us/them" kind of way, wherein the invading Chileans are conflated with the Spanish, during two different time periods: the Conquest and Independence. A border dispute did occur in the early 1930s, but it was on the northern, not southern, border, and the dispute was with Colombia, not Chile (see Deeds n.d.). The current border between Peru and Chile was established only in 1929 and remains a point of contention between the two countries.

6. *Earth Shade wouldn't have swallowed him up:* "Earth Shade" is our gloss for *pachatierra*: "Malevolent and perverse deity who inhabits the lower world" (Valderrama and Escalante 1977). Allen defines *pachatierra* as the "malevolent aspect of Pacha Mama" (1988:261), linking it to the two-sided nature—generative and destructive—of many earth, mountain, and ancestor spirits in Andean culture. She notes that the term seems redundant since *tierra* is the Spanish word for earth, but adds that *tierra* and *pacha* are not true synonyms, since *pacha* "denotes a temporal dimension that *tierra* lacks" (1988:48). According to the original editors, Earth Shade, in addition to being a malignant and possessive female deity that resides in the earth, is more localized than Earth Mother (see Chapter 1, note 30), a protective deity providing fecundity and reproduction. That is, while Earth Mother is more abstract (see also Allen 1988:49), residing in all the earth, but especially cultivated fields, Earth Shade resides in determined places, which explains why people become ill after falling to the ground or after falling asleep in a certain locale. Earth Shade can be placated by offerings (Valderrama and Escalante, personal communication 1993). Urton (1981:175) reviews different ethnographic instances of *pachatierra* in the Cuzco region and finds this term applied to "dark cloud constellations" which are considered female and which represent "a transitional, intermediate category of celestial phenomena" that provide a mirror image, a negative complement, to Earth Mother. For all of the above reasons, and because of the mirroring in the word *pachatierra* itself, Earth Shade seems an appropriate gloss.

7. *the Chileans were advancing up the coast of the sea lake:* "The coast of the sea lake" is our gloss for *La Mar* (Sp.) *Quchaq* (Q.)*kantun* (Sp. and Q., from the Spanish *canto*). *Mar Qucha* is translated as "The Sea" in the original glossary (Valderrama and Escalante 1977), and although it is clear that Gregorio refers here to the Pacific Ocean, his understanding of this body of water is mediated through highland concepts of lakes and water. For example, his use of "La Mar" rather than the generally masculine gender of the sea in Spanish ("El Mar") is consistent with Quechua notions that lakes are feminine (e.g., the Mother Lake; see Chapter 4, note 14). See, among others, Sherbondy (1982) on highland concepts of water and the relationship between highland lakes, subterranean filtration, and the ocean.

8. *who knows how San Martín's fellow comrades thought this up:* "Fellow comrades" is our gloss for *paisanokuna* (Sp. and Q.:-*kuna* is the pluralizer in Quechua) in this case. See the Introduction for a discussion of *paisano*, which we generally gloss as "villager" or "fellow villager." Although this passage is ambiguous, it seems that, given the context, Gregorio is using *paisano* here in the sense of "fellow countryman" or "comrade."

9. *the figure of the llama is a charmed amulet used on coins and matchboxes:* "Charmed amulet" is our translation of *illa* (Q.): "A figure or representation of animals or other beings carved in stone and which are used for magical ends or as amulets" (Valderrama and Escalante 1977). See Allen (1988) and Salomon (1991) for interesting discussions of *illa* and related concepts.

4. Earth Mother, Cropkeeper, and the Three Brothers

1. *by trading labor in ayni:* See Glossary for *ayni* (Q.). There is a large literature on reciprocity and cooperative labor in the Andes and on the key role that symmetrical and asymmetrical forms of exchange play within highland social life (e.g., Alberti and Mayer 1974, Allen 1988, Collins 1986, Núñez del Prado 1973, Van Den Berghe and Primov 1977). We have supplied the phrase "trading labor" in a couple of instances here. See also Chapter 1, note 9, on *faena,* as well as *mink'a* in the Glossary.

2. *a plot of land in one of the laymi sectors:* See Glossary for *laymi* (Q.): There is a large literature on *laymis* and other sectoral fallowing systems (e.g., Brush 1977, Godoy 1984, Orlove and Godoy 1986, Guillet 1981). This is just one of many agricultural and pastoral strategies used in the Andes (see, e.g., Shimada 1985). We have supplied the word "sector" and have also used it as a substitute for *laymi* in some parts of this passage.

3. *the Fieldmaster, reading coca leaves or the stars:* "Fieldmaster" is our translation of *Chakrakamayuq* (Q.): "Literally, he who orders in the cultivated fields. It is the person who is knowledgeable and well versed in climatological phenomena. Generally this person is also a ritual specialist who reads the movement of certain stars through coca leaves so as to determine the days in which the whole community should plant or harvest" (Valderrama and Escalante 1977). Those who undertake such important communal responsibilities are generally well-respected *paqus* (see Chapter 2, note 5), that is, diviners and spiritists. See Chapter 13, note 9, for the importance of coca leaf in Andean society.

4. *when the Fieldmaster said, "It's hail":* "Hail" is our translation of *chikchi* (Q.): "Literally, hail stones. The term also refers to the three masculine deities endowed with malevolent and terrible knowledge and power" (Valderrama and Escalante 1977). Later in the chapter, there is a vivid portrayal of these characters, who are intimately associated with sterility and crop failure.

5. *Such is life for the runa peasant:* "Peasant" is our translation of *chacarero,* which occurs just twice in the narratives; peasant should be read in the colloquial sense of "peasant farmer" or "smallholder." Gregorio makes it clear that he is talking about relatively powerless *runa* peasant farmers.

6. *being the host of a work party in the fields:* This is our translation of *chakrakuy* (Q.): "Literally, he who works the field. Title that is given to the owner of a field who has set a special date to work his land with the reciprocal aid of other peasants. This is done only among indigenous peasants" (Valderrama and Escalante 1977). Generally, the person sponsoring a work party—often with several different *ayni* partners at once, or in *mink'a*—must furnish food as well as coca, cigarettes, cornbeer, or liquor to those who attend. See also *ayni* and *mink'a* in the Glossary.

7. *Each year on Carnival Monday, a Cropkeeper was chosen:* "Cropkeeper" is our translation of *arariwa* (Q.): "Caretaker of the crops" (Valderrama and Escalante 1977). See Allen (1988) and Sallnow (1987) for descriptions of the ritual obligations and activities undertaken by the *arariwas* in other communities of the Cuzco region. By "Carnival Monday," Gregorio refers to Shrove Monday, that is, the Monday before Ash Wednesday. The same is true of Carnival Tuesday (Shrove Tuesday) mentioned elsewhere in this chapter.

8.   *it's said that Saint Ciprian's prayers make the hail go away:* Legend has it that Saint Ciprian was a sorcerer of black magic who later converted to Christianity and who turned his evil powers to good. Peasants throughout much of the southern Andes use his prayers to ward off evil.

9.   *That's the lightning bolt:* This is our translation of *illapa* (Q.): "Lightning bolt. Mythical figure that transmits the decisions of the major deities" (Valderrama and Escalante 1977). In highland culture, *illapa* refers both to the physical phenomenon itself and to the god of thunder and lightning. *Illapa* has been a central figure in Andean religious traditions since time immemorial (see, among others, Demarest 1981, MacCormack 1991, Salomon and Urioste 1991, Silverblatt 1987, and especially Gade 1983). Yet the term does not seem to have any overt religious significance in this particular passage. Rather, it exemplifies the way in which climatological phenomena—lightning, hail, and snow in this passage—are often anthropomorphized in contemporary highland culture.

10.   *the baby of the family, is Chanaku:* Not just a proper name, *chanaku* (Q.) is the "Quechua kinship term used to differentiate the youngest son from the rest of the male siblings because of his economic importance, that of maintaining the parents when they grow old" (Valderrama and Escalante 1977).

11.   *Their mother is the snow:* "Snow" is our translation of *rit'i* (Q.): "Literally, snow. It refers to the feminine deity that resides in the snow" (Valderrama and Escalante 1977).

12.   *Please, ma'am, put me up for the night:* "Ma'am" is our translation of *mamitay* (Q. and Sp.) and is, like "papa," a respectful familiar. See also Chapter 1, note 8.

13.   *I'll cover you up with this clay basin:* "Clay basin" is our translation of *raki* (Q.): "Large earthen vat with a wide mouth used for fermenting cornbeer" (Valderrama and Escalante 1977).

14.   *The hail's home is Mother Lake:* The latter is our translation of *Mama Qucha* (Q.): "Lake. Feminine deity who inhabits lakes" (Valderrama and Escalante 1977). See Chapter 1, note 12; Chapter 3, note 7.

15.   *those runas who've been struck and killed by lightning:* We have left *runa* untranslated here, although Gregorio may be referring to people in general (see Chapter 2, note 2). This chapter, however, is about village life, which suggests that he is talking about *runas* in the sense of peasant villagers.

5. The Barracks

1.   *Sánchez Cerro:* Sánchez Cerro was assassinated August 31, 1933, and the government was taken over by Benavides (see Chapter 1, note 17).

2.   *There inside the barracks:* "Barracks" is our gloss for *cuartel* (Sp.). Gregorio also uses the latter to refer to the "army" more generally (occasionally he uses the word *ejército*, Sp.), and we use this gloss when appropriate. In this passage, it is clear that he is talking about *cuartel* in the more specific sense of "barracks."

3.   *three clean hankies: one for dancing with your girlfriend:* The use of handkerchiefs here most likely indicates that they are dancing *marinera* (Sp.), a dance that is associated with the Spanish-speaking "criollo" and mestizo cultures of the coast and highlands (see also Mendoza-Walker 1993). Dance is one of the cultural forces used by the domi-

nant society in Peru to reform the behavior of its cultural majority. Forced recruitment of Andean peasants by the army, seen earlier in this narrative, is still widespread in southern highland communities. For a vivid evocation of the cultural politics of army life in Peru, see Francisco Lombardi's 1988 film, *The Mouth of the Wolf*.

4. *What's more, those fellow soldiers of mine were all Indian runas just like me, because there weren't any mistis:* This is the only place in the narrative where Gregorio self-identifies as an "Indian" (*indio*). By implicating his fellow *runas* here, his account suggests ways in which the categories of the dominant society, hatred of one's own cultural identity, and assimilation are inculcated through different means. See also Chapter 1, note 8; Chapter 6, note 1.

5. *one night around Independence Day:* "Independence Day" is our gloss for *28 de Julio*, that is, July 28, the day that San Martín declared independence from Spain, in Lima in 1821.

6. *So we're going to war over those bitches?:* "Bitches" is our translation of *arrechas* (Sp.). The original bilingual edition glosses this word as "Addicted to sexual pleasures" (Valderrama and Escalante 1977). In colloquial Spanish, *arrecho/arrecha* is used as an adjective or noun to mean "lustful" or "lustful person." However, as used by Gregorio and Asunta (see Chapter 16, notes 3, 7), the term is applied solely to females and appears to have not so much a sexual connotation as to refer to a haughty, ill-tempered, agitated, unruly, and generally animal-like behavior or person. This would correspond to the second usage given by the *Diccionario de la Lengua Española* (1984:129), that of "haughty, arrogant" and to the related word *arrechucho*, which can be translated as "outburst," "fit of anger," or "flying off the handle." The fact that Asunta applies this term to herself reinforces this interpretation (see Chapter 16, note 7).

7. *whoever enters the army unable to see, comes out with their eyes open and knowing how to read. And those unable to speak also come out with Spanish flowing off their tongues:* Although we have coordinated the parallelisms in this paragraph with those of the next, we have changed them somewhat in the next paragraph, substituting "dribbling" for "flowing" to strengthen the contrast. See Chapter 1, note 5; Chapter 2, note 7.

8. *those lieutenants and captains didn't want us speaking the runa tongue:* "Runa tongue" is our translation of *runa simi:* "Literally, the language of humans. It refers to the Quechua language" (Valderrama and Escalante 1977).

6. *"The Army Isn't Christian"*

1. *Damn good cholo!:* See Glossary for *cholo*, a key term in what Bourricaud (1975) has called "the Peruvian system of stratification." The latter is characterized by a strange combination of great rigidity and great fluidity (see also Tomoeda and Millones 1992). As Fuenzalida (1971:20) puts it, "The higher one is on the social ladder, the whiter one appears; the lower one is, the darker." As seen in Chapter 5, note 4, Gregorio considers his fellow soldiers to be Indian *runas* like himself. These terms, then, must be understood in the context of the people doing the labeling. Ethnic stratification and the politics of cultural pluralism are intimately linked. The ways in which colonial categories have been internalized by Andean peasants is joined to the process whereby the cultural frameworks that Andean peoples use to assert their own sense of identity are marginalized by the dominant society. Colonial categories and racist attitudes that were closely

tied to tribute in colonial times have survived with incredible virulence (Gelles 1992). See also Chapter 1, note 8; Chapter 5, note 4.

2. *He must be one of the damned, a suffering soul wandering inside Qurupuna Mountain:* "One of the damned, a suffering soul" is our gloss for *condenado penante* (Sp.), which combines the concept of "suffering lost soul" (see Chapter 1, note 7) with that of "the damned." The image of the latter, as Allen (1988:259) succinctly puts it—and as Gregorio's narrative in chapter 8 vividly illustrates—is of a "cannibalistic soul . . . trapped in a rotting corpse." One must suffer (*penar*) for one's sins after death, and those people who commit certain horrible sins, such as incest (see Asunta's narrative, Chapter 15), turn into "one of the damned." *Penante,* then, is a more inclusive category than *condenado* in that it connotes sufferers in general, including those possibly working off their sins in purgatory. Qurupuna Mountain, one of the highest snow-capped peaks in the central Andes (6,425 meters above sea level), is conceptualized as the abode of the dead in other regions of southern Peru (Arguedas 1985:187, Valderrama and Escalante 1992:252). Other mountain glaciers in the Cuzco region are also considered the abode of the damned (see Allen 1988:197). For an insightful examination of the concepts *condenado* and *penante,* see González (1994).

3. *while I'm lugging goods around as a strapper:* This is our gloss for *q'ipishaspallan* (Q.), a more literal rendering of which would be "while I am carrying." However, because this is the first time that he mentions his work, we have supplied "strapper" to signal the nature of his occupation, referred to elsewhere in the original text as *cargador* (Sp.). See Introduction, note 1.

4. *The Government, Velasco in Lima:* Juan Velasco Alvarado, a Peruvian military and political figure, led the military overthrow of the Peruvian government in 1968 and headed the country until 1975. He brought about radical social change, instituting one of the largest land reforms in Latin American history, nationalizing many of Peru's economic resources, and reforming the army (see, among others, Philip 1978, Lowenthal 1975). See Chapter 11, note 7.

5. *I went to a healer several times, and he'd make offerings to those souls:* "Healer" is our translation of *hanpiq* (Q.): "Healer. Person who cures people using traditional medicine and magical ceremonies" (Valderrama and Escalante 1977). "Offerings" is our translation of *alcanzo:* "Ritual offering made to Andean deities in exchange for favors and benefits that one expects to receive from them" (Valderrama and Escalante 1977).

6. *owned a cornbeer tavern:* "Cornbeer tavern" is our translation of *aqha wasi* (Q.), as well as for *chichería* (Sp.) elsewhere in the text. These small drinking establishments, which can vary in size from a side room in someone's home to a full-fledged restaurant, often serve food as well as cornbeer (see Chapter 1, note 23). In some places in the narratives, the term "cornbeer tavern" is used interchangeably with "cookhouse." The latter is our translation of *picantería,* a place where spicy dishes are served. See Chapter 8, note 9; Chapter 9, note 4; Chapter 14, note 6.

7. *we'd take them to the people selling cooked corn:* "Cooked corn" is our translation of *mut'i* (Q.), which is in fact boiled maize kernels, or hominy.

7. Inkas and Spaniards

1. *Túpac Amaru was from Tungasuca; he was one of our people, son of Inkas:* Túpac Amaru (José Gabriel Condorcanqui), a wealthy Indian merchant and ethnic chieftain

(*kuraka*) who claimed to be a descendant of Inka nobility, led a rebellion against the Spaniards from 1778 to 1781. He was captured and executed in Cuzco in 1782. "One of our people" is the gloss that we have given *paisano* in this context (generally translated as "villager"). The use of *paisano* here expresses an affinity that Gregorio, as a *runa*, feels toward a past leader of his people. Throughout this short chapter, Gregorio is claiming a historical kinship between Inkaríy, Túpac Amaru, and contemporary *runas*. For studies of historical consciousness and its relationship to resistance in the Andes, see, among others, Flores Galindo (1987) and the collected articles in Stern (1987).

2. *Even right now, this light here comes from the waters of Calca:* Here Gregorio refers to the interview context. In this passage, we have translated *luz* (Spanish for "light)" both as "light" and as "electricity," as this is a common usage in Peru, as in "to pay the electric bill" (*pagar la luz*). He uses the word in this way when talking about the lack of electricity in his house in Chapter 10.

3. *We are Peruvians, native people:* We are using "native people" as a translation of *indígenas* (Sp.). This is the only time the word is used in the narratives, and like "Indian" (*indio*), it has a greater top-down and imposed feel to it than other self-defining terms, such as *runa* or "villager" (*paisano*). Until the late 1960s, when they were renamed "Peasant Communities," the official designation for rural communities legally recognized by the Peruvian state was *Comunidad Indígena*, or Indigenous Community. Yet it is clear that Gregorio appropriates the official designation of *indígena* here to make the point that his are the autochthonous people, the true "Peruvians." See also Chapter 1, note 8.

4. *And he flung the paper to the ground:* This image of conquest expresses the cultural difference between the literate invaders and the Inkas, who had other means of communicating, such as by *qhipu* (see Ascher and Ascher 1981, Julien 1982), the knotted cords that Gregorio mentions. Gregorio is speaking here of a much commemorated encounter between Atahuallpa, one of the heirs to the Inka throne, and his Spanish captors. Atahuallpa was held for a huge ransom (rooms full of gold and silver), and once this was paid, the Spaniards garroted him. Throughout the Andes, this event is remembered in both written and oral histories, as well as in poetry and nonverbal forms of history making, such as dance plays. For various analyses of the ways in which contemporary highlanders' interpretations of history bolster cultural identities and are used for current political projects, see, among others, Beyersdorff (1988), Mannheim (1991), Rappaport (1994), and Wachtel (1977). For an accessible overview of the events of the Conquest, see Hemming (1970).

5. *The Inkas Wayna Qhapaq and Inka Ruka had been his uncles, and Inka Rumichaka was his brother:* Here, Gregorio's narrative moves easily between what we would call "myth" and "history" and shows the immediate kinship between the cultural hero *Inkaríy* and the pre-Columbian Inka nobility. Wayna Qhapaq (often written Huayna Capac) was an Inka king who died around 1525 and who fathered the two sons, Atahuallpa and Huáscar, who were engaged in a civil war for the Inka throne when the Spaniards arrived in 1532. See also Chapter 1, note 11.

6. *What would the Spaniards say if our Inka was to return?:* The myth of *Inkaríy* (see Glossary) and of his return is widespread in the Andes and is part of a messianic tradition; there are many variants of this myth (see, among others, Arguedas 1985 [1964], Getzels 1983, Ortiz 1973, Ossio 1973, Pease 1982). See also Chapter 1, note 11.

8. Stories from Jail

1. *But I didn't know anything about the craft of spinning or weaving:* Cloth has always figured importantly in Andean society, and though both women and men spin wool and weave in the highlands (this varies from region to region), these skills are generally considered women's work, and women are the most skilled weavers. Cloth was a basic tribute item during the Inka Empire, and the Spaniards later created workshops (*obrajes*) that specialized in producing cloth. For the importance of cloth during Inka times, see Murra (1980), and for its contemporary significance, see, among others, Cereceda (1987), Zorn (1987), and Femenias (1991).

2. *near mountain lord Apu Ausankati:* Mountain worship, like worship of the Earth Mother (see Chapter 1, note 30), is a fundamental part of native Andean religious practices (see, among others, Allen 1988, Bastien 1978, Isbell 1978, and Reinhart 1985). Humans must revere and make offerings to these deities who give fertility and life, as well as sickness and death, to their human charges. Throughout this passage, the fertility-giving nature of mountains—as in the bountiful flocks of cattle found inside the *apu*—could not be clearer. See *apu* in Glossary, as well as Chapter 1, notes 12, 35.

3. *a runa dressed in the local garb of the region approached him:* Here we have left *runa* to signal that, like the clothes he wears, this man appears as a local "Indian," in contrast to the *wiraqucha* he addresses. Clearly, this parable-like account of mountain lords, fertility, and marriage concerns not just the importance of making the proper offerings and libations to mountain lords, but also *runa-misti* relations. Thus, stories about the misguided behavior of *mistis* who do not observe or understand Andean ritual practices, like "portraits of the white man" elsewhere (Basso 1979), are reminders of how one should *not* behave.

4. *she wanted him to make offerings of its essence to her:* "Offerings of its essence" (and further below in this passage, "libations") is our gloss for *samincha:* "Ritual that consists of offering small portions of the foods and liquids that are to be consumed, by sprinkling or blowing them toward the deities" (Valderrama and Escalante 1977). Allen, who defines the root word here, *sami*, as "animating essence" (1988:262), provides examples of this concept in different ritual contexts and finds that, whether burning coca leaf or making libations, the purpose of *samincha* is to share the food or drink being consumed (see also Harrison 1989:94). The fragrance of the burning leaves is blown toward a given mountain lord or the Earth Mother; in the case of drink offerings, people blow across the top of the drink or purposively spill or flick the liquid in the direction of the deity while invoking its name. Elsewhere in the text, we also use "libations" to gloss *ch'allay*, which is a ritual aspersion of liquids (see also Chapter 10, note 6, for the related concept of *t'inka*).

5. *a farm servant, tending the drying shed:* This is our gloss for *pongo* (Q.) *tendalero* (Sp.). The *pongo tendalero* is a farm servant responsible for overseeing the drying shed (*tendal*). There are different forms of servitude carried out by peasants for hacienda owners in exchange for the right to cultivate a small parcel of hacienda land. See Asunta's account of these obligations in Chapter 13. For more information on this exploitive, semifeudal system, see Chapter 13, notes 4, 5.

6. *This Ccamaran was in jail for stealing a llama herd—he'd gone and done that to his wedding compadre:* Gregorio uses the term *compadre* to mean "godfather" (*padrino*)

when speaking of his own wedding (Chapter 10), and this may be the meaning here as well. Gregorio's statement that the Ccamaran "had gone and done that to his wedding *compadre*" can be read as evidence that the Ccamarans were really tough and treacherous: stealing from a *compadre* or *comadre* is one of the worst kinds of betrayal. However, *compadrazgo* relationships often involve an asymmetrical relationship between *mistis* and *runas*, and the Ccamaran may have been challenging a relatively powerful *misti*, one who happened to be his *compadre*. Cattle rustling has been linked to social banditry and resistance movements, and cattle rustlers are both hated and admired in Andean society. While communal patrols or *rondas* have been instituted in many parts of the Andes to control rustling (see Starn 1992), and harsh punishments are meted out to rustlers, there is a certain fearful admiration for the wild and authority-defying trickster figure of the rustler. Gregorio, in recounting several of the Ccamarans' exploits, obviously delights in this cattle-rustling people. Some regions in the southern Andes have entire communities that specialize in cattle rustling. See, among others, Aguirre and Walker (1990), Orlove (1980), Poole (1990), and Valderrama and Escalante (1992); the latter is a wonderful bilingual Quechua-Spanish edition of two testimonials taken from cattle rustlers in the Cotabambas region.

7. *jumped up on the main rafter and clung to it like a big dark butterfly:* "Big dark butterfly" is our gloss for *taparaku* (Q.): "Nocturnal butterfly. When it enters a house it indicates misfortune" (Valderrama and Escalante 1977). Lira (1982) gives this definition: "Large black butterfly with white splotches on the wings. It is thought to be a bad omen and to presage death when it appears."

8. *because that's the star they were born with:* See Chapter 1, note 13.

9. *a house that had the little cornbeer-for-sale flag outside:* Private houses that sell cornbeer indicate that they currently have cornbeer for sale by displaying small, pennant-sized flags on a little pole by their doorways. See Chapter 1, note 23; Chapter 6, note 6.

10. *the crying might be coming from a little gold idol of the ancients:* The "ancients" is our translation of *ñawpa machu:* "The humans who lived in the epoch prior to our own" (Valderrama and Escalante 1977). See Allen (1988:54–57) for a discussion of this term, which she describes as a "gigantic race who lived by moonlight in an age before the current Sun existed" (1988:54). This "displaced race" occupies a shadowy world parallel to that of living humans, and these ancestral spirits are viewed as very much influencing the human world and as having a dual nature, that is, possessing malevolent as well as benevolent aspects. The little golden idol that the peons expect to find is a type of sacred object known as *encanto* (Sp.), which are thought to cross over from the shadow world of the ancients into our own. See Chapter 1, note 16; Chapter 11, note 10.

9. Rosa, Josefa, and Miracle Shrines

1. *I met my first wife, Rosa Puma:* As discussed in the Introduction, "wife" in this case—and wherever it does not appear as "lawfully married"—should be read as "common-law wife."

2. *She was a food vendor:* "Food vendor" is our translation of *chupi qhatu* (Q.): "Woman who has a business selling meals at cheap prices" (Valderrama and Escalante 1977). *Qhatu* means vendor, peddler, or "woman who works selling things or prepared foods to passersby" (Lira 1982:161). These vendors usually sell their goods on tiny side-

walk food stands, calling out and cajoling potential customers as they pass in the street. *Chupi*, in the strict sense of the word, is "a soup made with potatoes, meat, vegetables, and spices" (Lira 1982:56), but in the context of these food stands refers to other dishes as well. Asunta describes this occupation, with its attendant troubles and travails, in Chapter 16. For discussions of market women in other parts of the highlands in Ecuador, Peru, and Bolivia, see Babb (1989), Femenias (1991), Seligmann (1989, 1993), Sikkink (1994), and Weismantel (1988).

3. *she caught an ill wind and couldn't walk*: "Ill wind" is our translation of *mal viento* (Sp.); Asunta, in her account, calls this illness simply "wind" (*viento*). It should be understood that this does not refer to a "chill," but rather to an "evil breeze," that is, a kind of sickness that moves through the air itself and that is generated by malignant spirits, such as those "exhaled" from the body of the recently deceased or from ancient tombs. See, among others, Allen (1988), Bastien (1978), Lira (1985), and Stoner (1989) for spirited discussions of these and related beliefs.

4. *There was a little cookhouse*: "Cookhouse" is our translation of *picantería* (Sp.), small eateries that specialize in spicy dishes. In her translation of José María Arguedas' *Deep Rivers*, Barraclough defines *picantería* as "a place where hot, peppery food is sold; for instance a *chicha* bar" (Arguedas 1978:247). As a passage further below shows, corn-beer taverns and cookhouses are often one and the same (Chapter 14, note 6). See also Chapter 6, note 6.

5. *tending the good Lord's garden, there where the qantu flowers turn into high-neck jugs*: The *qantu* flower (*Cantua buxifolia*; also spelled *cantu, kantu, k'antu, kkantu* in other texts) is a much celebrated flower in the highlands. Allen states, "Red, bell-shaped *qantus*, consecrated to the dead since pre-Spanish times, are a dry season, cold weather flower" (1988:17). Lira (1982) describes it in his dictionary as a bush with "beautiful red and orange flowers that are bell-shaped and come in clusters. The flower held symbolic importance for the Inkas, the reason for which it is also called 'The Inka's Flower.' Many vases from the imperial era have stylized decorations of the Kkantu." In his *Medicina andina*, Lira adds that "in the highlands, we are accustomed to putting branches of these flowers in holy water for All Saints Day, from the first to the third of November, with our faith that the souls of purgatory drink water from this sacred flower which has the shape of small bells or little cups" (1985:65). The fact that the *qantu* is the national flower of Bolivia and that some have proposed that it be the national flower of Peru (Pulgar Vidal 1987:82) also attests to the deep Andean roots and symbolic importance of this flower. See also Beyersdorff (1984:26) and Arguedas (1985:196).

6. *Limbo is down in the underworld*: See Chapter 1, note 16, for a discussion of the underworld. Limbo is defined by Webster's Dictionary (1990:693) as "an abode of souls that are according to Roman Catholic theology barred from heaven because of not having received Christian baptism." Yet, while limbo is clearly a Christian concept, Gregorio's mention of the *qantu* flower and the underworld provides contrasting images taken from native Andean religion. And while his use of "upperworld" later in this passage is obviously a reference to "heaven" (where the good Lord lives), the indigenous categories of upperworld and lower world encompass many other states and beings than those given in Catholic theology. See Chapter 1, note 16; Chapter 3, note 6; Chapter 9, note 5.

7. *but my blood would no longer take hold inside her belly*: "Take hold" is our translation of *hap'iy*, which could also be translated as "to kindle" or "to spark," in the sense

of "to start up." For Andean conceptions of the body, fertility, and life processes, see Bastien (1978), Lira (1985), Stoner (1989), and Crandon-Malamud (1991).

8. *some herbal teas—such as radishes, dog thorn, sharp sowthistle, soft sowthistle, ribwort, and ox tongue:* The latter are our glosses for the following medicinal herbs and plants: *rábanos, alqu kiska, kiska qhana, llamp'u qhana, saqarara,* and *wakaq qallun.* Andean peoples have a vast store of medicinal lore and plant knowledge. In the case of dog thorn (*alqu kiska*), Lira (1985:5) reports that a small cup of the boiled-down essence of this herb, taken while fasting, "helps the liver, spleen, and kidneys." See also Stoner (1989).

9. *But the essence of those herbs must've passed through my bones to the marrow, destroying it:* The notion of "essence" pervades Gregorio's narrative, whether he is speaking of the essence of the stolen cow in Chapter 8, the concept of *sami* and offerings to the deities (Chapter 8, note 4), or the "spirit" of the plants that is stolen by the hail (Chapter 4). See, among others, Allen (1988), Bastien (1978), and Harrison (1989), for detailed discussions of the notion of animating essence in Andean culture.

10. *Four days after the Lord of Pampamarca's octave:* "Octave" is our translation of *octava* (Sp.): "A space of eight days, during which the Church celebrates a solemn fiesta or commemorates the object of this fiesta" (*Diccionario de la Lengua Española* 1984: 969). The ritual sponsorship of fiestas in the Andes, as well as the ritual washing of the clothes of the dead, are organized in terms of this eight-day cycle. See also Chapter 13, note 2; Chapter 14, note 1.

11. *That wiraqucha is incredibly miraculous:* Wiraqucha was the name of the Inka's supreme deity, and the fact that Gregorio speaks of the Lord of Pampamarca (*Señor de Pampamarca*) as "that *wiraqucha*" could suggest that the term *wiraqucha* here—like the words "good Lord" (*Taytacha*) and "Lord" (*señor*) that he applies to this shrine holder—retains an aura of the sacred. However, a few lines down, this *wiraqucha* is identified as a *misti,* and it appears that the term refers here to the social-racial notion of *wiraqucha,* that is, to the "white," upperclass, non-*runa* aspect of the person who was miraculously transformed. See Chapter 9, note 18 for the miraculous nature of these shrines.

12. *they still come and do the Qanchi, Chilean-foe, tilt-step, and windmill dances:* These are our glosses for certain stylized dances—*Qanchi, awqachileno, k'achampa,* and *molino-tusuq* respectively—that are common in the Cuzco area; competing dance troupes assemble for important festivals and pilgrimages in the region (see, among others, Allen 1988, Mendoza-Walker 1993, and Sallnow 1987).

13. *the boy used to dwell right there at the earth shrine on Atas Pass:* "Right there at the earth shrine on Atas Pass" is our gloss for *kikin Atas apachitapis* (Q.), which indicates that the boy lived right around, and possibly in, the cairn itself. Here, as elsewhere in the narratives, these mountain passes and their earth shrines embody various types of sacred power. See Chapter 1, note 35.

14. *a man on the trail who was very ill with syphilis:* "Syphilis" is our translation of *wanthi.* In their Spanish glossary, the original editors translate *wanthi* as "bubonic plague" (*buba*), but after a more in-depth study, they find that it means "a syphilitic in the last stages of the disease" (Valderrama and Escalante, personal communication 1993). This is confirmed by Lira (1985:154), who describes *wanthi* as a "vapor exhaled by the earth after hailstorms and snowfall, and some strong rainstorms, because it is through these gases that such diseases are transmitted . . . This also comes from a con-

tagious disease, which is surely syphilis." The next line in Gregorio's narrative mentions that this man has two wives, and the fact that he is reprimanded for this by the Lord of Huanca reinforces this interpretation of *wanthi*.

15.   *That sick man was Pedro Arias, a wealthy prospector:* "Prospector" is our translation of *macuquero* (Sp.), which is a rustic miner who searches out and gleans over abandoned mines using rudimentary tools and pack animals (Valderrama and Escalante, personal communication 1993). The *Diccionario de la Lengua Española* (1984:853) defines *macuquero* as, "He who, without the knowledge of the authorities, devotes himself to extracting ore from abandoned mines."

16.   *he stayed at a rooming house in San Blas:* "Rooming house" is our gloss for *tampu* (Q.), which has often been translated in the literature as "inn." Yet, as commonly used in English, "inn" is inappropriate for describing the rundown places and destitute people that Gregorio refers to here and elsewhere when speaking of *tampus*.

17.   *a man who belonged to a community from the Huanca-Huanca region:* Gregorio introduces a new term here, that of *comunero* or "community member." *Comuneros* are also *runas* and villagers. But the term *comunero* emphasizes membership in, and identification with, a specific community. This relationship consists of, among other things, a series of rights and obligations between the *comunero* and the larger community. A *comunero*, for example, has access to communal resources such as irrigation water, grazing lands, firewood, medicinal plants, and fiesta celebrations. In return, the *comunero* must pass certain *cargos* (see glossary) and participate in the communal work parties known as *faena* (see Chapter 1, note 9).

18.   *his other brother is Quyllur Rit'i:* The annual pilgrimage to the mountain shrine of Quyllur Rit'i is one of the largest collective rituals in the southern Andes. For wonderful evocations of this pilgrimage see Allen (1988) and Sallnow (1987). These shrines, like *apachitas* and other sites of sacred power in the Andes (see Chapter 1, note 35), combine images from both native Andean religion and Catholicism. As Sallnow, generalizing about the kinds of shrines discussed in these passages, puts it, "The shrine has an illustrious past, historically accessible and embellished by myth. . . . Though Christian, served by priests and a lay staff, it may well hallow a pagan sacred site, or it may have direct associations with a native, non-Christian cosmology . . . the shrine marks an irruption of history, the entry of the divine into the temporal as well as the spatial order of reality. By approaching it, pilgrims seek to tap its still active power, to draw this into their lives and thereby to induce existential change" (1987:2–3). These shrines, and the pilgrimages made by peasants to ask for special favors or to fulfill a vow, are thus joined to two types of divine power. While nominally Christian, most of these miraculous shrines are established around "lithic images on rocks or crags. In fact they pertain to the same religious topography, the same religious landscape, as the *apus* themselves. In the locations, histories, and cosmologies of miraculous shrines, native and non-native religious traditions are brought into direct relation" (1987:3).

19.   *warm up the cornbeer's bottommost dregs:* "Cornbeer's bottommost dregs " is our gloss for *qunchu* (Q.): "Cornbeer sediment" (Valderrama and Escalante 1977). In contrast to strained cornbeer slag, or *sut'uchi* (see Chapter 10, note 1), *qunchu* is what remains at the bottom of the glass, that is, the settlings. Lira (1985:76) also cites *qunchu* as a cure, but for stomach inflammation; here it is also used as a kind of plaster, but one that is applied externally.

20.   *accompanied by six of my people:* "My people" is a more intimate and fitting

gloss for *paisano* than "fellow villager" in this context, especially considering Gregorio's recent and bad experiences with people other than his own. See also Chapter 7, note 1.

10. Life with Asunta

1. *so they'd sell me the strained cornbeer slag:* "Strained cornbeer slag" is our translation of *sut'uchi* (Q.): "Leftover slag that results from straining ground corn sprouts, barley, or *chuño* for beer (*chicha*)" (Valderrama and Escalante 1977). As stated in Chapter 1, note 23, the alcoholic beverage known as *chicha* can be made out of crops other than maize. The leftover slag is nutritious and is used to fatten different animals, such as guinea pigs, chickens, and pigs.

2. *they told me "anger spells":* This is our translation of *colerina* (Sp.), one of the major health problems caused by emotions in the southern Andes: "This condition develops following an argument or heated discussion, generally with a close family member. The individual who feels anger (*cólera*) in the context of the disagreement may experience nausea, vomiting, diarrhea, and severe abdominal cramps. *Colerina* may be quite serious, requiring bedrest. . . . The most important component of therapy is to determine the source of the anger and to resolve the disagreement between parties, if possible" (Stoner 1989:100). This kind of illness is found in other parts of Latin America.

3. *But then you'll be my wedding compadre:* Gregorio uses *compadre* here instead of *padrino* or "godfather," which is the proper term for the relationship he describes. Indeed, the original editors have translated it as *padrino* in their Spanish translation. We have supplied "wedding" here to differentiate Leocadio's current *compadrazgo* relationship with Gregorio (based on his having baptized his son), from the new type of godparenthood relationship that Gregorio proposes.

4. *But Asunta used to know a lot of the people:* Here and in other places in this section, "Asunta" has been supplied in place of "my wife" to avoid confusion over the terms "wife" and "married."

5. *his wife, my comadre, was also a mestiza:* In this passage, the words "mestiza" and *misti* are used interchangeably. See Glossary and Chapter 1, note 8.

6. *Hey, I'd like you to be my compadre—well then, let's drink a toast, compadre:* "Toast" is our translation of *t'inka:* "Ritual offering; an affectionate toast to demonstrate fondness" (Valderrama and Escalante 1977). While *t'inka* (and the verb *t'inkay*) generally refers to a kind of libation to the deities in which cornbeer, wine, or hard liquor is ceremonially dripped, splashed, or sprinkled onto the earth or in the direction of a given mountain (see, among others, Candler 1993, Valderrama and Escalante 1976, Paerregaard 1989), here Gregorio is simply referring to a toast made to seal a *compadrazgo* commitment (Valderrama and Escalante, personal communication 1993). The term *t'inka*, then, connotes sharing liquids to confirm a relationship between humans (a toast) and between humans and nature spirits (libations). And while this passage may not directly refer to libations to nature spirits, almost any kind of toast in highland society involves a few drops for Earth Mother. See also Chapter 8, note 4.

7. *she'd go around like a haughty little snob, better than the rest:* "Little snob, better than the rest" is our gloss for *dáme* (Sp.) *lawa* (Q.): "Insult. Disparaging term that is given to an indigenous woman who adopts *mestiza* attitudes" (Valderrama and Esca-

lante 1977), that is, someone who is pretentious and false (Valderrama and Escalante, personal communication 1993). *Dáme lawa* literally means "give me soup," and this term probably refers to people who imperiously demand soup in Spanish from the food vendors there.

8. *the Law of the New Town came around:* There has been a huge demographic shift in Peru from rural to urban areas over the last thirty years, and during this period, large squatter settlements secured through massive land invasions have arisen around most of Peru's major cities. The Law of the New Town (Ley de Pueblo Joven, Sp.) granted ownership rights to the members of these squatter colonies. See, among others, Altamirano (1984), Mangin (1970), and Mitchell (1991).

9. *so one of them, all by himself, began whistling and jeering:* In fact, Gregorio just says "whistling" here. Whistling is often used as a form of jeering in Latin America, and since it often marks approbation in the English-speaking world, we have supplied "jeering."

11. The Factory

1. *I responded in the runa tongue:* "*Runa* tongue" is our translation of *runa simi* (see Chapter 5, note 8). With this statement Gregorio is apparently emphasizing that, although Emiliano was an important man, he was also one of "his people."

2. *So that's how I ended up taking the place of a fellow factory worker who'd died:* According to the Preliminary Note, Gregorio started working there in January 1943.

3. *The factory's closing down:* According to the Preliminary Note, the factory shut down in March 1967.

4. *that's how he died:* According to the Preliminary Note, he died in January 1964.

5. *from the time of Odría to that of Belaúnde:* Several political figures appear in these next passages: José Luis Bustamante was elected president in 1945, but in 1948 was overthrown by a military coup led by Manuel A. Odría, who then assumed the presidency from 1948 to 1956. Víctor Raúl Haya de la Torre founded the Alianza Popular Revolucionaria Americana and ran for president several times. Fernando Belaúnde Terry was elected president in 1963 and served until 1968, when he was ousted from office by a military coup led by Juan Velasco Alvarado (see Chapter 6, note 4). The latter served as president until 1975, when he was replaced by another general (Francisco Morales Bermúdez).

6. *they dressed him up as a lovely lady:* According to the Preliminary Note, the incident that Gregorio's recollection is based on concerned General Vargas Dávila and occurred in April 1958. It began with a gasoline strike.

7. *he's helping the poor by getting rid of the haciendas:* Velasco instituted a number of other important social reforms in the rural countryside, such as making it easier for peasant communities to gain official recognition. For the effects of these reforms, see Long and Roberts (1978), Seligmann (1995), and Skar (1982). See also Chapter 6, note 4.

8. *Long before the Agrarian Reform Law was ever even discussed, people began talking about Hugo Blanco:* Børn in 1934, Hugo Blanco led the peasant movement in the Cuzco region beginning in 1959. He was captured in 1963 and condemned to twenty-five years in prison; he was pardoned and exiled from the country. He later returned to Peru and became a senator. The Agrarian Reform Law was instituted in 1969 (see also Chapter 6,

note 4). Over the next several years, many resident and nonresident tenant laborers of the Cuzco region were awarded ownership of their plots (Sallnow 1987:114). For the effects of this law in the Cuzco area, see, among others, Seligmann (1995).

9. *just like any other tenant farmer:* "Tenant farmer" is our translation of *arrendire* (Sp.): "Peasant who uses a parcel of land that is the property of the *hacienda* owner, in exchange for which he must provide a certain number of days of unpaid labor each month for the hacienda owner's direct benefit" (Valderrama and Escalante 1977). Asunta, in Chapter 13, provides a good description of the land and labor arrangements found in this exploitive system. See Chapter 13, note 4.

10. *he was holed up in a cave on top of a mountain peak, like an ancestral spirit:* "Ancestral spirit" is our translation of *gentil* (Sp.) *machu* (Q.): "Masculine. They are malignant spirits that reside in old dwelling places of pre-Columbian origin. They are identified with mummies" (Valderrama and Escalante 1977). Ancestor worship is a well-documented phenomenon for the colonial period in Peru (see, e.g., Salomon 1987). Caves were used as burial sites for mummies, which were revered by their descendants long after death. In contemporary Andean culture, mountain caves—while not the focus of mummy worship as in the past—are still considered the abode of ancestor spirits. In their most recent book, the original editors define *gentil* as "Spirit that inhabits the subsoil in certain places. It is conceived of as the being that resided in these lands before the human race. Generally malignant, it is the owner of the place where it resides. To obtain favors or to placate its anger, they are given offerings" (Valderrama and Escalante 1992). In this same text, *machu* is defined as "Spirit that resides in or near the ruins of pre-Columbian origin. They are identified with the bones of the mummies. They are conceived as having a lot of power and influence over our lives" (ibid.). Thus *gentil machu*, though quite similar to the concept *ñawpa machu* (Chapter 8, note 10), is more localized and has a more malignant character. See also Allen's (1988) rich description of *machu* and its different manifestations.

11. *to Frontón Prison out in the sea lake:* "Sea lake" is our gloss for La Mar Qucha (see Chapter 3, note 7).

12. We Strappers

1. *You can make twenty to twenty-five soles a day, and sometimes even up to seventy:* Given the exchange rate for the time (see *sol* in Glossary), Gregorio was making between fifty cents to a dollar and seventy cents a day.

2. *carrying three blocks of ice:* "Of ice" supplied. Gregorio confirmed to the original editors that he was talking about blocks of ice (Valderrama and Escalante, personal communication 1993).

3. *she must be blessed by offerings:* "Offerings" is our translation of *despacho* (Sp.): "Ritual offering to the deities. It is synonymous with *alcanzo* [see Chapter 6, note 5], offering bundle, and payments to the earth" (Valderrama and Escalante 1977). "Blessed" is our translation of *curado* (Sp.), which refers to the ritual activity itself, that is, the making of the offerings, and to the blessings, good luck, and material benefits that these bring about. The worldview that concerns fertility and abundance in the realm of rural agropastoral production is easily transferred to the urban cash-based economy.

4. *the offerings that've been made to my guardian spirit:* "Guardian spirit" is our

gloss for *marka* (Q.): "An individual's personal protector deity" (Valderrama and Escalante 1977). Lira (1982:190) defines it as "protector, defender, advocate."

5. *As an old-timer who has been lugging for a long time, I'd like all of us strappers living here in Cuzco, young and old alike, to get together and form a union so we don't have to live this kind of life.* Gregorio's wish was fulfilled. In fact, it was his very narrative here that led to the creation of a strappers' union (see Postscript). See also Introduction, note 1, for more information on this kind of work.

ASUNTA

13. Running Away from the Hacienda

1. *a man who belonged to the community of Rondobamba:* Our gloss for Rutupanpa (Q.) *comunero* (Sp.). See Chapter 9, note 17.

2. *so he could be there for the octave and wash the clothes of the deceased:* See Chapter 9, note 10, for the concept of "octave." In many parts of the Andes, the clothes of the deceased are washed eight days after the burial.

3. *My father spread his fever to our little old grandmother, my mother's mother:* The Quechua transcription of this passage is flawed. We have followed the Spanish version for these two lines.

4. *the tenant farmers there in the hacienda all had to do labor service:* See Chapter 11, note 9, for an explanation of "tenant farmer," our translation of *arrendíre* (Sp.). "Labor service" is our translation of *condición* (Sp.): "Term that refers to the different kinds of servitude that the *hacienda* owner imposes on the peasants that are dependent on his *hacienda*" (Valderrama and Escalante 1977). "Labor service," then, refers to the general agreement or contract between bondsman and lord, and thus encompasses the unpaid work carried out on the hacienda lands, as well as "manor service" (*pongueaje*; see Chapter 13, note 5). Land and labor arrangements such as those described here were common in the semifeudal haciendas found throughout the southern highlands until the 1970s (and in some places are still in use today). The nature of these arrangements, however, varied from one community to the next. Sallnow, for example, distinguishes between haciendas established during colonial times and those originating during the republican period, between those haciendas whose subject communities retained a degree of independence and others that were either privatized or converted en bloc into haciendas, and between haciendas that relied on resident tenant labor and those that relied on nonresident tenant labor (Sallnow 1987:112–113, 169–174; see also Mallon 1983). Asunta's description makes it clear that her family's status was that of nonresident tenant farmer, that is, while they depended on the lands of the hacienda for their sustenance, they did not actually live there. Vivid descriptions of hacienda life can be found in Manrique (1988) and in many of Arguedas' novels (e.g., 1978, 1986).

5. *you'd also have to do a month of manor service each year:* "Manor service" is our translation of *pongueaje* (Q. and Sp.), and "manor servant" and "servant" are, in this passage, our translations for *pongo* (Q.): "Peasant who provides personal services in the house of the *hacienda* owner" (Valderrama and Escalante 1977). Similarly, Barraclough defines *pongo* as "an *hacienda* Indian who is obliged to work as an unpaid servant in

the landowner's house" (Arguedas 1978:247). We have defined this as "manor" rather than "house" servant because there are different forms of "servant" (*pongo*) that appear in the narratives. As Asunta says, "In the hacienda, there were servants for everything." Besides the house servants (such as housemaids, sweepers, and cooks), the narrators mention servants who watch over drying sheds (*pongo tendalero*; see Chapter 8, note 5) and others who milk cows (*lechero pongo*). The figure of the *pongo* has been well portrayed in the novels of José María Arguedas (e.g., 1978) and in his wonderful "El sueño del pongo." In this short story, which was told to him by a peasant from the Cuzco region, a manor servant dreams that he and his hacienda master find themselves before Saint Francis in Heaven, where each receives his just desserts. See also Chapter 1, note 26; Chapter 8, note 5; Chapter 13, note 4.

6. *since we were all girls, none of us were able to work as peons:* The relatively low valuation of female labor compared to that of the labor of men, whether in ayni and mink'a labor exchanges, in debt peonage relationships, or in wage labor is well documented (e.g., Bourque and Warren 1981).

7. *the work of the blessed souls no doubt:* Asunta's narrative, as expressed by her Christian metaphors, displays a different notion of "fate" than that of Gregorio (see Chapter 1, note 13). This is probably the result of her early years on the priests' hacienda, the fact that she grew up in and around the large city of Cuzco, and her years as a maid in a mestizo household (unlike Gregorio, who grew up and lived his formative years in country villages). On the whole, Asunta's life was more urbane than that of Gregorio, something that is reflected in her language and worldview.

8. *my sufferings continued:* Asunta's suffering is not an isolated event. The wrenching testimonies of twenty-three domestic servants can be found in Sindicato de Trabajadoras del Hogar de Cuzco (1982).

9. *coca leaf:* Coca (*Erythroxylum coca*), an indigenous crop in the Andes, has been an important part of social relations, diet, and religious ceremony for millennia, and its importance remains undiminished in countless thousands of highland communities. See Allen's (1988) evocative ethnography of coca and cultural identity; see also Martínez's (1994) film on the production and politics of the coca leaf, *Mamacoca: The Other Face of the Leaf.*

10. *and have those same students of hers take the sacks to the Urcos train station:* This section of Asunta's narrative is another illustration of *runa-misti* relations in the countryside and shows the way in which schools and other government institutions help to underwrite these exploitative relations. See also John Cohen's 1979 film, *Q'eros: The Shape of Survival*, which depicts the cultural chasm that exists between rural schoolteachers and indigenous people in another region of Cuzco.

11. *that's why she had many community members as her godchildren:* "Community members" is our gloss for *comuneros* in this instance (see Chapter 9, note 17; Chapter 13, note 1).

14. Eusebio

1. *it was the octave of the Corpus Christi Fiesta in San Cristóbal:* Corpus Christi falls in late May or June, on the Thursday after Trinity Sunday. This ostensibly Roman Catholic ritual has been linked to highland agricultural cycles and native Andean religious celebrations for over four centuries. MacCormack states that in the early colonial

period, "the Catholic festival of Corpus Christi, with its elaborate procession of the Eucharistic host, resonated in Andean perceptions with the Inca Inti Raymi, which had been celebrated around the same time of year" (1991:180). Rituals from Inti Raymi were incorporated into Corpus Christi, and "the festival that in Catholic Europe epitomized the theological position of the post-Tridentine church became encrusted with a variety of Andean associations and accretions" (1991:421). Sallnow (1987), who traces the transformation of this fiesta from the early colonial period to modern times, says that today, "Only three saints from outside the city attend, all from within a ten-kilometer radius: Santa Bárbara from Poroy to the northwest and the eponymous patrons of San Jerónimo and San Sebastián to the southeast, the latter pair traditionally engaging in a race to see which will arrive first in Cuzco. . . . They enter the cathedral on the eve of Corpus and the next day circuit the Plaza de Armas to the accompaniment of fireworks, rockets, and pealing bells, the Eucharist following behind. . . . They then return to the cathedral, where they remain until the octave of the feast. . . . They return to their parishes one at a time, in a sequence of eight day periods beginning with the octave, each being honored on its homecoming with yet another fiesta" (Sallnow 1987:164). See Chapter 9, note 10, for a discussion of the term "octave."

2.   *In the month of June, there's a big fiesta to make the sheep merry:* Pastoral rituals oftentimes directly involve the animals being celebrated, whether these be alpacas, llamas, sheep, or others. That is, the animals not only have libations and offerings made to them but are also force-fed liquor (see also John Cohen's 1979 film *Q'eros: The Shape of Survival* for a wonderful portrayal of this). These rituals generally have as their object the fertility of the animals, and in many such rituals, the mountains that nourish and protect these animals are "paid." The fertility-oriented nature of the rite is exemplified by the ritual embrace between male and female sheep in this passage. For the lives of pastoral peoples and their rituals, see, among others, Flores Ochoa (1977), Valderrama and Escalante (1992), Orlove (1980), and Webster (1983).

3.   *that's how I learned what men are like:* As several authors have shown, Andean women suffer a double burden of racism and sexism, and these work together in often extremely brutal ways. For a suggestive overview of changing gender ideologies during the Inka and colonial periods, see Silverblatt (1987). For descriptions of Andean women and the patriarchal nature of highland society for the modern period, see, among others, Andreas (1985), Babb (1989), Belote and Belote (1988), Bourque and Warren (1981), Barrios de Chungara and Viezzer (1979), Femenias (1991), Harrison (1989), Harvey (1994), Kirk (1992), Lynch (1991), Seligmann (1989), Skar (1981), Sikkink (1994), Sindicato de Trabajadoras del Hogar (1982), Wasserstrom (1985), and Weismantel (1988).

4.   *Since you don't want to talk, it must be the wiraqucha's:* Here *wiraqucha* refers to the "master of the house," that is, Mrs. María's husband (whom Asunta surely addresses as "*wiraqucha*").

5.   *when our son Marianito was about a year old, he caught a bad cough that killed him:* As revealed in Asunta's account, most of her children died before they were one year old, and only one of the seven children to whom she gave birth reached adulthood. Peru has one of the worst infant mortality rates in the world. Indeed, "half of all deaths are of children under five. In Peru it is more common to die in infancy than old age" (Roddick 1988:167).

6.   *Stories began coming into that cornbeer tavern:* Cookhouse and cornbeer tavern are used interchangeably in this passage. See Chapter 6, note 6; Chapter 9, note 4.

7. *he traveled to the Yauri area for Carnival:* In the Roman Catholic religious calendar, *Carnaval* (Sp.) is held on the three days that precede Ash Wednesday (between Epiphany and Ash Wednesday) and involves a popular celebration. Allen (1988: 182–187) describes the ludic nature of this celebration, one which has little Christian imagery and which is a time of sexual play, ritual fighting, dancing, singing, and fertility rites. During these celebrations, itinerant peddlers gather in the streets, markets, or central squares of rural towns and villages to sell their products.

8. *he'd see blue devils:* This refers to extreme intoxication, a hallucinatory state in which the drunk person is completely out of control.

15. *"I Stopped Bearing That Cross"*

1. *with all the sin that exists in the world, to live this life is to suffer:* So begins one of the most reflective passages in the book, one that again portrays the ways in which different religious elements from both native Andean and Christian belief systems—including "sin," the Christian God, and Judgment Day, on the one hand, and mountain lords, upperworld, lowerworld, and Sun Father, on the other—form a seamless whole for the narrator, a worldview that is both Christian and distinctly Andean (see Chapter 1, notes 16, 35; Chapter 9, note 18). As discussed in Chapter 1, note 16, we have generally translated the word *vida* (Sp.) as "world" rather than "life" in the text. In this passage, however, we alternate "this life" and "the other life" with "this world" and "the otherworld" as glosses for *kay vida* and *huk kaq vida.*

2. *Yet, everybody, from the tiniest moth to the mountain lord's fearsome puma:* "Mountain lord's fearsome puma" is our translation of *manchana puma awki* (Q.): "The puma as a sacred animal of the *Apus*" (Valderrama and Escalante 1977). Other animals, such as condors, are also viewed by highlanders as embodying the spirit, and being agents, of the mountain lords.

3. *when the dead soul's kinfolk know about his dirty deeds:* We have cast this phrase in the masculine—"*his* dirty deeds"—because, although Quechua is gender neutral, the incestuous act occurs with a daughter or wife. However, while the perpetrators of this particular type of damnable sin are, judging by Asunta's account, generally men, "the damned" include women as well.

4. *Once we'd arrived, they also gave us a little hut to live in:* For a vivid evocation of the extreme living and working conditions of highland mines, see the testimonials of Domitila Barrios de Chungara (Barrios de Chungara and Viezzer 1979) and Juan Rojas (Nash 1992) from Bolivia. See also the vivid evocations of life in the mines by Arguedas (1986) and Nash (1979). These mines are generally located over the 14,000-foot mark in desolate, mountainous regions and have few amenities.

5. *it's un-Christian of the mistis here in the city to look down on and sneer at such delicious meat:* In the highlands, meat of any kind is highly valued by rural villagers, and to be able to consume it frequently as Asunta does in the mining region—because of the proximity of herding communities—is something of a luxury. Food, as Weismantel has shown in the Ecuadorian Andes, is an important symbolic means for expressing and distinguishing ethnic, class, and gender identities. Chicken and rice, for example, are iconic of "white" cuisine, while their "Indian" counterparts are guinea pig and potatoes (1988:34); these and other "Indian" foods, such as the llama meat that Asunta mentions, are regarded with utter disdain by the dominant society in Andean countries.

6. *her father stole her away from me:* The labor value of children is very high in the Andes, and conflict between different family members over the control of this labor is not uncommon. This passage also speaks to *runa-misti* relations, as Asunta is virtually powerless to reclaim her child from her husband's mestiza *comadre.*

7. *Who knows what else he said, feeding her liquor to convince her:* Another gloss would be: "Who knows what else he said, convincing her to accept some liquor." It is unclear whether he used liquor to break down her will power—and Asunta makes several mentions in her narrative about the abuses committed by, and lack of willpower of, people under the influence—or whether this refers to Andean drinking etiquette. In the latter, accepting a drink from someone signals an ongoing relationship. If that were the case, then by accepting the liquor he offered, Asunta's mother may have obligated herself to speak to Asunta on his behalf.

16. Life with Gregorio

1. *from the moment I'd arrived, he was checking me out:* It is interesting to compare Gregorio's and Asunta's versions of the events in this chapter. These versions reveal differences, among other things, in their application of ethnic categories and in the way that they view their relationship.

2. *But we didn't go to either San Jerónimo or San Sebastián's Corpus Christi that day:* See Chapter 14, note 1.

3. *But when that uppity, hot-headed pig grew a bit bigger:* "Uppity, hot-headed" is our gloss for *arrecha* (Sp.), which has the colloquial meaning of "lustful" (see Chapter 5, note 6). While Asunta may mean that the pig was in heat and ran away, she is probably referring to a certain agitated and unruly quality.

4. *two or three large glasses of strawberry beer:* The latter is our translation of *frutillada* (Sp.), which is a beer made of *frutilla*, a large yellowish strawberry native to the Americas.

5. *They were Mrs. Mercedes' clients, and they worked as food vendors at central market:* For the term "food vendor" (*chupi qhatu*), see Chapter 9, note 2.

6. *to gather forage for guinea pigs:* Guinea pigs (*Cavia porcellus*), known as *quwi* (Q.) in the highlands and *cuy* (Sp.) in the literature, are livestock raised at home for their meat. They have been an important part of Quechua cuisine since time immemorial and are used for special occasions and ritual meals. See Morales (1994) and Weismantel (1988).

7. *That soldier's wife was a raving bitch who liked to pick fights:* "A raving bitch who liked to pick fights" is our translation of *arrecha pendenciera* (Sp.). The fact that Asunta applies this term to herself in the passage reinforces our interpretation of *arrecha* (see Chapter 5, note 6)—that it is used to refer to the agitated and unruly, rather than sexual, quality of the person being described.

8. *and a wiraqucha gringo, who must've taken pity on me when he saw me there sobbing:* Note that in Chapter 10 Gregorio describes this person as a *misti* (and as a "foreigner named Repeto"), whereas Asunta describes him as a *wiraqucha gringo*, showing more subtle distinctions in her classification of *mistis*. This is perhaps due to her greater urban experience. Asunta apparently uses the term *wiraqucha gringo* to speak of someone who is not from Cuzco, though perhaps from Lima. He "is *wiraqucha* because he was surely well-dressed in occidental-style clothes giving off a wealthy

appearance, because he has the power to decide about the lands of Coripata, because he is white, and because he is compassionate" (Valderrama and Escalante, personal communication 1993). See Glossary and Chapter 1, note 8.

9. *Go live in shed:* When imitating the speech of the *wiraqucha gringo*, Asunta made it clear to the original editors that she could not understand his Spanish well, probably because he was a foreigner or was a monolingual Spanish speaker (Valderrama and Escalante, personal communication 1993). See Chapter 16, note 8.

10. *buying used clothes from wealthy professionals:* "Wealthy professionals" is our translation of *doctores* (Sp.). As used in the highlands, this term refers to urban-based, wealthy *mistis*, that is, those who have high-status, professional white-collar jobs (e.g., lawyers, professors, and engineers).

11. *one must work the needle carefully:* Besides being a reference to the need for being careful with even the smallest of actions, this reference to needles may have to do with witchcraft. Some stores in Andean communities prohibit the sale of certain goods—including sewing needles—after certain hours of the night because of their potential use in witchcraft. Thus, this phrase may refer to inadvertently doing harm to someone by such carelessness.

POSTSCRIPT

1. For more information on this organization, contact:
Proyecto "Casa del Cargador"
Asociación Civil "Gregorio Condori Mamani"
Apartado 1075
Cuzco, Peru

2. For more information on this organization, contact:
"Programa de Alfabetización Bilingüe Intercultural de Anta y Chumbivilcas"
Centro Andino de Educación y Promoción "José María Arguedas"
Calle Saphi 808
Cuzco, Peru

GLOSSARY

This glossary was written for the English edition, with the exception of some glossary definitions taken from the original bilingual edition, and which are cited in the following manner: Valderrama and Escalante (1977). In several instances, we reference a specific endnote where the interested reader can find more information on the glossary term. The origin of the word is marked by either "Q." for Quechua or "Sp." for Spanish. Only italicized words that appear in *the narratives themselves* are found in the glossary.

apu (Q.): "Literally, lord. Refers to a powerful Andean deity that resides in peaks and mountains and that goes by the name of the mountain it lives within. It is the protector of the people, animals, and crops in its territory, or of those who appeal to it" (Valderrama and Escalante 1977). *Apus* go by other names in other Andean regions, such as *wamani* and *cabildo*. See Chapter 8, notes 2, 4.

awki (Q.): "A category of mountain spirit, which is of a lower rank than *apu*. They go by the names of the mountains in which they reside" (Valderrama and Escalante 1977).

ayni (Q.): "Reciprocity: fundamental principle of Andean socioeconomic organization that consists of the reciprocal exchange of goods and services" (Valderrama and Escalante 1977). This institution is widespread in the Andes and is used in many social domains (e.g., fiesta sponsorship, agricultural labor). *Ayni* generally refers to the equal exchange of a given good or service; in agricultural labor, it usually refers to the exchange of a day of work between two parties. *Ayni* is one of many different forms of mutual aid in the Andes. See also *mink'a* and Chapter 4, note 1.

cargo (Sp.): "Religious obligation that consists of ceremonies organized, paid for, and carried out by a member of the community" (Valderrama and

Escalante 1977). *Cargo* can also refer to political offices undertaken by a member of the community. Undertaking a certain number of *cargos*, whether these be religious or civil, is generally obligatory for individual members of a community. Religious *cargos* often involve the organization and sponsorship of a religious festival in honor of a particular saint in the Roman Catholic pantheon. Political *cargos* are often a type of civic duty or community service in which townspeople are appointed or volunteer to fulfill a town office. See Chapter 1, notes 10, 26.

centavo (Sp.): A monetary unit equivalent to one-hundredth of a *sol*. For the sake of readability, and to avoid the proliferation of monetary terms, we have translated the monetary value of other subunits that appear in the text—such as *real* (ten *centavos*) and *warku* (eighty *centavos*)—into *centavos*. See *sol*.

cholo, chola (Sp.): A denigrating term sometimes translated as "half-breed," "mestizo," or "civilized Indian," it is often applied to a transculturated "Indian." There is often a sense of liminality implied by the term, as if the person being so described is between cultures and somehow inauthentic. As with other terms, such as *runa* or *misti*, the term *cholo* is part of a racial idiom used to express class and ethnic differences. See Chapter 1, note 8; Chapter 6, note 1.

chuño (Q.): A type of freeze-dried potato that is processed at high altitudes by Andean peasants and that can be stored for long periods of time. This is accomplished by a process that alternates freezing the potatoes at high altitudes during the night and then dehydrating them with the sun's rays during the day, taking advantage of the severe temperature fluctuation in the high reaches.

compadre, comadre (Sp.): Co-father, co-mother. Name used to express the relationship between the godparents and parents of godchildren. *Compadrazgo* is an important institution used throughout the Andes in a wide variety of social fields. The most important instances of *compadrazgo* are baptism and marriage. In his narrative, Gregorio occasionally uses the term *compadre* to refer to his *padrino* or godfather. See Chapter 8, note 6; Chapter 10, note 3.

gringo, gringa (Sp.): Foreigner. This category refers to people foreign to the Cuzco area and who are even more culturally dissimilar to *runas* than local *mistis*; the term also implies whiteness. While the term is often applied to Europeans and North Americans in colloquial Spanish, highlanders in Peru also apply it to "white" monolingual Spanish speakers from Lima. It thus overlaps with *misti* to a certain degree (see Chapter 16, note 8). See also Chapter 1, note 8; Chapter 6, note 1.

hacienda (Sp.): Large landed estate. In the case of the Andes, haciendas include not only agricultural lands but vast areas of highland pastures where large herds of cattle, alpacas, llamas, and sheep are kept and where many other resources, such as wood and medicinal herbs, are obtained. These landed estates often have subject communities and employ different forms of coercion and exploitation, including indentured servitude. See Chapter 8, note 5; Chapter 13, notes 4, 5.

Inka (Q.): "Mythic figure that represents the era before the Spanish conquest" (Valderrama and Escalante 1977). Inka has varied meanings in the text: sometimes it is used in the foundational sense of mythic creator gods and culture heroes (e.g., as in the skirmish between Inka and Inka Qulla) and is synonymous with Inkaríy. In other cases, it refers to a class of ruler (as in Wayna Qhapaq) or a people (those who preceded the Spaniards, the true "Peruvians"). The different meanings associated with Inka overlap in complex ways. See Chapter 1, note 11; Chapter 7, note 5.

Inkaríy (Q. and Sp.; *ríy* is from *rey*, Spanish for "king"): "Mythic figure that symbolizes a unitary principle that will return one day to restore the order that was lost during the Conquest; this will be accomplished by a symmetrical inversion of the present order. With the Spanish Conquest of the Tawantinsuyu (the Inka Empire), the indigenous peoples lost their privileged position; with the return of Inkaríy they would recover their previous status" (Valderrama and Escalante 1977). See Chapter 1, note 11; Chapter 7, note 5.

laymi (Q.): "Parcels of land that are cultivated on a rotating basis" (Valderrama and Escalante 1977). These communal lands, often parceled out to members of the community on an individual basis, are managed by a sectoral fallowing system in which parcels of land are fallowed and cultivated on a rotating schedule. Decisions regarding these fields are usually made by communal authorities. See Chapter 4, note 2.

lisa (Sp.): Short for *papa lisa*, a common name for *olluco* (*Ullucus tuberons*), a variety of Andean tuber.

mestizo, mestiza (Sp.): See *misti*.

mink'a (Q.): "Exchange of labor for labor" (Valderrama and Escalante 1977). Festive labor, exchange labor, peonage. The term *mink'a* designates different kinds of labor arrangements from one region to another. Sometimes it denotes a form of peonage; other times, a replacement worker for an *ayni* debt; and other times, the collective and festive labor used in activities such as roofing a house, working a field, and so on. Andean peoples pool their labor in different ways, and *mink'a* is a generic name for several of these. See also *ayni* and Chapter 4, note 1.

misti (Q.): "Mestizo, nonindigenous person" (Valderrama and Escalante 1977). Derived from the Spanish word *mestizo*, *misti* is the term used by indigenous peasants in the southern Peruvian highlands to refer to nonindigenous peoples. The term has variable meanings in different parts of the Andes; Asunta and Gregorio use this term in opposition to the social group that they identify with, *runa*. As with other terms, such as *runa* or *cholo*, *misti* is part of a racial idiom used to express class and ethnic differences. See Chapter 1, note 8; Chapter 6, note 1.

moraya (Q.):   A special kind of *chuño*, that is, freeze-dried potato that is white in color.

oca (Q.):   *Oxalis tuberosa*: A variety of Andean tuber.

pampa (Q.):   The extensive, generally grass-covered plain of the high reaches.

pisco (Q.):   A clear grape brandy made on the Peruvian coast.

qulla (Q.):   "Indigenous person from the high plateau" (Valderrama and Escalante 1977). This term refers to the indigenous inhabitants of the altiplano of Peru and Bolivia, which lies to the southeast of the Cuzco region.

rocoto (Q.):   *Capsicum baccatum*: An indigenous hot pepper.

runa (Q.):   "Indigenous person of the Quechua culture" (Valderrama and Escalante 1977). While the word is sometimes used by the narrators to mean "human being" (or even "living being") in a generic sense, it often refers exclusively to the social group that Gregorio and Asunta closely identify with, that is, Quechua-speaking indigenous people of peasant origin. As with such terms as *cholo* or *misti*, *runa* is part of a racial idiom used to express class and ethnic differences. See also Chapter 1, note 8; Chapter 16, note 8.

sol (Sp.):   The *sol*, or "sun," is a monetary unit equal to 100 *centavos*. Its value has changed tremendously over time. The following equivalences in U.S. dollars and cents are approximate. From 1900 to 1918, the sol was worth 49 cents; from 1919 to 1930, 37 cents; from 1933 to 1939, 23–25 cents; from 1939 to 1945, 14–16 cents; from 1950 to 1956, 8–10 cents; from 1973 to 1976, 2–3 cents.

soltero (Sp.):   A highland dish that consists of green broad beans, cheese, tomatoes, kelp, and onions.

tarwi (Q.):   (*Lupinus mutabilis*): A white bean.

tumbo (Q.):   (*Passiflora quadrangularis*): A green fruit that is yellowish orange on the inside, with many seeds.

tupu (Q.):   Agrarian measure of land that is approximately eighty-eight by forty-four yards.

vicuña(Q.):   (*Lama vicugna*): A type of fine-wooled, undomesticated camelid.

wiraqucha (Q.):   "Literally, 'sir.' A term used by *runas* when addressing or referring to a *mestizo*" (Valderrama and Escalante 1977). Originally the name of the supreme deity of the Inkas, *wiraqucha* is today used as a term of deference that connotes race, ethnic, and class differences between *runas* and *mistis*. Used both as adjective and noun, *wiraqucha* has different valences in the text, but generally refers to the power, wealth, "whiteness," and sometimes compassion and benevolence, of a non-*runa* (*misti, mestizo,* or *gringo*). The term connotes "whiteness," not just in terms of perceived race, but also in the sense of being wealthier, more urbane, speaking Spanish, and wearing Western clothes (e.g., shoes rather than tire sandals). This is an ideal type, however, and the term expresses different degrees of hierarchy and cultural distance in different contexts. See Introduction and Chapter 1, note 8; Chapter 6, note 1; Chapter 16, note 8.

BIBLIOGRAPHY

Ackerman, Raquel
1988 "Rhetorics of Power among the Quechua." Paper presented to the Forty-sixth International Congress of Americanists.

Adorno, Rolena
1986 *Guaman Poma: Writing and Resistance in Colonial Peru.* Austin: University of Texas Press.

Aguirre, Carlos, and Charles Walker
1990 *Bandoleros, abigeos y montoneros: Criminalidad y violencia en el Perú, siglos XVIII–XX.* Lima: Instituto de Apoyo Agrario.

Alberti, Giorgio, and Enrique Mayer
1974 *Reciprocidad e intercambio en los Andes peruanos.* Lima: Instituto de Estudios Peruanos.

Albó, Xavier
1973 *El futuro de los idiomas oprimidos en los Andes.* La Paz: Centro de Investigación y Promoción del Campesinado.

Allen, Catherine
1988 *The Hold Life Has.* Washington, D.C.: Smithsonian Press.

Altamirano, Teófilo
1984 *Presencia andina en Lima metropolitana: Un estudio sobre migrantes y clubes de provincianos.* Lima: Pontificia Universidad Católica del Peru.

Andreas, Carol
1985 *When Women Rebel: The Rise of Popular Feminism in Peru.* Westport, Conn.: Lawrence Hill and Company.

Arguedas, José María
1978 [1958] *Deep Rivers.* Trans. Frances Horning Barraclough. Austin: University of Texas Press.
1985 [1941] *Yawar Fiesta.* Trans. Frances Horning Barraclough. Austin: University of Texas Press.
1985 [1964] "Puquio: A Culture in Process of Change." In *Yawar Fiesta.* Trans. Frances Horning Barraclough. Pp. 149–192. Austin: University of Texas Press.
1986 *Todas las sangres.* Lima: Editorial Horizonte.

Ascher, Marcia, and Robert Ascher
1981 *Code of the Quipu: A Study in Media, Mathematics, and Culture.* Ann Arbor: University of Michigan Press.
Babb, Florence E.
1989 *Between Field and Cooking Pot: The Political Economy of Marketwomen in Peru.* Austin: University of Texas Press.
Barrios de Chungara, Domitila, and Moema Viezzer
1979 *Let Me Speak! Testimony of Domitila, a Woman of the Bolivian Mines.* Trans. Victoria Ortiz. New York: Monthly Review Press.
Basso, Ellen B., ed.
1990 *Native Latin American Cultures through Their Discourse.* Bloomington: Folklore Institute, Indiana University.
Basso, Keith H.
1979 *Portraits of "the Whiteman": Linguistic Play and Cultural Symbols among the Western Apache.* New York: Cambridge University Press.
Bastien, Joseph
1978 *The Mountain of the Condor.* New York: West Publishing Company.
Bauer, Brian
1992 *The Development of the Inca State.* Austin: University of Texas Press.
Belote, Linda, and Jim Belote
1988 "Gender, Ethnicity, and Modernization: Saraguro Women in a Changing World." In *Multidisciplinary Studies in Andean Anthropology.* Ed. Virginia J. Vitzthum. Pp. 101–117. Ann Arbor: University of Michigan Press.
Beverley, John
1992 "The Margin at the Center: On *Testimonio* (Testimonial Narrative)." In *De/Colonizing the Subject: The Politics of Gender in Women's Autobiography.* Ed. Sidonie Smith and Julia Watson. Pp. 91–114. Minneapolis: University of Minnesota Press.
1993 *Against Literature.* Minneapolis: University of Minnesota Press.
Beyersdorff, Margot
1984 *Léxico agropecuario quechua.* Cuzco: Centro de Estudios Rurales Andinos "Bartolomé de las Casas."
1986 "La tradición oral quechua vista desde la perspectiva de la literatura." In *Revista Andina* 4:213–236.
1988 *La adoración de los Reyes Magos: Vigencia del teatro religioso español en el Perú andino.* Cuzco: Centro de Estudios Rurales Andinos "Bartolomé de las Casas."
Bolton, Ralph
1980 "Nine Quechua-Qolla Narratives: Peruvian Folktale Texts." *Anthropos* 75(1–2): 140–162.
Bolton, Ralph, and Enrique Mayer
1977 *Andean Kinship and Marriage.* Washington, D.C.: American Anthropological Association.
Bourque, Susan, and Kay Warren
1981 *Women of the Andes: Patriarchy and Social Change in Two Peruvian Towns.* Ann Arbor: University of Michigan Press.
Bourricaud, Francois
1975 "Indian, Mestizo, and Cholo as Symbols in the Peruvian System of Stratification."

In *Ethnicity: Theory and Experience,* ed. Nathan Glazer and Daniel P. Moynihan. Pp. 350–387.

Brody, Jill
1994 "Performance and Discourse: Transcribing Latin American Languages and Cultures." *Latin American Research Review* 29(3):249–256.

Brush, Stephen
1977 *Mountain, Field, and Family.* Philadelphia: University of Pennsylvania Press

Candler, Kay.
1993 "Place and Thought in a Quechua Household Ritual." Ph.D. diss., University of Illinois at Urbana-Champaign.

Cereceda, Verónica
1987 "Aproximaciones a una estética andina: De la belleza al *Tinku.*" In *Tres reflexiones sobre el pensamiento andino.* Ed. Thérèse Bouysse-Cassagne, Olivia Harris, Tristan Platt, and Verónica Cereceda. Pp. 133–231. La Paz: Hisbol.

Cerrón-Palomino, Rodolfo
1987 *Lingüística quechua.* Biblioteca de la Tradición Oral Andina 8. Cuzco: Centro de Estudios Rurales Andinos "Bartolomé de las Casas."

Chirinos Rivera, Andrés
1994a *Ñawpaq Timpumanta: El tiempo antiguo.* Cuzco: Centro Andino de Educación y Promoción "José María Arguedas."
1994b "Normas empleadas para la escritura quechua." In *Asuntapa kawsayninmanta.* Ed. Ricardo Valderrama and Carmen Escalante. Pp.58–60. Cuzco: Centro Andino de Promoción y Educación "José María Arguedas."

Classen, Constance
1993 *Worlds of Sense: Exploring the Senses in History and Across Cultures.* New York: Routledge.

Clifford, James, and George Marcus
1986 *Writing Culture.* Berkeley: University of California Press.

Cohen, John
1979 *Q'eros: The Shape of Survival.* Berkeley: Center for Media and Independent Learning.

Collins, Jane
1986 "The Household and Relations of Production in Southern Peru." *Comparative Studies in Society and History* 28(4):651–671.

Condori, Bernabé, and Rosalind Gow
1982 *Kay pacha.* Cuzco: Centro de Estudios Rurales Andinos "Bartolomé de las Casas."

Crandon-Malamud, Libbet
1991 *From the Fat of Our Souls: Social Change, Political Process, and Medical Pluralism in Bolivia.* Berkeley: University of California Press.

Cusihuamán, Antonio G.
1976 *Diccionario Quechua Cuzco-Collao.* Lima: Ministerio de Educación/Instituto de Estudios Peruanos.

Davies, Carol Boyce
1992 "Collaboration and the Ordering Imperative in Life Story Production." In *De/Colonizing the Subject: The Politics of Gender in Women's Autobiography.* Ed. Sidonie Smith and Julia Watson. Pp. 3–19. Minneapolis: University of Minnesota Press.

Deeds, Eric
n.d. "A Chronology of the Life Histories of Gregorio Condori Mamani and Asunta Quispe Huamán." Manuscript, University of California at Berkeley.

de la Cadena, Marisol
1991 "'Las mujeres son más indias': Etnicidad y género en una comunidad de Cusco." *Revista Andina* 9(1):7–29.

Demarest, Arthur A.
1981 *Viracocha: The Nature and Antiquity of the Andean High God*. Cambridge: Peabody Museum Monographs, Harvard University.

Dillon, Mary, and Thomas Abercrombie
1988 "The Destroying Christ: An Aymara Myth of Conquest." In *Rethinking History and Myth: Indigenous South American Perspectives on the Past*. Ed. Jonathan D. Hill. Pp. 50–77. Chicago: University of Illinois Press.

Dover, Robert V. H., Katherine E. Seibold, and John H. McDowell, eds.
1992 *Andean Cosmologies through Time*. Bloomington: Indiana University Press.

Earls, John
1971 "The Structure of Modern Andean Social Categories." *Journal of the Steward Anthropological Society* 3(1):69–106.

Femenias, Blenda
1991 "Regional Dress of the Colca Valley, Peru: A Dynamic Tradition." In *Textile Traditions of Mesoamerica and the Andes: An Anthology*. Ed. Margot Blum Schevill et al. Pp. 179–204. New York: Garland Publishing.

Flores Galindo, Alberto
1987 *Buscando un Inca: Identidad y utopía en los Andes*. Lima: Instituto de Apoyo Agrario.

Flores Ochoa, Jorge A.
1977 "Pastores de puna: Uywamichiq punarunakuna. Lima: Instituto de Estudios Peruanos.
1985 "Interaction and Complementarity in Three Zones of Cuzco." In *Andean Ecology and Civilization: An Interdisciplinary Perspective on Andean Ecological Complementarity*. Ed. Shozo Masuda et al. Pp. 251–276. Tokyo: University of Tokyo Press.

Flores Ochoa, Jorge A., and Juan V. Núñez del Prado B., eds.
1983 *Q'ero: El último ayllu inka*. Cuzco: Centro de Estudios Andinos.

Fuenzalida, Fernando
1970 "La matriz colonial." *Revista del Museo Nacional* (Lima) 35:92–123.
1971 "Poder, etnia y estratificación en Perú rural." In *Perú: Hoy*. Pp. 8–86. Madrid: Siglo XXI.

Gade, Daniel
1983 "Lightning in the Folklife and Religion of the Central Andes." *Anthropos* 78:770–787.

Gelles, Paul H.
1992 "'*Caballeritos*' and *Maíz Cabanita*: Colonial Categories and Andean Ethnicity in the Quincentennial Year." *Kroeber Anthropological Society Papers* 75–76:14–27. Oakland: GRT Press.
1995 "Equilibrium and Extraction: Dual Organization in the Andes." *American Ethnologist* 22:4, in press.

Getzels, Peter
1983 "Los ciegos: Visión de la identidad del runa en la ideología del Inkarrí-Qollari."
In Q'ero: El último ayllu inka. Ed. Jorge Flores Ochoa and Juan Núñez del Prado.
Pp. 170–201. Cuzco: Centro de Estudios Andinos.
Godenzzi, Juan Carlos, ed.
1992 El Quechua en debate: Ideología, normalización y enseñanza. Cuzco: Centro de Es-
tudios Rurales Andinos "Bartolomé de las Casas."
Godoy, Ricardo
1984 "Common Field Agriculture: The Andes and England Compared." Cambridge:
H.I.I.D. Press.
González Jiménez, Odi
1994 "El condenado o alma en pena en la tradición oral andina." B.A. thesis, Univer-
sidad Nacional de San Agustín, Arequipa.
Gugelberger, Georg, ed.
Forthcoming The Real Thing: Testimonial Discourse and the Americas. Durham: Duke
University Press.
Gugelberger, Georg, and Michael Kearney
1991 Introduction. "Voices for the Voiceless: Testimonial Literature in Latin America."
Latin American Perspectives, issue 70, 18(3):3–14.
Guillet, David
1981 "Land Tenure, Ecological Zone, and Agricultural Regime in the Central Andes."
American Ethnologist 8(1): 139–155.
Harris, Olivia
1985 "Ecological Duality and the Role of the Center: Northern Potosí." In Andean
Ecology and Civilization. Ed. Shozo Masuda et al. Pp. 311–336. Tokyo: University
of Tokyo Press.
Harrison, Regina
1989 Signs, Songs, and Memory in the Andes. Austin: University of Texas Press.
Harvey, Penelope
1994 "The Presence and Absence of Speech in the Communication of Gender." In Bi-
lingual Women: Anthropological Approaches to Second Language Use. Ed. Pauline
Burton, Ketaki Kushari Dyson, and Shirley Ardener. Pp. 44–64. Oxford: Berg
Press.
Hemming, John
1970 The Conquest of the Incas. New York: Harvest.
Hendricks, Janet Wall
1993 To Drink of Death: The Narrative of a Shuar Warrior. Tucson: University of Ari-
zona Press.
Hughes, Robin R.
1987 "Birdlife in the Colca." In Discovering the Colca Valley. Ed. Mauricio de Romaña,
Jaume Blassi, and Jordi Blassi. Barcelona: Francis O. Patthey and Sons.
Isbell, Billy Jean
1974 "Kuyaq: Those Who Love Me": An Analysis of Andean Kinship and Reciprocity
within a Ritual." In Reciprocidad e intercambio en los Andes peruanos. Ed. Giorgi
Alberti and Enrique Mayer. Pp. 110–152. Lima: Instituto de Estudios Peruanos.
1978 To Defend Ourselves: Ritual and Ecology in an Andean Village. Austin: University
of Texas Press.

Julien, Catherine J.
1982 "Inca Decimal Administration in the Lake Titicaca Region." In *The Inca and Aztec States, 1400–1800.* Ed. George Collier, Renato Rosaldo, and John Wirth.

Kaplan, Caren
1992 "Resisting Autobiography: Out-law Genres and Transnational Feminist Subjects." In *De/Colonizing the Subject: The Politics of Gender in Women's Autobiography.* Ed. Sidonie Smith and Julia Watson. Pp. 115–138. Minneapolis: University of Minnesota Press.

Kirk, Robin
1992 *Untold Terror: Violence against Women in Peru's Armed Conflict.* New York: Human Rights Watch.

Kristal, Efraín
1987 *The Andes Viewed from the City. Literary and Political Discourse on the Indian in Peru, 1848–1930.* New York: Lang Publishing.

Latin American Perspectives
1991 "Voices of the Voiceless in Testimonial Literature," issues 70–71, 18(3–4).

Lira, Jorge A.
1982 *Diccionario Kkechuwa-Español.* 2d ed. Bogotá: Editora Guadalupe Ltda.
1985 *Medicina andina: Farmacopea y rituales.* Biblioteca de la Tradición Oral Andina 6. Cuzco: Centro de Estudios Rurales Andinos "Bartolomé de Las Casas."

Lombardi, Francisco
1988 *The Mouth of the Wolf.* New York: Cine Vista.

Long, Norman, and Bryan R. Roberts, eds.
1978 *Peasant Cooperation and Capitalist Expansion in Central Peru.* Austin: University of Texas Press.

Lowenthal, Abraham F.
1975 *The Peruvian Experiment: Continuity and Change under Military Rule.* Princeton: Princeton University Press.

Lynch, Barbara
1991 "Women and Irrigation in Highland Peru." *Society and Natural Resources* 4:37–52.

MacCormack, Sabine
1991 *Religion in the Andes.* Princeton: Princeton University Press.

Mallon, Florencia
1983 *The Defense of Community in Peru's Central Highlands: Peasant Struggle and Capitalist Transition, 1860–1940.* Princeton: Princeton University Press.

Mangin, William, ed.
1970 *Peasants in Cities: Readings in the Anthropology of Urbanization.* Boston: Houghton Mifflin Company.

Mannheim, Bruce
1985 "Southern Peruvian Quechua." In *South American Indian Languages, Retrospect and Prospect.* Ed. Harriet E. Manelis Cline and Louisa R. Stark. Pp. 481–515. Austin: University of Texas Press.
1991 *The Language of the Inka since the European Invasion.* Austin: University of Texas Press.

Manrique, Nelson
1988 *Yawar Mayu: Sociedades Terratenientes Serranas, 1879–1910.* Lima: DESCO.

Marcus, George, and Michael Fischer

1986 *Anthropology as Cultural Critique.* Chicago: University of Chicago Press.

Martínez Escobar, Gabriela

1993 *Ch'ullacuy.* Berkeley: Center for Media and Independent Learning.

1994 *Mamacoca: The Other Face of the Leaf.* Berkeley: East Bay Media Center.

Marzal, Manuel

1977 *Estudios sobre Religion Campesina.* Lima: Pontificia Universidad Católica del Peru.

1985 *El Sincretismo Iberoamericano.* Lima: Pontificia Universidad Católica del Peru.

Mason, Otis

1887 "The Human Beast of Burden." In *Annual Report of the Board of Regents of the Smithsonian Institution, Part II.* Pp. 237–295. Washington, D.C.: Government Printing Office.

Matos Mar, José, and Jorge A. Carbajal

1974 *Erasmo: Yanacón del valle de Chancay.* Lima: Instituto de Estudios Peruanos.

Maybury-Lewis, David

1989 "The Quest for Harmony." In *The Attraction of Opposites: Thought and Society in the Dualistic Mode.* Ed. David Maybury-Lewis and Uri Almagor. Pp. 1–18. Ann Arbor: University of Michigan Press.

Mayer, Enrique

1991 "Peru in Deep Trouble: Mario Vargas Llosa's 'Inquest in the Andes' Reexamined." *Cultural Anthropology* 6(4):466–504.

Menchú, Rigoberta, with Elisabeth Burgos-Debray

1984 *I, Rigoberta Menchú: An Indian Woman in Guatemala.* Trans. Ann White. London: Verso.

Mendoza-Walker, Zoila

1993 "Shaping Society through Dance: Mestizo Ritual Performance in the Southern Peruvian Andes." Ph.D. diss., Department of Anthropology, University of Chicago.

Mitchell, William P.

1991 *Peasants on the Edge: Crop, Cult, and Crisis in the Andes.* Austin: University of Texas Press.

Montoya, Rodrigo

1987 *La cultura quechua hoy.* Lima: Hueso Húmero Ediciones.

Montoya, Rodrigo, Edwin Montoya, and Luis Montoya

1987 *La sangre de los cerros: Urqukunapa yawarnin: Antología de la poesía quechua que se canta en el Perú.* Lima: Centro Peruano de Estudios Sociales.

Morales, Edmundo

1994 "The Guinea Pig in the Andean Economy: From Household Animal to Market Commodity." *Latin American Research Review* 29(3):129–142.

Morote Best, Efraín

1988 *Aldeas sumergidas: Cultura popular y sociedad en los Andes.* Cuzco: Centro de Estudios Rurales Andinos "Bartolomé de las Casas."

Moseley, Michael

1992 *The Incas and Their Ancestors: The Archaeology of Peru.* London: Thames and Hudson.

Muratorio, Blanca
1991 *The Life and Times of Grandfather Alonso: Culture and History in the Upper Amazon*. New Brunswick: Rutgers University Press.

Murra, John
1980 *The Economic Organization of the Inka State*. Greenwich, Conn.: JAI Press.
1982 "The Cultural Future of the Andean Majority." In *The Prospects for Plural Societies*. Ed. David Maybury-Lewis. Pp. 30–39. Washington, D.C.: American Ethnological Society.

Nash, June
1979 *We Eat the Mines and the Mines Eat Us: Dependency and Exploitation in Bolivian Tin Mines*. New York: Columbia University Press.
1992 *I Spent My Life in the Mines: The Story of Juan Rojas, Bolivian Tin Miner*. New York: Columbia University Press.

Núñez del Prado, Oscar
1973 *Kuyo Chico: Applied Anthropology in an Indian Community*. Trans. Lucy White Russo and Richard Russo. Chicago: University of Chicago Press.

Oré, Teresa
1983 *Memorias de un viejo luchador campesino: Juan H. Pévez*. Lima: Tarea.

Orlove, Benjamin
1980 "The Position of Rustlers in Regional Society: Social Banditry in the Andes." In *Land and Power in Latin America: Agrarian Economies and Social Processes in the Andes*. Ed. Benjamin S. Orlove and Glynn Custred. Pp. 179–194. New York: Holmes and Meier Publishers.

Orlove, Benjamin, and Ricardo Godoy
1986 "Sectorial Fallowing Systems in the Andes." *Journal of Ethnobiology* 6(1):169–204.

Ortiz, Alejandro
1973 *De Andaneva a Inkarrí: Una visión indígena del Perú*. Lima: Ediciones Retablo de Papel.

Ossio Acuña, Juan M.
1973 "Guamán Poma: Nueva corónica o carta al Rey: Un intento de aproximación a las categorías del pensamiento del mundo andino." In *Ideología mesiánica del mundo andino*. Ed. Juan Ossio. Pp. 153–213. Lima: Edición Ignacio Prado Pastor.
1980 "La estructura social de las comunidades andinas." In *Historia del Perú*. Vol. 3. Lima: Editorial Mejía Baca.
1992 *Parentesco, reciprocidad y jerarquía en los Andes: Una aproximación a la organización social de la comunidad de Andamarca*. Lima: Pontificia Universidad Católica.

Paerregaard, Karsten
1989 "Exchanging with Nature: *T'inka* in an Andean Village." *Folk* 31: 53–73.

Palomino, Salvador
1984 *El sistema de oposiciones en la comunidad de Sarhua*. Lima: Pueblo Indio.

Patterson, Thomas
1991 *The Inka Empire: The Formation and Disintegration of a Precapitalist State*. New York: Berg Press.

Payne, Johnny
1984 *Cuentos cusqueños*. Cuzco: Centro de Estudios Rurales Andinos "Bartolomé de las Casas."

Pease, Franklin

1981 "Ayllu y parcialidad: Reflexiones sobre el caso de Collaguas." In *Etnohistoria y antropología andina*. Ed. Amalia Castelli, Marcia Koth de Paredes, and Maríana Mould de Pease. Pp. 19–34. Lima: Aguarico.

1982 *El pensamiento mítico: Antología*. Lima: Mosca Azul Editores.

Philip, George D. E.

1978 *The Rise and Fall of the Peruvian Military Radicals, 1968–1976*. London: Athlone Press of the University of London.

Platt, Tristan

1982 *Estado boliviano y ayllu andino: Tierra y tributo en el norte de Potosí*. Lima: Instituto de Estudios Peruanos.

1986 "Mirrors and Maize: The Concept of *Yanantin* among the Macha of Bolivia." In *Anthropological History of Andean Polities*. Ed. John V. Murra, Nathan Wachtel, and Jacques Revel. Pp. 228–259. Cambridge: Cambridge University Press.

Poole, Deborah

1990 "Ciencia, peligrosidad y represión en la criminología indigenista peruana." In *Bandoleros, abigeos y montoneros*. Ed. Carlos Aguirre and Charles Walker. Pp. 335–368. Lima: Instituto de Apoyo Agrario.

Pratt, Mary Louise

1992 *Imperial Eyes: Travel Writing and Transculturation*. London: Routledge.

Preuss, Mary H., ed.

1989 *"In Love and War: Hummingbird Lore" and Other Selected Papers from Laila/Alila's 1988 Symposium*. Culver City, Calif.: Labyrinthos.

1990 *Laila Speaks! Selected Papers from the VII International Symposium on Latin American Indian Literatures*. Culver City, Calif.: Labyrinthos.

Pulgar Vidal, Javier

1987 *Geografía del Perú*. Lima: Peisa.

Rappaport, Joanne

1994 *Cumbe Reborn: An Andean Ethnography of History*. Chicago: University of Chicago Press.

Rasnake, Roger

1988 *Domination and Cultural Resistance: Authority and Power among an Andean People*. Durham: Duke University Press.

Real Academia Española

1984 *Diccionario de la Lengua Española*. Madrid: Editorial Espasa-Calpe, S.A.

Reinhart, Joseph

1985 "Chavin and Tiahuanaco: A New Look at Two Andean Ceremonial Centers." *National Geographic Research Reports* 1(3):395–422.

Roddick, Jackie

1988 *The Dance of the Millions: Latin America and the Debt Crisis*. London: Latin American Bureau.

Rostworowski, María

1988 *Historia del Tahuantinsuyo*. Lima: IEP.

Rowe, John

1982 "Inca Policies and Institutions relating to the Cultural Unification of the Empire." In *The Inca and Aztec States, 1400–1800, Anthropology and History*. Ed. George Collier et al. New York: Academic Press.

Sallnow, Michael
1987 *Pilgrims of the Andes: Regional Cults in Cusco*. Washington, D.C.: Smithsonian Institution Press.

Salomon, Frank
1987 "Ancestor Cults and Resistance to the State in Arequipa, ca. 1748–1754." In *Resistance, Rebellion, and Consciousness in the Andean Peasant World, Eighteenth to Twentieth Centuries*. Ed. Steve J. Stern. Pp. 148–165. Madison: University of Wisconsin Press.

1991 Introduction. In *The Huarochirí Manuscript: A Testament of Ancient and Colonial Andean Religion*. Ed. Frank Salomon and George Urioste. Pp. 1–38. Austin: University of Texas Press.

Salomon, Frank, and George L. Urioste
1991 *The Huarochirí Manuscript: A Testament of Ancient and Colonial Andean Religion*. Austin: University of Texas Press.

Seligmann, Linda
1989 "To Be in Between: The *Cholas* as Market Women in Peru." *Comparative Studies in Society and History* 31(4):694–721.

1993 "Between Worlds of Exchange: Ethnicity among Peruvian Market Women." *Cultural Anthropology* 8(2):187–213.

1995 *Between Reform and Revolution: Political Struggles in the Peruvian Andes, 1969–1991*. Stanford: Stanford University Press.

Sherbondy, Jeanette
1982 "El regadío, los lagos y los mitos de origen." *Allpanchis* (Cuzco) 17(20):3–32.

1986 "Los Ceques: Código de Canales en el Cusco Incaico." *Allpanchis* (Cuzco) 27:39–74.

Sherzer, Joel, and Greg Urban, eds.
1986 *Native South American Discourse*. New York: Mouton de Gruyter.

Shimada, Izumi
1985 Introduction. In *Andean Ecology and Civilization*. Ed. Shozo Masuda, Izumi Shimada, and Craig Morris. Pp. xi–xxxii. Tokyo: University of Tokyo Press.

Sikkink, Lynn
1994 "House, Community, and Marketplace: Women as Managers of Exchange Relations and Resources on the Southern Altiplano of Bolivia." Ph.D. diss., University of Minnesota, Minneapolis.

Silverblatt, Irene
1987 *Moon, Sun, and Witches: Gender Ideologies and Class in Inca and Colonial Peru*. Princeton: Princeton University Press.

Silverman-Proust, Gail
1983 "Motivos Textiles en Q'ero." In *Q'ero: El último ayllu inka*. Ed. Jorge Flores Ochoa and Juan Núñez del Prado. Pp. 87–105. Cuzco: Centro de Estudios Andinos.

Sindicato de Trabajadoras del Hogar
1982 *Basta: Testimonios*. Cuzco: Centro de Estudios Rurales Andinos "Bartolomé de las Casas."

Skar, Harold
1982 *The Warm Valley People: Duality and Land Reform among the Quechua Indians of Highland Peru*. New York: Columbia University Press.

Skar, Sarah

1981 "Andean Women and the Concept of Space/Time." In *Women and Space*. Ed. Shirley Ardener. Pp. 35–49. New York: St. Martin's Press.

Smith, Sidonie, and Julia Watson, eds.

1992 *De/Colonizing the Subject: The Politics of Gender in Women's Autobiography*. Minneapolis: University of Minnesota Press.

Spalding, Karen

1984 *Huarochirí: An Andean Society under Inca and Spanish Rule*. Stanford: Stanford University Press.

Starn, Orin

1991 "Missing the Revolution: Anthropologists and the War in Peru." *Cultural Anthropology* 6(1):63–91.

1992 "I Dreamed of Foxes and Hawks: Reflections on Peasant Protest, New Social Movements, and the Rondas Campesinas of Northern Peru." In *The Making of Social Movements in Latin America: Identity, Strategy, and Democracy*. Ed. Arturo Escobar and Sonia E. Alvarez. Pp. 89–111. Boulder, Colo.: Westview Press.

Stern, Steve

1987 "New Approaches to the Study of Peasant Rebellion and Consciousness: Implications of the Andean Experience." In *Resistance, Rebellion, and Consciousness in the Andean Peasant World, Eighteenth to Twentieth Centuries*. Ed. Steve J. Stern. Pp. 3–25. Madison: University of Wisconsin Press.

Stoner, Bradley Philip

1989 "Health Care Delivery and Health Resource Utilization in a Highland Andean Community of Southern Peru." Ph.D. diss., Indiana University.

Tedlock, Dennis

1983 *The Spoken Word and the Work of Interpretation*. Philadelphia: University of Pennsylvania Press.

1985 *Popul Vuh: The Mayan Book of the Dawn of Life*. New York: Simon and Schuster.

1993 *Breath on the Mirror: Mythic Voices and Visions of the Living Maya*. New York: Harper Collins.

Tomoeda, Hiroyasu, and Luis Millones, eds.

1992 *500 años de mestizaje en los Andes*. Lima: Talleres de Artes Gráficas Espino.

Urbano, Henrique, ed.

1991 *Modernidad en los Andes*. Cuzco: Centro de Estudios Regionales Andinos "Bartolomé de las Casas."

Urton, Gary

1981 *At the Crossroads of the Earth and the Sky*. Austin: University of Texas Press.

1990 *The History of a Myth: Paqaritambo and the Origin of the Inkas*. Austin: University of Texas Press.

Valderrama Fernández, Ricardo, and Carmen Escalante Gutiérrez.

1976 "*Pacha t'inka o la t'inka a la Madre Tierra en el Apurimac.*" *Allpanchis* 9:177–192.

1988 *Del Tata Mallku a la Mama Pacha: Riego, sociedad y ritos en los Andes peruanos*. Lima: DESCO.

Valderrama Fernández, Ricardo, and Carmen Escalante Gutiérrez, eds.

1977 *Gregorio Condori Mamani: Autobiografía*. Edic. Bilingüe Quechua-Castellano. Cuzco: Centro de Estudios Rurales Andinos "Bartolomé de las Casas."

1992 *Nosotros los humanos (Nuqanchik runakuna): Testimonio de los quechuas del siglo XX*. Edición bilingüe Quechua y Castellano. Biblioteca de la Tradición Oral Andina 12. Cuzco: Centro de Estudios Rurales Andinos "Bartolomé de Las Casas."

Other editions and translations of Valderrama and Escalante (1977):

1979 *Gregorio Condori Mamani: Autobiografía*. Segunda Edición popular en Castellano. Cuzco: Centro de Estudios Rurales Andinos "Bartolomé de las Casas."

1981 *Asunta og Gregorio Condori Mamani: Indianarliv i Peru*. Oslo: Edic. det Norske Samlaget.

1982a *Gregorio Condori Mamani*. Ed. bilingüe Quechua-Castellano 3a edic. Cuzco: Centro de Estudios Rurales Andinos "Bartolomé de las Casas."

1982b *Gregorio Condori Mamani*. Frankfort: Ed. Suhrkamp Verlag.

1983a *De nosotros los runas: Gregorio Condori Mamani*. Madrid: Ed. Alfaguara.

1983b *Asunta: Frauen in Latinamerika: Erzählungen und Berichte*. Munich: Deutscher Taschenbuch Verlag dtv.

1985 *Gregorio Condori Mamani*. Amsterdam: Ediciones Meulenhoff Nederland Bv.

1987 *Gregorio Condori Mamani: Autobiografía*. Havana: Edición Arte y Literatura.

1992 *Gregorio Condori Mamani: Autobiografía*. Edición bilingüe. Cuzco: Municipalidad Provincial del Qosqo.

1994 *Asuntapa kawsayninmanta*. Cuzco: Centro Andino de Promoción y Educación "José María Arguedas."

Van Den Berghe, Pierre L., and George P. Primov

1977 *Inequality in the Peruvian Andes: Class and Ethnicity in Cuzco*. Columbia: University of Missouri Press.

Wachtel, Nathan

1977 *Vision of the Vanquished*. New York: Barnes and Noble.

Wasserstrom, Robert

1985 "'Libertad de mujeres': A Savings and Loan Cooperative in the Bolivian Andes." In *Grassroots Development in Latin America and the Caribbean*. Pp. 42–68. New York: Praeger.

Watson, Julia, and Sidonie Smith

1992 "De/Colonization and the Politics of Discourse in Women's Autobiographical Practices." In *De/Colonizing the Subject: The Politics of Gender in Women's Autobiography*. Ed. Sidonie Smith and Julia Watson. Pp. xiii–xxxi. Minneapolis: University of Minnesota Press.

Webster, Steven S.

1983 "Ritos del ganado." In *Q'ero: El último ayllu inka*. Ed. Jorge Flores Ochoa and Juan Núñez del Prado. Pp. 131–142. Cuzco: Centro de Estudios Andinos.

Weismantel, Mary J.

1988 *Food, Gender, and Poverty in the Ecuadorian Andes*. Philadelphia: University of Pennsylvania Press.

Zimmerer, Karl S.

1994 "Transforming Colquepata Wetlands: Landscapes of Knowledge and Practice in Andean Agriculture." In *Irrigation at High Altitudes: The Social Organization of Water Control Systems in the Andes*. Ed. William Mitchell and David Guillet. Pp. 115–140. Washington, D.C.: American Anthropological Association.

Zorn, Elayne

1987 "Encircling Meaning: Economics and Aesthetics in Taquile, Peru." In *Andean Aes-*

thetics: Textiles of Peru and Bolivia. Ed. Blenda Femenias. Pp. 67–79. Exhibition catalog, Elvehjem Museum of Art and Helen Allen Textile Collection. Madison: University of Wisconsin.

Zuidema, Tom

1977 "The Inca Kinship System: A New Theoretical View." In *Andean Kinship and Marriage*. Ed. Ralph Bolton and Enrique Mayer. Pp. 240–281. Washington, D.C.: American Anthropological Association.

1990 *Inca Civilization in Cuzco*. Trans. Jean-Jacques Decoster. Austin: University of Texas Press.

INDEX